"Grounded in African consciou
Dr. Fanny Brewster has writte
compelling examination of Afric ... .c, uccply
thoughtful book explores the dreams voices of African people: our identity,
freedom, struggle, lineage, and legacy. Dr. Brewster's gift for storytelling,
handed down to her from her maternal grandmother, illuminates each page,
weaving scholarly research with a re-telling that touches the heart and
soul. Our dreams are our legacy, and our hope and Dr. Brewster captures
them with exquisite clarity and compassion."

Valerie Brown, *JD, MA, PCC, Co-Director, Georgetown University,*
Institute for Transformational Leadership, Buddhist Dharma
Teacher and Author Hope Leans Forward *and* Braving Your
Way toward Simplicity, Awakening and Peace

"Throughout reading this work, I was reminded of my African American
grandmother who would look forward to our deceased relatives visiting her
because somehow, she knew of the West African belief that people did not
truly die until they were forgotten. Addressing the long-neglected dream life
of people of African descent, Dr. Brewster's landmark work takes a deep
dive into African philosophy and mythology and its relevance to people of
the African Diaspora in terms of their culture, psychology, and ultimately
their dream life. It then weaves it all into the development of psychoanalysis
and dream analysis and is nothing short of brilliant, culminating in case
material that is fresh and relevant. Destined to become a classic, *Race and
the Unconscious: An Africanist Depth Psychology Perspective on Dreaming*
will need to be incorporated into the curriculum of psychoanalytic institutes
worldwide."

Kim Arrington, *Director of Psychological Services,*
Garnet Health Medical Center Faculty and Supervisor,
Metropolitan Institute for Psychoanalytic Psychotherapy,
New York, NY

"With great pleasure I endorse Fanny Brewster's new book on the African
psyche. She brings a magnifying lens to images on philosophy, mythology,
stories, and dreams, that challenges the Eurocentric blindness of African
values and its effect on Black people in the Americas. I commend the reading
of this book to old and new generations in the spirit of balancing social
psychic energy and embracing healing in the world."

Carmen Ada Gonzalez, *Ed.D, Jungain Analyst, C.G. Jung*
Institute, San Francisco, Recipient of the 2000 Peace
and Justice Award from the City of Cambridge

"Extraordinarily well researched and heartfelt, *Race and the Unconscious: An Africanist Depth Psychology Perspective on Dreaming* fills many long-standing gaps in the clinical practice and theory around African Americans in Jungian psychology. Practitioners and clients from all backgrounds will once again benefit from Dr. Brewster's insight. A powerful and incredible book."

Satya Doyle Byock, *Director of The Salome Institute of Jungian Studies and author of* Quarterlife: The Search for Self in Early Adulthood

"In *Race in the Unconscious*, Dr. Fanny Brewster provides a "Literary dreamlife voice for the African Diaspora" to the reader who is a serious seeker of truth and understanding. This work offers a way to move beyond those historical descriptions of African people which were based more on projections from the European imagination than upon factual information, making them invisible both consciously and unconsciously, without any understanding of their rich inner life and dreams. This book will transform that landscape."

Catherine Meeks, *Executive Director Absalom Jones Center for Racial Healing, Atlanta, GA*

Race and the Unconscious

Race and the Unconscious: An Africanist Depth Psychology Perspective on Dreaming engages the archetypal African consciousness that enriches our knowledge regarding the foundational mythopoetic of Africanist dreaming.

Featuring crucial historical context, Jungian and post-Jungian theory, clinical case studies, and dream series interpretations, the book offers readers a rich framework for exploring and understanding the language, images, and symbols of African and African American dreamlife. It expands the modern understanding of dreaming with the inclusion of Africanist perspectives, philosophy, and mythology while emphasizing the potential for and process of psychological healing through dreamwork.

Race and the Unconscious: An Africanist Depth Psychology Perspective on Dreaming is a must-read for Jungian analysts and analytical psychologists in practice and in training, as well as anyone interested in understanding psychological processes inclusive of those of African descent and their culture, including academics and students of sociology, anthropology, African American studies, and African diaspora studies.

Fanny Brewster is a Jungian analyst and a Professor at Pacifica Graduate Institute. She is the author of the *Racial Complex: A Jungian Perspective on Race and Culture*.

Race and the Unconscious

An Africanist Depth Psychology Perspective on Dreaming

Fanny Brewster

Routledge
Taylor & Francis Group

LONDON AND NEW YORK

Designed cover image: © Daniele Hunter

First published 2023
by Routledge
4 Park Square, Milton Park, Abingdon, Oxon OX14 4RN

and by Routledge
605 Third Avenue, New York, NY 10158

Routledge is an imprint of the Taylor & Francis Group, an informa business

British Library Cataloguing-in-Publication Data
A catalogue record for this book is available from the British Library

ISBN: 978-1-032-11449-1 (hbk)
ISBN: 978-1-032-11448-4 (pbk)
ISBN: 978-1-003-21996-5 (ebk)

DOI: 10.4324/9781003219965

Typeset in Times New Roman
by MPS Limited, Dehradun

Dedicated to Grandmother Rebecca — My First Dream
Teacher

Contents

Acknowledgments

I wish to acknowledge and thank individuals from different parts of life who have contributed to my always-developing knowledge and understanding of dreams and the dream life. First, I will thank and give respect to my paternal grandmother who taught me from an early age that dreams were a natural aspect of my being. She taught me that they were gifts from the Sacred.

Thank you to Sylvia Perera for the wonderful years of dreamwork teaching that I experienced through our work together.

I deeply appreciate the teachings I have acquired through spiritual teachers from different traditions. They have helped me to understand that dreams can influence my life as part of a natural path—sometimes mysterious, and always with more to be discovered.

Deep gratitude to the three women, Rae, Liz, and Kyesha who shared their dreams and worked with me to better understand our Africanist cultural dreaming lives.

Thank you to the supervising Jungian analysts at the C.G. Jung Institute of New York who gave much time to supporting me in deepening my understanding of dreamwork during my psychanalytical training.

My appreciative thanks to the 12 Dream Circle participants who kept the energy field of our work present as I completed the revisions on the book.

Stephen Eisenstadt, the author of *Dreamtending*, was my first dream teacher in my doctoral program. It was and continues to be an amazing journey into the dreaming archetypal—thank you.

I am appreciative of the editorial guidance and direction provided by Alexis O'Brien and Katie Randall at Routledge, and to Susannah Frearson for having a vision for the publication of this book.

Foreword

I had just finished reading Fanny Brewster's book T*he Racial Complex: A Jungian Perspective on Culture and Race* (2020), a subject too long neglected in analytical psychology and was looking forward to her keynote address at a conference of the Inter-Regional Society of Jungian Analysts in Minneapolis, Minnesota. There I was, standing in the hotel lobby in front of a set of three elevators when one of the doors opened and who do I see standing before me but Fanny, in all her unassuming and yet commanding presence! In an embarrassingly spellbound moment, and out of sheer enthusiasm, all I could think to say was, "I just read your book!" to which Fanny gracefully replied, "Which one?"

Fanny Brewster has gifted us with groundbreaking works: *African American and Jungian Psychology: Leaving the Shadows* (2017), *Archetypal Grief: Slavery's Legacy of Intergenerational Child Loss* (2019), and now with *Race and the Unconscious: An Africanist Depth Psychology Perspective on Dreaming (2022)*. Dismayed by a lack of literature on the study of dreams of Africans and African American women in particular, Brewster, herself a woman of African heritage, turns her attention to African cultural dreaming, a "literary dreamlife voice for the African Diaspora." *Race and the Unconscious: An Africanist Depth Psychology Perspective on Dreaming* explores the dreamlife of three African American women and uncovers a rich African philosophy that frames the structure of her work. African mythology, cosmology, spiritual customs, and healing practices come out of the shadows to reframe and set straight what white anthropologists, Christian missionaries, and social scientists got wrong. Poetically weaving a narrative of both respect for analytical psychology and a healthy critique of Jung's racialized writings, Brewster's words provide a refreshingly new understanding of an African dreaming unconscious.

Brewster's voice is a breath of modern 21st-century fresh air that breathes new life into dated and dusty psychological theories. Her words stand side by side with Maya Angelou, Henry Louis Gates, Isabel Allende, and other prominent authors who speak of their own dreams and bring African mythological figures out of the past to sit aside Greek myths and Greek gods. Emerging from her work it is evident that a meaningful reciprocal exchange can exist among Jungian theory and African American philosophic traditions. Including African American and people of color's cultural symbols, mythological motifs, and dreamwork as a collective experience will enrich the Jungian cultural body of knowledge. She challenges analytical psychology to claim Jung's shadow so that it can become a more inclusive and equitable community better poised to attract African Americans and people of color into analysis and training.

Focusing primarily on African Americans, much of what Brewster reveals can also be applied to indigenous people and people of color in general. Her masterful research exposes the challenges African American and indigenous people face when their cultural symbols are not acknowledged, recognized, or are (mis)interpreted exclusively through a western lens. Brewster's work speaks to me as an indigenous woman. I couldn't help but notice the commonalities our communities share. Like African traditions and African American communities, tribal people also recognize the spirit in all things; extended family, kin, and community provide the basis for our identity; we suffer intergenerational trauma from boarding schools that broke our family structures, and we continue to value our spiritual healers who have retained, against all odds, sacred knowledge shared by our ancestors and other spirit beings. This work reaches across cultures and provides an essential model for others to build on.

For practitioners working with African Americans, this work is essential. Deepening Jung's classical theory of dreamwork, readers are introduced to traditional African healing practices, the importance of the physical body, and how creativity and the imaginal influence the work of dream interpretation. Brewster includes some of her own dreams and poetry showing a creative process intertwined with self-reflection that comes with working with dreams. Analysts, therapists, and training programs are cautioned, particularly as it pertains to clinical practice, that to do cross-cultural work of this nature will require a careful ethical deconstruction of Jung's racialized writings and theoretical framework that keep people of color at arm's length.

Race and the Unconscious: An Africanist Depth Psychology Perspective on Dreaming, and all of Brewster's works, come at an important time. We are in a moment of history when the country is awakening to race and the power it holds in our lives. The need couldn't be greater to better connect unconscious content with conscious understanding. There simply is not enough literature on the study of dreams of African Americans or people of color and the literature that does exist is offensive and racially biased. Brewster's voice speaks *from* rather than *about* African American cultural dreaming and brings to center stage cultural values critical to understanding and working with African Americans in a therapeutic setting. We are called to listen, to be open, to dare to ask difficult questions, and perhaps most of all, to stay engaged when what we learn reveals some of our most painful collective shadows.

This book has something for everyone. Whether your interest is in dream-work, the feminine, mythology, philosophy, racism, archetypal theory, or therapeutic practice, you will not be disappointed. This work should be a required reading in the curriculum for psychology training programs across the nation. Especially for those programs earnestly seeking to build a more inclusive and diverse membership.

Jeanne A. Lacourt, Ph.D.
Diplomate Jungian Analyst
Saint Cloud, Minnesota
September 2021

Part I

Historical Foundation

Introduction

Race and the Unconscious: An Africanist Depth Psychology Perspective on Dreaming explores aspects of historical and contemporary Africanist dreams and cultural dreaming. The book provides a literary dreamlife voice for the African Diaspora. The relationship between this psychological dreamlife and an African American foundational cultural unconscious has been mostly uninvestigated. There has also been a lack of examination of Africanist dreamlife in much of the American Psychology literature on dreaming. Through the decades, in the development of American Psychology, and especially Jungian psychology literature—the *Collected Works*, Africanist people have remained in the shadows except as designated inheritors of poor intellect and lowered consciousness. A "hierarchy of consciousness" was developed by the early creators of modern psychology—Sigmund Freud and C.G. Jung and other European men. Their promotion and development of theories, through their "discovery" of Africa, *invented* "primitive" thinking and consciousness theories about Africans, and later the African Diaspora. This idea regarding lack of consciousness went directly to Jung's theory of the unconscious, including his theories regarding dreams and dreaming. However, Jung himself has stated in speaking of his dreams and the guidance he gets from them: "I am as primitive as any nigger, because I do not know!" (CW18: 286, para. 674) In his way, Jung indicates that he, like Africans, are guided by dreams and his skin color does not assure him of having prior knowledge. The racialized undercutting of phrasing in Jung's language speaks to the important necessity for including a more modern and 21st-century interpretation of our understanding of the Africanist dreamlife and an African unconscious.

Race and the Unconscious: An Africanist Depth Psychology Perspective, explores the dreams of three African American women and the historical foundation of an African dreaming unconscious. This is accomplished through discussions of African mythology, philosophy, and religion, thereby providing the basis for a better understanding of Africanist cultural dreaming within an African-centric model. This model considers psychological group cultural influences as well as intergenerational trauma.

DOI: 10.4324/9781003219965-2

Prior to beginning doctoral studies, I participated in workshops and activities related to the study of dreams. As I progressed with these studies, I increasingly read more literature regarding dreams and dreaming. As a woman of African ancestry, I was particularly interested in the literature relevant to this heritage. I had recorded my own dreams for decades and looked forward with excitement to exploring the African cultural dream life. Unfortunately, since many details of African cultural dreaming had not been retained, I found relatively sparse literature on Africanist dreams and beliefs regarding dreaming as given by Africans. Although the 1920s through the 1950s were times of intensive European anthropological "research" in Africa (Hambly, 1937), these ethnographic "studies" only superficially mention, the dreams of Indigenous people. In addition, the more I read, the more obvious it became that the few studies that were available about Africans, were racially biased. It proved disappointing for me, as I progressed through my doctoral program, to find negative accounts of Africanist people and their dreaming traditions.

Christian missionaries, European politicians, and anthropologists had set about determining the "identity" of native people. Dreams, though minimally examined, were yet another avenue to negatively define Africa's people. It seemed obvious to me that missionaries and social scientists alike tended to emphasize the negative symbology of the dreams, as interpreted by Christian doctrine or Sigmund Freud's *Interpretation of Dreams* (1900/1965), rather than honor the manifest and thematic richness of African dreams themselves. I found scarce reporting of African philosophical concepts and theories regarding Africans reporting on their own dreaming lives. This is so although dreams are very significant in the traditional healing practices of many Africans (Buhrmann, 1986).

The word "primitive" has been used in the early development of the field of Modern Psychology to mean *undeveloped*—lacking something.

The comparison was between native, Indigenous people, and Caucasians. As a rule, the word carries a negative connotation. Often it is placed opposite a strong, developed ego in the theories of hierarchy of psychological development. *Primitive*, as a general term, according to some, is applicable to any person or circumstance that is ancient or original. Even today, Indigenous people all over the world can still be referenced as *primitive*. In fact, European writers in the first half of the 20th century consistently referred to Africanist peoples, Native Americans, and other Indigenous groups as "primitives." While the term may have initially suggested ancient or original, it more clearly over time connoted uncivilized, unintelligent, and even ignorant, in other words, the supposed exact opposite of European civilization, intelligence, and knowledge. Because of this cultural bigotry, Christian missionaries attempted to dissuade African people from their own ancient cosmological beliefs in a life continuum with spiritual beings and ancestors. Europeans, and American Christian missionaries, tried to turn Africans away from their ancestor reverence, healing traditions (which almost always included divination and dreams), and spiritual practices that honored goddesses and gods.

Indigenous African spiritual customs and healing practices were very much intertwined. Sickness and spirituality were integral aspects of a single cosmology.

Knowledge of dream interpretation and the understanding of dream imagery was essential to traditional African healing practices. The traditional healer's divination could ascertain the divine, ancestral cause of sickness and prescribe a healing solution. Into this ancient well-integrated cultural ethos, Europeans brought the priest, the confessional, and the concept that sickness was caused by germs or offending the white God the Father. Absolution and healing were now in the hands of the priest or the European doctor. Fortunately, in the same way that African American slaves never relinquished the idea of freedom, Africans never completely gave up their cosmological view of life. Even today, decades after the end of colonialism, Africans and the Diaspora continue with traditional healing practices, divination, and belief in the gods. Christianity has impacted African life, but it has failed to eradicate an African consciousness that saw no Cartesian division of mind and soul, no reason to cease spiritual rites nor to stop the telling of myths.

Modern depth psychology used selected cultural Africanist attributes to which Freud, Jung, and other early depth psychologists were recipients. Though Freud, like many others of his day spent no actual time with Indigenous people, and conducted no "analysis" with them, he found that he was able to write *about* their psychology in *Totem and Taboo* (1913). Freud and others were assisted by anthropologists such as Levy-Bruhl, Levi-Strauss, and Mircea Eliade, men who built their professional careers writing *about* Indigenous peoples. Because of the writings of these men, and others like them, V. Y. Mudimbe (1996) says in *The Idea of Africa,* it was determined how Africa would be imaged and projected onto world consciousness—namely, that Africa and Africans, were to be seen as pre-logical, uncivilized, and of low intellect. This racist conception exists in one form or another in most of the social sciences from early missionary studies of Africans in such early books as *Bantu Philosophy* through and including literature of the 20th century, for example, The *Bell Curve: Intelligence and Class Structure in American Life.*

C.G. Jung, psychiatrist and founder of Analytical Psychology, spent many years analyzing the dreams of Europeans. His theory of the collective unconscious was tied to his proposition that archetypes existed within human consciousness. Formerly a close colleague of Freud, Jung eventually broke with him developing psychological theories which explored human consciousness and the unconscious through non-drive/biological theories. Jung began his early work with mentally ill patients at Burgholzli Hospital in Zurich. Eventually, he developed a private practice in which archetypal psychology, with its focus on dream analysis and issues of transference/countertransference, came to dominate his work. Unlike Freud, Jung held that dreams could not always be interpreted in the same manner based on the same "signs" of the dream, applicable to all dreamers with little variation.

Jung's dreamwork anticipated that there would be what he terms *uncertainty*—an essential element of the work. His theory of *compensation* was an attempt to complement Freud's wish-fulfillment dream theory. Taking dream imagery past the point of mere wish-fulfillment, Jung saw dreams as part of a necessary psychic functioning aimed at the assimilation of both conscious and unconscious material in support of psychological healing and wellness.

Jung's desire to have his theory of archetypes accepted is understandable. However, the universality that he attributes to the archetypes of the collective unconscious and therefore the dreamlife, has not been equally applied to Africans and their mythology, their philosophy or generally to human protentional for psychological growth in a fair, unbiased manner.

Chapter 1 of *Race and the Unconscious: An Africanist Depth Psychology Perspective on Dreaming* is titled *African Philosophy: Identity,* and begins the book's narrative by exploring how an individual's culture is inseparable from learned beliefs—including philosophy. This is discussed as the grounding for all that lives and emerges through culture, laws, and societal rituals.

The guidance of wisdom provided by previous generations is explored to understand the resiliency of African spirituality as an aspect of philosophy and the survival of Indigenous spirituality in African post-colonialism. The influence of European culture on the identity and very existence of Africanist life is not underestimated. This includes theories and biased rules of raciality that helped shape our understanding of philosophy that includes Africanist dreaming and the dreamlife.

Chapter 2 centers on how the introjection of European colonialism into African culture created a rupture in the philosophical underpinnings causing a question even as to the existence of an African philosophy. What does an African philosophy consist of, and could it exist without a European philosophical mirror upon which to reflect itself? Doubt regarding the preposition of free-willed African societies is discussed as an aspect of thinking about the presence of colonialism and its impact on what holds a country together at its cultural roots—values, beliefs, all tied to philosophy.

The ways that mythologies are an intricate part of the lives of all people, no matter their ethnicity, is discussed in Chapter 3. There is a close reading of the writing of Karla Holloway, who considers black women and their connection to the story and spirituality/goddess at the center of these writings.

Reading through an African Bemba myth in this chapter provides a context for finding the relationship between the dream and mythology from an Africanist point of view.

Chapter 4 continues an exploration of African mythology looking at it in a comparative way to those white anthropologists who had created early theories of African mythology and their interpretation for Africans of their myths. Anthropologist Levy-Bruhl and his relationship to C. G. Jung is discussed in terms of a theoretical approach that was a major influence on

Jung's Analytical Psychology. This informed his construct of Africanist people functioning within his psychological model. In the re-framing of African mythology, considering it from an Africanist perspective, a discussion is offered through the work of Henry Gates and his interpretation of Esu, Yoruba Trickster god and that of authors presented in *Esu: Yoruba God, Power, and the Imaginative Frontiers*.

Chapter 5 opens *Part II*, the *Practice* section of the book and reviews classical Jungian theories. This chapter offers an opportunity to develop a deeper understanding of Jung's early theories and their impact on the development and study of dreams as well as the practice of Jungian dreamwork in America.

In Chapter 6, the discussion focuses on ways of healing practices, including dreamwork that are a part of African culture. The chapter reviews traditional African healing practices and accepts the foundation for understanding the strength of an African philosophy that underpins dreamwork as an essential aspect of healing practice.

Chapter 7 connects dreamwork together with creativity, two aspects of the Imaginal. *Dreaming as a Creative Process* anticipates that the unconscious imagery that comes in the dream is created by the archetypal, a goddess, Soul, the Divine—in service of deepening consciousness towards changes of the personality, of the ego-life. The narrative within this chapter engages the voices of writers such as Maya Angelou and Isabel Allende who are interviewed and speak of their dreams and how influential they are in their creative processes. The significance of self-reflection and intertwining between these two creative aspects of the unconscious are discussed throughout the chapter.

Chapter 8 creates a narrative regarding the importance of the physical body and the dream body. The chapter discusses the pioneering work of Arnold Mindell, an early explorer of how the body and dreams work together in understanding the meaning of dreams, especially ones that indicate when physical healing needs to take place. Robert Bosnak's book titled *Dreaming with an Aids Patient* is also explored for its contribution to understanding the dreaming body. A third significant aspect of the chapter's discussion relates to trauma as recollected and held within the dreaming body and how healing can be possible. This is important toward any discussion of intergenerational trauma. *Bodydreaming in the Treatment of Developmental Trauma* by Marian Dunlea is explored in the chapter's discussion of dreaming and trauma. The theme of the book and its details relate well to the understanding of how somatic psychology matters in the wake state as well as on the dream body landscape.

Chapter 9 details the dreams of three women, and is titled, *African American Dreamer Dialogue Portraits*. The chapter shows a one-year dream study and interviews with three African American women who reveal their dreams, their thoughts about their dreams and suggest the importance of formulating a theory regarding the nature of dreaming by women of color. Considering the place of the feminine in African American women's psyche is in keeping with the importance of the feminine in Africanist culture and feminist thought in general.

In African societies, in those religious rituals that have not been taken over by the men—and even in some of these—the presence of the feminine is strong. The strength of this presence continued among Africans first brought to this country in slavery.

Classical Jungian psychology conceives of the feminine in a variety of ways but takes its early lead from the definitions provided by Jung and Erich Neumann. The content of these definitions contains some of what is true of the feminine but also puts forth biases and rigid concepts that continue to envision women as being weaker, like children, and dependent on men. This is being challenged by feminist revisionists from African as well as American perspectives with a view to discredit past patriarchal theories and concepts that devalued women. The following quote is from *The Invention of Women: Making an African Sense of Western Gender Discourses* by Oyeronke Oyewumi (1997):

> The histories of both the colonized and the colonizer have been written from the male point of view—women are peripheral if they appear at all. While studies of colonization written from this angle are not necessarily irrelevant to understanding what happened to native females, we must recognize that colonization impacted males and females in similar and dissimilar ways. Colonial custom and practice stemmed from *a world view which believes in the absolute superiority of the human over the nonhuman and the subhuman, the masculine over the feminine ..., and the modern or progressive over the traditional or the savage.* (p. 121) (Italics from Ashis Nandy, *The Intimate Enemy: Loss and Recovery of Self under Colonialism*, Oxford University Press, *1983*)

American feminist theorists wrote about Jungian psychology and its relationship to the Feminine. The following was one such writing: In *Jung and Feminism: Liberating Archetypes* (1987), Demaris S. Wehr stated:

> The androcentric nature of the prevailing symbol systems—from which Jung derives his theory of the collective unconscious—prevent feminists from claiming full allegiance to or responsibility for them as they are presented to us. This is why many feminists have gone on a search for pre-patriarchal systems or of the goddess in pre-patriarchal history hoping to find historical remnants of a worldview that reflect women's consciousness. (p. 23)

In considering the application of Jungian psychology to African American women, the ideas, images, and psychological stance of the two may hold opposite tensions that require careful discernment. In African American women, there is a presence that speaks of necessary strength and ability due to multiple factors of being African American and female in this society that itself emerged from British colonization. Jungian psychology will have to re-frame its concepts to include many factors that connect with this as well as American slavery, the American psyche as related to racism, and the position of the Africanist female in American collective consciousness.

Chapter 10 discusses the dreams of the three women and the relevance of their dreams to the archetypal and to mythology and mythological imagery that appeared in their dreams. I believe that archetypal patterns do exist, and as humans we all have the potentialities of all the archetypes. However, my dis-agreement regarding the archetypes and a Jungian claim of universality of these archetypes, occurs when the people of origin, on whom much of "primitive" theory and psychology is based, are only included by way of a deprivation and hierarchical model. This has meant that Africanist archetypes have had no place in the universality of the archetypal pantheon. The images that one is asked to accept from Jungian psychology predominantly reflect Western culture. Analytical psychology as it has developed in the United States has been very reluctant to include imagery that is African—except for Egyptian imagery. The inclusion of Egyptian imagery has been "acceptable" only because historically, many Europeans and Americans do not consider Egyptian culture to *be* African.

Chapter 11 includes the dreams of participants with an Africanist per-spective on reviewing the dreams. The discussion focuses on how important it is to be inclusive of Africanist dreams and African centrist interpretations in the literature as well as clinical practice of psychoanalysis.

Chapter 12 reviews the author's personal dream drawing a connection between the dream images and the Feminine. There is also a connection developed that sees the relationship between how the unconscious material of dreams influence wake state conscious awareness.

The Concluding chapter indicates the importance of cultural symbols to the Africanist dreamer. Africanist culture belongs within depth psychology literature on dreaming, in a positive vein, as dreaming and the dreamlife has existed as an important topic within previous psychological writings that focused only on whites and their dreamlife. The discussion of culture within dreaming is highlighted in the chapter.

Race and the Unconscious: An Africanist Depth Psychology Perspective on Dreaming, through exploration of African American women's dreams, opens a discussion regarding the political and societal relevance of the humanity of this most important part of life—the dreamlife. This part of the psycholog-ical, cultural, and spiritual, belongs equally to people of color. Though the historical psychological literature makes little space for the positive presence of an African and African Diaspora dreamlife, it is significantly important to find a place of inclusion for their dreamlife in post-colonial, 21st-century depth psychology literature.

Chapter 1

African Philosophy
Identity

Philosophy and Culture

African culture has a deep and long-abiding respect for dreams and dreaming. Unfortunately, African methods and beliefs about dreams and dreaming have gone mostly underreported in written form. African mythology, philosophy, cultural rites, and social customs will serve as the basis for my writing regarding the significance of dream images, language, and states of conscious awareness present in Africanist dreaming. The importance of dreaming to our human life has been considered through Psychology, spiritual customs, and various cultures for centuries. Identity as a psychological aspect of being human encompasses the dreamlife. Dreams, culture, and the need to understand dreams are all interwoven with the philosophic beliefs, values, and morals of a society. This chapter considers Africanist identity within varying philosophies discussed by African philosophers.

In *African Philosophy: Myth and Reality* (1983), Paulin Hountondji proposed that history and culture determine the form that philosophical thought assumes. Hountondji stated, "Hegel's philosophy of history remains the most exalted statement of European self-affirmation in opposition to other races, the most elaborate rationalization of European ethnocentrism" (p. 5). In referencing Levy-Bruhl, Hountondji noted that it was during the greatest thrust of European expansion that anthropology gained the status of a "science." Levy-Bruhl and others like him compared the European mind with "primitive mentality." Ordinary features of Western logic, causality, and time were compared with the prelogical mental status of Indigenous peoples. "More generally speaking, Levy-Bruhl's contribution to anthropology and to European ideas was posited on an explicit hierarchy of values for which the Western serve as an absolute reference" (p. 13). Following World War II, a cultural pluralism and relativity came to dominate anthropology. In 1945, with the introduction of Temple's work in proposing "native" logic, the period of classical anthropology ended.

Hountondji (1983), in reviewing this post-war time discussed the development of Senghorian thought ("Emotion is African, as Reason is Hellenic")

DOI: 10.4324/9781003219965-3

(Hountondji, p. 16) and the writings of David Diop, which both sought to define the African identity. Hountondji quoted Frantz Fanon's *The Wretched of the Earth* (1961) in support of the theory of the unworthiness of the oral tradition as a basis for African philosophy: "Culture will take shape around the struggle of the people, not around songs, poems or folklore" (Hountondji, p. 23). Hountondji (1983) defined African philosophy as a set of texts written by Africans, and his goal was to analyze the literature of African philosophers from the previous 38 years. In seeking to do this, Hountondji said, "Our philosophy consists essentially in the process of analysis itself" (1983, p. 33), meaning that African philosophy has evolved from the text *Bantu Philosophy* and latter-day ethnophilosophers. He stated, for example, that philosophy is a history, not a closed knowledge system but a discontinuous evolution, and that African philosophy is in its first "decisive mutation." It is an error to think that "African philosophy [is] construed as a spontaneous, unreflective, collective world view" (p. 76). He reinforced his belief that there is and must be a plurality of opinions, not just collective thought through one view. Quoting Radin, Hountondji also maintained that verbal arts—storytelling, singing, and myth-telling—are artistic endeavors, unlike philosophy, which is scientific.

Author Bayo Akomolafe, in *These Wilds Beyond Our Fences: Letters to my daughter on Humanity's Search for Home* (2017), uses the form of letter writing to speak philosophically about being human and a person of color. This style of writing reminds me of the storytelling and oral tradition that seems to still belong to contemporary Africanist thinking. Our art *is* our philosophy, and it remains "scientific" because it provides the boundaries and borders of an interconnected Africanist life that offers us definition. When we cross these boundaries, we can become lost in the "wilds" where we become "Other." What then happens to our voice of expressing, in a creative way, our own cultural stories? Is this not the painful history of colonization that we continue to work at repairing?

Akomolafe says:

> So I sometimes walk about stiffly when your mother sends me down the road to the local store. I would put on an affected Americanized accent, or say I was from South African when people ask what part of the world I was from. It's true. I hardly feel at home in my own skin—which seems like a necessary prerequisite to fashioning new settlements and new ontologies of home. If your own skin repels you, then where might you live? (*These Wilds beyond our Fences*, p. 138)

In contrast to Hountondji, I believe that cosmological beliefs help establish the value of life events, supporting the development of concepts that produce certain patterns of behavior and the formulation of ideas. Hountondji's rejection (1983) of verbal arts appears as a basic rejection of his own cultural identity. In his search for identification with science, he has sacrificed the oral tradition. I perceive his rejection of verbal arts and oral tradition as negating a most important aspect of African culture. Instead, I find myself agreeing with Tsenay Serequeberhan, who explained that "philosophical discourse itself originates from and is organically linked to the concrete condition-of-existence ... out of which it is formulated" (Serequeberhan, 1994, p. 15).

God and African Spirituality

African spirituality is a necessary aspect of any debate or discussion regarding African philosophy and its significance as a part of establishing self and community identity. European missionaries affected the ability of Africans to observe spiritual practices within their own societies. Traditional African spiritual practices amongst Africans and African American slaves were changed to accommodate European religious rites. The religion of Santeria and some African American congregations combine African traditional spirituality and Catholicism. Many Africanist people have converted to non-Traditional European-established religions. How does this affect the understanding of African philosophical thought?

For those who have eliminated the tension by a practice of Santeria, it is anticipated that philosophical answers come easier. However, many African Americans are claiming allegiance to no particular church because of a sense of isolation in adopting European spiritual practices. Jung drew many of his theories regarding religion and dream symbolism from the Judeo-Christian tradition.

It is my understanding of Jungian psychology theory that archetypical patterns remain constant, but the historical/cultural images produced by the archetypes change once emerging into the specific cultural moment. Religion in African culture, unlike any other area for potential philosophical discussion, has been the focus of much research, primarily because of the European fanaticism brought to Africa in the name of God under missionary "guidance." God, human relationship to God and creation, and all that these entailed have had numerous interpretations by individuals of many religious disciplines.

In his text *Cultural Universals and Particulars* (1996), Kwasi Wiredu discussed religion within the context of the commonality that binds us as a species, but also keeps us separate—the particulars of our individual cultural philosophies. His expressed concern was with philosophical universals and the particulars of religion, morality, and language. Wiredu asked whether the word "religion" in English had applicability to African thought or life. He then stated that in Akan there was no single word for "religion." The word *anyamesom*, meaning in the "service of the Supreme Being," was chosen by missionaries to mean "religion." However, Wiredu explained that the word meant "Christian." In choosing a word to describe the *religion* of the Africans, missionaries chose the word *abosomsom*, that meant literally "service of stones," because Indigenous people were thought by missionaries to worship stones.

According to Wiredu, Africans were thought by Europeans to lack spirituality and morality, because of the absence a God-Father figure in African religions, as witnessed by Europeans. In response, Wiredu described Akan belief that is not tied to the worship of God, but rather to knowing what is expected within the realm of human behavior. Because there is no concept of heaven or hell as such, positive and negative behavior are answerable by individuals *within themselves*, and to the community in which they reside, and is based on responsibility—not on anticipation of punishment from an omnipotent God.

The Supreme Being described by Akans was different than the Christian God in that He was known not to have created something (what we know as life) out of nothing. This Being was part of a hierarchy of existence, *wo-bo*, which included all of life, inanimate objects, the dead (ancestors), the living, and the Supreme Being himself. *Quasi-material beings*, also known as gods or goddesses, were also a part of this hierarchy, but were not viewed in a religious way as has been presupposed by most European missionaries. Rather, they were valued in a purely "utilitarian" way, as noted by Wiredu (1996). If they did not produce the desired results for the humans who sacrificed and communicated with them, then they ceased to be important and lost their significance to the human community.

"The Akan worldview then involves no sharp ontological cleavages such as the Cartesian dichotomy of the material and the spiritual" (Wiredu, 1996, p. 98). For the Akan individual, spirituality was very much related to space. Everything held space. The material—water, cloth, the river—held space. The quasi-material—the ancestors, gods—once held space in this realm and now hold space in a parallel location.

That something could exist and not have a specific location was unacceptable to the Akan. According to Descartes and Christianity, the spiritual is unseen and immaterial. Such a thing did not exist in Akan thinking. Throughout the text, Wiredu (1996) showed and emphasized the importance of language in the conceptual formation of ideas. The importance of language was stressed in that "any unexamined use of a foreign language in philosophical work is a mark of the colonial mentality" (1996, p. 148).

Wiredu argued that the use of English and French languages has within them, as any language does, a predisposition toward a selected way of thinking. As examples, the author provided rather detailed and consistent analogies from the Akan linguistic system of Ghana, of which he is a native. He compared the logic, metaphysics, and reasoning of Descartes with Akan philosophy in predetermining meaning and obtaining meaning in philosophical thought. "In my opinion, the agenda for contemporary African philosophy must include the critical and reconstructive treatment of the oral tradition and the exploitation of the literary and scientific resources of the modern world in pursuit of a synthesis" (p. 113). It was Wiredu's belief that it is crucial to study the oral tradition of African countries.

He found the two sources most available in the traditional reports of communal philosophy: first, through proverbs, tales, myths, poetry, and the art motifs of a people. Second, he referred to Indigenous thinkers as a source for relating African philosophy. Referencing Okura in the latter circumstance, Wiredu reminded us that the elders, especially in an oral tradition society, hold a key position in informing those of us in contemporary life regarding philosophical history, past, and present. An idea that was very important to Wiredu was what he called "conceptual decolonization." It was essential to rethink how one thought if one was to achieve success in formulating thoughts and ideas beneficial to African society without what he described as "colonial mentality."

Said Wiredu, "The problem is that thinking *about* them [universal concepts] in English almost inevitably becomes thinking *in* English about them ... one thinks most naturally in the language of one's education and occupation. But in our case, this means thinking along the lines of conceptual frameworks which may be significantly different from those embedded in our indigenous languages" (1996, p. 137).

I believe the problem Wiredu (1996) cited regarding language and how one comes to form concepts touches on the historical debate in American society regarding Ebonics. We can see how this is not a problem of the past but one that continues even today.

In her essay, "Afrocentricity and the Critical Question of African Agency," author Ama Mazama in speaking of the racialized bias of international language ordering says the following:

> Although linguistics officially claims that all languages are equal, Language Planning Studies, a field within sociolinguistics whose aims are to address the "language problems " of developing countries," postulates nonetheless a linguistic hierarchy reminiscent of the hierarchies established in other social sciences. At the very bottom of the continuum, one finds "preliterate languages," followed by "unstandardized languages," "young standard languages," "archaic standard languages," "fully developed small group standard languages," and finally, at the top, "mature standard languages" (Kloss, 1968:82). Needless to say, most Western European languages, the so-called world languages, belong to the last category. (*We Will Tell Our Own Story: The Lions of Africa Speak!* 2017, p. 59)

African American language structure is originally different from that of Caucasian Americans. The former structure is based primarily on West African linguistic systems. Although African Americans speak "standard" English, most learn Ebonics or Black English at home as a first language. There is still debate regarding the value, significance, and/or feasibility of supporting Ebonics in public school education. Those who support Ebonics would agree with Wiredu. Africans as well as African Americans, have a native language that is not without English influence. Can there be a precise determination of the degree or existence of conceptualization problems created by the construct of English and African-derived linguistics spoken by African Americans? What would be the conceptual framework when both are present in the language of African Americans? I believe these are difficult questions to answer. They are questions unique to the African American experience. How are these questions to be held within the context of Africanist philosophy and dreaming?

Wiredu (1996) believed that "professional" philosophy of Africa does allow for the necessary "reflection" on African and non-African influences. He considered it important that this occurs in the vernacular of Africans. He proposed a formula that the first course of action is to determine if there is an African solution or alternative to a Western-proposed idea. He noted that urbanization has required most philosophical writing to be in French or English. However, he stressed the necessity of the use of African vernacular in thinking through concepts to determine the true nature of a philosophical dilemma or problem. Is something a dilemma because of its nature, requiring a philosophical focus, or is it a dilemma because of the nature of its linguistic structure, highlighting the natural difference and conflict between two systems of thought? Wiredu showed by example how this may exist in the situation of Akan and English. He stressed that it is up to the *truthfulness of the philosopher* to investigate and report findings, in relationship to Indigenous ideas and linguistic considerations.

Clearly, not all Blacks are Africans, and not all Africans are Blacks. But it matters little where they are located. As objects of discourse and objects of knowledge, Africa and Blackness have, since the beginning of the modern age, plunged the theory of the name as well as the status and function of the sign and of representation into deep crisis .... Every time it confronted the question of Blacks and Africa, reason found itself ruined and emptied, turning constantly in on itself, shipwrecked in a seemingly inaccessible place where the language was destroyed and words themselves no longer had memory. Language, its ordinary functions extinguished, became a fabulous machine whose power resided in its vulgarity, in its remarkable capacity for violation, and in its indefinite proliferation. Still today, as soon as the subject of Blacks and Africa is raised, words do not necessarily represent things; the true and the false become inextricable; the signification of the sign is not always adequate to what is being signified. It is not only that the sign is substituted for the thing. Word and image often have little to say about the objective world. The world of words and signs has become autonomous in such a degree that it exists not only as a screen possessed by its subject, its life, and the conditions of its productions but as a force of its own, capable of emancipating itself from all anchoring in reality. That this is the case must be attributed, to a large extent, to the law of race .... It would be a mistake to believe that we left behind the regime that began with the slave trade and flourished in plantation and extraction colonies (Achille Mbembe, *Critique of Black Reason*, 2017, p. 12).

Claiming an African Philosophy

In his opening discussion of African philosophy, Odera Oruka, the author of *Sage Philosophy* (1990), recounted what he considered to be the brief history of African philosophical thought. In the 1960s, African thought developed with the influence of anthropologists and theologians. According to Oruka, John Mbiti's book *African Religion and Philosophy* followed this trend, which was later known as ethnophilosophy. As a result, Oruka believed that Africans have been designated as a people incapable of forming a philosophy due to an inability to reason. He stated that the purpose of his study "was to help substantiate or invalidate the claim that traditional African peoples were innocent of logical and critical thinking" (p. 5).

Oruka (1990) proceeded to discuss the various "trends" that he found in African philosophical thought. Of the four that he named, he considered himself to be among the group known as *professional philosophers*. Members of this group were usually trained in the study of philosophy in Western universities and were usually considered to be a part of what Oruka defined as the rationalist school. This group held that African philosophy must have critical thinking as a necessary element to consider itself a philosophy. The ethnological school considered the communal knowledge of mythology and religion as essential to African philosophy. Oruka, in his study of sagacity, explored a third avenue. In conducting interviews with individuals, he defined them as either philosophical or folk sages, he said, "Sage philosophy in my usage consists of the expressed thoughts of wise men and women in any given community and is a way of thinking and explaining the world that fluctuates between popular wisdom and didactic wisdom" (1990, p. 28). Oruka interviewed 12 Kenyans—11 men and 1 woman—for his study. It was his belief that *philosophical sages* existed as a "second order" in that they reflect on the wisdom of their culture, unlike *folk sages* who do not expand on what are usually well-known and widely held community beliefs. "Between philosophy and wisdom, there is an overlap which enables some philosophers to have wisdom and some wise men to be philosophers. Within this overlap, both the philosopher and the wise man have the same function: they employ abstract reasoning for the understanding and solution of the basic questions of human life and nature.

Our concern is to look for philosophy within sagacity, i.e., to get to their overlap" (1990, p. 36). The sages spoke for themselves in Oruka's text. His questions addressed primarily the topics of God and religion, with explorations of related areas. Folk sages tend not to question the basis of their wisdom or knowledge. They acknowledge what they consider to be the facts and suggest there is no need for revision.

A part of Oruka's task as he saw it was to act as protagonist, in drawing out the interviewee; as Oruka said, "to help the sage give birth to his full views on the subject under consideration" (p. 43). Oruka's study (1990) showed the difference that exists between those who hold to tradition and keep sacred the philosophical wisdom of proverbs, myths, and tales, and those who succeed in adding their own voices of change to communal philosophical ideas. He presented a variety of voices, some who agree with the "rationalist" stance and others who do not. Of special interest to me was the chapter written by an African American author, Lucius Outlaw. Outlaw discussed what he terms the "deconstructive challenges" of African philosophy.

"African philosophy involves efforts to displace the dominant Greco-Eurocentric notions of man and civilized human by expanding their denotative ranges, or by redefining these notions, in part by particularizing them to African peoples such that it becomes possible to distinguish them from peoples of European descent and culture in non-trivial ways" (1990, p. 72). It was Outlaw's belief that there is no reason to debate the existence of African philosophy. This debate originated with Europeans or European-trained African philosophers who were caught in a useless argument based on a European ideal—*logos* or *nous.*

> African people have often been made invisible by 500 years of Eurocentric oppression and suppression. Eurocentrism, for the sake of our discussion here, is defined as the interpretation of all reality from the Western perspective, especially as it emerged during the so-called European Enlightenment period. This perspective developed both internally, with the development of a meta-paradigm specific and relevant to Europe; and externally, in opposition to "others," especially African people. Thus there are four assumptions of that European meta-paradigm which have played a major and negative role as far as African people are concerned: (1) all human beings evolve along the same line; (2) the European experience is universal; (3) Europeans are superior; and (4) "others" are defined by their experiences with Europeans .... European social sciences, informed as they are by Eurocentric assumptions have played a major role in making Africans secondary, even to themselves (Mazama, 2017, pp. 57–58).

M. Makinde, in his monograph *African Philosophy, Culture, and Traditional Medicine* (1988) raised several key questions that have dominated academic conversation as it relates to African philosophy. Most important was the question of the actual existence of African philosophy. Makinde, who was trained in the tradition of Western philosophy via the British system of thought, explored the question of who can truly *be* an African philosopher and what constitutes African philosophical thought.

According to Makinde (1988), there were three stages in the development of African philosophical thought. He described the first stage as the *unwritten* phase. This was based on oral tradition, which was an intricate part of African life. Makinde related that the first written thoughts of Africans were carried by outsiders: missionaries and anthropologists. These authors wrote of African thought as only a collective experience, ignoring whatever individualism may have existed at the time. Makinde named the second stage *colonial ethnophilosophy*. This stage was supported in its development by written works of men such as Levy-Bruhl, Placide Temple, and later native Africans such as Mbiti and Kagame. The third stage was described by Makinde as a reaction by contemporary philosophers against ethnophilosophy. Makinde considered himself to be in this third stage.

In discussing whether there is an African philosophy—based solely on the existence of written philosophy—Makinde (1988) referred readers to men who were written about but who never themselves wrote. He included Buddha, Confucius, and Socrates in this list of "sages." He asked the question: *Why not for Africans?* It was his belief that African philosophy cannot be declared nonexistent because it did not originate as a written form.

Related to the issue of the written form, Makinde (1988) entered discussion of language and culture.

He claimed that the linguistic-philosophical heritage of African philosophers is European, most usually British, or French. In recognizing this, Makinde asked us to look at the influence of language on how we develop our thinking ability, noting the cultural biases that come with any language and the mutual effects of the circumstances between the development of language and philosophy. His argument was that it is difficult for any philosopher to identify as an African philosopher without considering the linguistic influences—the overlay of an "acquired" language superimposed on the native language.

Makinde asked: How can native African philosophers, trained in the language and philosophical traditions of Western philosophy, converse, and find meaning in African philosophy? Is it perhaps this *conflict* that continues to prompt the problematic question of the existence of African philosophy?

"We cannot and must not use the analytic rigor as the telescope and yardstick through which we look for and by which we measure the existence of African, Oriental, or any non-Western philosophy" (Makinde, 1988, p. 40). Makinde believed that it was not analytical thought that African philosophy should model itself. He was also opposed to using a strictly traditional model, as did the ethnophilosophers. This, he believed, prevented the continuation of current explorations into contemporary philosophical issues.

He appeared hopeful that through a combination of approaches that were already available and in use (i.e., logic, analytical thought, traditional African medicine, and contributions of contemporary cultural sages), African philosophic thought might emerge that proved meaningful, and deepened the further development of African thought. If it is true that cultural circumstances determine philosophy and vice versa, then the differences that exist between pre- and postcolonial Africa and the effects of colonialism on African society, even the language and consideration of "pre" and "post" colonial, the consistency of such designations, have been influential circumstances in supporting a particular line of African philosophic thought. I believe the question regarding the existence of African philosophy would seem to answer itself. The idea of some members of a society, that other cultural groups may have philosophic thought, and they themselves do not, only reiterate the degree of struggle present in attempts at Africanist self-identification.

It is my belief that the issue of self-identification exists in a similar manner for African Americans. The evolving labels of Africanist peoples from *slave* to *African American* reflects the societal problem and issue of identification. This problem exists not only within the African American psyche but also in the larger behavioral society. Over centuries, we find that politics has resulted in increasingly positive names for the African diaspora. However, the "n" word continues to be used as a racial slur by some in America. The most recent American collective arguments of who and who cannot use the "n" word has occupied the American psyche and debates for several years now. I think there can be an internal struggle amongst African Americans who constantly strive for individual self-identification, cultural group identification, while always facing societal fluctuations controlled by race, gender, politics, and economic factors.

Akan Philosophy

In *An Essay on African Philosophical Thought* (1987), Kwame Gyekye discussed in detail the philosophical thoughts of the Akan people of Ghana. Through his writing, Gyekye responded to other African philosophers who have also written about Akan society.

Though he engaged and critiqued the work of Mbiti, Gyekye appeared more in line philosophically with Mbiti than with the previously mentioned African philosophers. Gyekye opened his discussion with a defense of traditional African thought as the necessary foundation of African philosophy. He declared the existence of an African philosophy foundation based on its tradition composed of culture, history, and language. He argued that African philosophy should not refer to the exclusive use of Western philosophical concepts and that geographical origin or conceptual tools are not the essential basis for philosophy.

Gyekye (1987) saw humanism and communalism as core African values. Through these, Africans may proceed in further development of African thought. Akan value of humanism determines its code of morality and helps to create dialogue related to concepts of truth, life, knowledge, and logic. However, Gyekye believed that Western emphasis on communalism in Africa went too far in eliminating individualism in Akan life. It was because of both communalism and individualism that Akan live at peace within their society. Each person in his or her own way expressed individualism and communalism.

Gyekye believed that one extreme or the other would create isolation, loneliness, or a fanatical group with no hope of privacy or individualism. It was the communalism, or idea of the "collective," of Africans and African Americans that has come under much European criticism. Europeans who first visited Africa and those that followed, including Levy-Bruhl, saw only the communalism of Africans and not the individualism. Communalism or collectivism was determined to be a negative aspect of African society by Western scholars. However, claiming extreme collectivism in Africa had more to do with creating an opposite to European existence. Lacking true actual knowledge of the features of communalism and individualism in African culture, European theoretical constructs were created from the most minimal *nonlived* experience concerning Africans.

The Akan theory of "being" was based on the lived experience, with a "Supreme Being" at the top. This vertical view of life encompassed God, deities, ancestors, humans and objects of nature from top to bottom. Every aspect of this vertical existence contained *sunsum*. Gyekye (1987) gave a very lengthy, detailed description of *sunsum*, stating that it was the spirit, or quality that exists in all things. As he progressed, Gyekye further detailed his definition of *sunsum* as a part of the *okra* (soul) that is also one's personality. He stated that the Akans concept of a person was dualistic and *interactionist*. There was no separation of body and soul as in the Cartesian model because both *okra* and *honam* (body) were joined together by the spirit of *sunsum*, which kept all things together.

This was important in considering the healing practices of the Akan community. "The belief in psychophysical causal interaction is the whole *asi* of spiritual and psychical reality in Akan communities" (p. 82). Thus, individuals in the community knew that they were more likely to be healed by the traditional healer than by the Western practitioner because of their spiritual belief. A sickness in the body was also a reflection of a sickness in the soul—both were treated by the traditional healer.

Gyekye (1987) gave an in-depth account of Akan proverbs and the relevance of such proverbs to Akan philosophical life. He used models from Socrates and other early Greeks to show that "fragments" (i.e., proverbs have existed and been meaningfully respected) were incorporated from other cultures and were a crucial and vital part of Akan philosophy. In this manner, Gyekye detailed Akan belief in the Supreme Being, responsibility, free will, and other concepts important to Akan society. The author pointed to the mythology and proverbs of the Akans as underpinnings in the philosophical tradition of this culture particularly concerning destiny and free will.

Like Gyekye, I believe that we can recognize our destiny from our lived experience. The author suggested that it is through individual reflection that one ascertains a direction for one's life, and this is very much tied in with free will. When we are truly experiencing free will we live active lives that are spontaneous. Living in the moment provides us with understanding the potentialities of our destiny. Repetition of behaviors, practiced in an unconscious manner, keeps us from knowing and living our destinies.

Failure to live in the moment creates an inability to discern one's destiny. Exercising free will means making the choice to practice awareness concerning one's life. This presupposes a willingness to take each lived experience on its own merit, understanding that each experience contributes to living one's destiny. These ideas then become parts of an individual's life philosophy. In turn, they are lived as aspects of the cultural group and their philosophical life point of view.

Achille Mbembe, in discussing Franz Fanon in his book, *Critique of Black Reason*, says:

> If we owe Fanon a debt, it is for the idea that in every human subject there is something indomitable and fundamentally intangible that no domination—no matter what form it takes—can eliminate, contain, or suppress, at least not completely. Fanon tried to grasp how this could be reanimated and brought back to life in a colonial context that in truth is different from ours, even if its double—institutional racism—remains our own beast. For this reason, his work represents a kind of fibrous lignite, a weapon of steel, for the oppressed in the world today. (p. 170)

Yoruba Language and Philosophy

Authors Barry Hallen and J. O. Sodipo, in *Knowledge, Belief and Witchcraft* (1986), provided an intricate and detailed description of selected Yoruba words for examination in comparison with the indeterminacy thesis of radical translation by W. V. O. Quine. This thesis held that each language has its own uniqueness and "complex theory for describing experiences that conveys its own ontology, which may be distinct from that of any other" (p. 16). Based on this, Quine argued that it is impossible to determine whether any given manual of translation is true or false. Hallen and Sodipo used Quine's thesis to explore *standing sentences*—those that derive truth value independent of current occasion—to establish the validity and applicability of universal propositions to Yoruba words. Hallen and Sodipo provided the reader with a comparison of two theories relevant to their study: coherence and correspondence theories. The former theory stated there are no basic truths that can be verified in isolation. The latter theory stated that truth "corresponds" to reality and every basic truth is reflected in our view of reality. We are constantly interacting with our environment and this interaction creates the "truth" of our present reality. The coherence theory relied on proof of its viability through comparison with and dependability on other truths.

In this way, one truth may be created or judged "truthful" because it relies on another that is considered to have the same quality of truthfulness. There was no way to establish a foundation of truth on which to build propositions.

The authors (1986) analyzed *mo*, which has been translated by anthropologists to mean "know," while *gbagbo* is translated as "believe." Hallen and Sodipo conducted interviews with *onisegun*, "masters of medicine"—not witch doctors—in Yoruba society.

The interviewers provided these interviewees with words such as *mo* and *gbagbo* and requested that they comment on the meanings of these words and provide their commentaries. Hallen and Sodipo argued in support of this interview technique, which they distinguished from the philosophical sagacity studies of Oruka. *They believed that one must align one's methodology with the tradition of the culture studied.* Since African philosophical thought proceeded from an oral tradition, the authors believed that a methodology that reflected this was essential. Hence, the decision for an interview format. The authors argued (1986) that *mo* meant first-hand knowledge rather than simply "knowledge." They went on to explain that knowing, in the sense intended by the Yoruba speaker, was inclusive of critiquing because this was a key aspect of *mo*. Non-native speakers, because of their phonetic background and their own cultural frames, missed the underlying subtle and nuance that occur when native speakers use their native language. *Gbagbo* was indicative of knowledge gained in a variety of ways. Possibilities included oral tradition as well as through formal education and daily communication with others. An important feature of *gbagbo* was that it distinguished among levels of communication—hearing, comprehension, and agreement or nonagreement with what is heard. *Mo* was direct experience of a communicative intent whereas *gbagbo* was secondary.

Descartes believed that reason was the lone determinant of "truth" (Hallen & Sodipo, 1986). He proposed that reason was the basis for all forms of knowledge. Within the Yoruba linguistic system, truth was aligned with reality for which experience must be firsthand.

Knowledge existed as an outgrowth of experience. Hallen and Sodipo did not believe that empirical methodology was appropriate for analyzing a traditional epistemological system such as the Yoruba, because such elements as symbolism, poetics, expressiveness, and the magical were overlooked.

In the second portion of their text, Hallen and Sopido (1986) analyzed the word *aje*, which in English has been defined as "witch." The authors offered a very detailed, insightful analysis of this word as considered in African society, as defined by non-Africans such as professor of comparative religions Geoffrey Parrinder, and as compared with the European concept of a witch. It is clear from their discussion and the depth of their study among the *onisegun* that the meaning of the word in describing African "witchcraft" has been superimposed on the meaning of *aje* as conceived and used by Africans. For instance, Parrinder stated (Hallen & Sodipo, 1986) that Western culture has "lost" most of its information regarding witchcraft and assumes that African society can provide that which is missing. Witchcraft, according to Parrinder, was developed from psychological diseases within the societies of Europe. He made this applicable to African society when he suggested that European witchery is the same as African witchcraft. With the input of the *onisegun*, the authors disavowed much of what Parrinder put forth in his description of "witches" in Africa. According to Hallen and Sodipo, Parrinder lacked understanding of the layered meanings contained in African words. They suggested that the personality of witches in Africa parallel so closely those of Europe because Europeans have a preconceived idea of a witch that was placed on the reality of the *aje* in African society. According to an African perspective, the *aje* may be either male or female, generally uses medicine in healing practices, and typically are not thought to be evildoers.

Hallen and Sodipo (1986) concluded their text by recommending that studies be conducted from a cross-cultural perspective rather than propositional universality and believed that it is impossible to translate another's language without "infecting" the information gained. They believed that the least amount of infection occurs when bilingualism is an option.

The authors have provided a most vital study of methodology and content for necessary cautions when performing conceptual analyzing in a language other than one's own.

In *Hermeneutics of African Philosophy* (1994), Serequeberhan argued for a hermeneutical approach in the contemplation and development of African philosophy and believed that because of the impact of European influence in pre- and postcolonial Africa, a deep involvement with and consciousness of history is crucial. This history was delineated primarily through European philosophers and African statesmen and philosophers. In referencing Senghor and Nkrumah, Serequeberhan illustrated the attitude of the former, which has promoted a reinforcement of Eurocentric superiority. Serequeberhan indicated that Nkrumah, though believing himself to be a supporter of African traditionalism and nationalism, added yet another European overlay by his support of Marxist-Leninism. Serequeberhan argued that Senghor and Nkrumah are not philosophically different. They paralleled the philosophical schools they criticized for using only "European universality" to describe or fill African needs.

Author and Psychologist Peter Onyekwere Ebigbo says "Indeed there is a psychic unity of mankind but the various languages and cultures make it imperative that an indigenization of universal knowledge be undertaken. It can only be so that people's mentality, belief systems, culture and indeed habit should be considered before a psychological test is developed, a psychotherapeutic method is formulated and even research undertaken" (Ebigbo, p. 227).

Serequeberhan's primary question (1994) was to discern what Africans were trying to free themselves from and what they were trying to establish. In response to this question, Serequeberhan reiterated that it is through recognition and adherence to the "interplay of horizon and discourse" that Africans may come to know themselves. Serequeberhan said that Descartes and modern European discourse developed in response to the advent of modern science. In quoting Zar'a Ya'qob, a 16th-century Arabic philosopher, Serequeberhan noted that it was a crisis of piety and faith that gave rise to a defense against Jesuit Christianity.

Serequeberhan argued that Africans, because of their history of colonialism and its aftermath—war, famines, poverty—can only immerse themselves in how they currently live to find the answers to their philosophical questions. This immersion must hold not only the horizon—in this case, colonialism—but also contain discourse, an examination and re-interpretation of its tradition. It is only through such a hermeneutical view that Africans will successfully develop an African philosophy that represents Africans differentiated from Eurocentric influence. Through confronting and destroying colonial and neo-colonialism influence, revealing its historical-political base, an African philosophical tradition will be re-established.

The question of freedom and the struggle for freedom continues to confront Africans as well as African Americans.

> The asceticism of crossing this way the land-sea that, unknown to you, is the planet Earth, feeling a language vanish, the word of the gods vanish, and the sealed image of even the most everyday object, of even the most familiar animal vanish. The evanescent taste of what you ate. The hounded scent of ochre earth and savannas (Edouard Glissant, *Poetics of Relation*, p. 7).

The end of the colonial period and of American slavery has not eliminated the question "What are Africanist people trying to free themselves from?" This is the third area of African philosophic thought, following identity and spirituality, that I believe requires continued discussion and development. Psychologically, many African Americans consider themselves to still be enslaved. The size of this group continues to grow, reflecting society's inability to resolve issues of individual and institutional acts of racism. In my view, it is the psychological structures of colonialism and slavery that Africans and African Americans need to dismantle. Can governmental laws eliminate the effects of slavery or the patterns of mental individual and group psychological enslavement?

I believe, as does Serequeberhan (1994), that philosophical fighting between ethnophilosophers and professional philosophers can be of value, but to what end? He said that it is a *xala* ("impotent") discussion. What does it matter? Importance must be placed on Africans and African philosophers engaged in philosophical reflection.

It defeats the purpose of Africa's future philosophy and undermines the strength of its historical positioning to dwell on differences between schools. The argument between the schools is itself caused by European influence and is another remnant of colonialism, as European-trained *rational* thinkers confront "Negro reason which is intuitive through participation" (Serequeberhan, 1994, p. 45).

George J. Sefa Dei, in his essay "Re-claiming Schooling and Higher Education in Africa" discussing an African-centered discursive framework says:

The African-centered paradigm provides a space for African peoples to interpret their own experiences on their own terms, worldviews and understandings rather than being forced through a Eurocentric lens. An African-centered perspective is about developing an African worldview. The worldview borrows from the Afrocentric perspective as a system of thought. It is shaped by the lens of Africology stressing the centrality of culture, agency, history, identity and experience. Consequently, African-centered, like Afrocentric education, stresses notion of culture, centering learners' histories, identities and experiences, focusing on the learner's agency to bring about change in personal and community lives. (*We Will Tell Our Own Story*, pp. 147–148)

Chapter 2

The Politics of African Philosophy

Survival and Identity

Africanist people are continuously viewing a horizon that reflects issues of identification, freedom, struggle, and survival. The problems that accompany these issues confront individuals as well as the communal group. The psychology of finding oneself first within the family, recognizing lineage and history, and then seeing one's individuality within the society is crucial in any psychological process. However, to reconcile European influence with Africanist values, philosophy, and identity is an ongoing issue not just for those remaining in Africa but also for the African Diaspora. A major theme of philosophic thought is group and cultural survival. I believe it is important to continuously define the word "survival." African Americans survived the Middle Passage, plantations, Reconstruction and Jim Crow. Yet, within this group, there is a sense of continued sense of enslavement and the push for survival on both an individual as well as a cultural group level. Questions remain continuously as to the nature and form of this group's survival, particularly African American men. The joining through the activities of racism and centuries of negative racial relationships, has reinforced the conscious, and I believe unconscious, connection between members of African societies and the African Diaspora. Through the centuries much was attempted through slavery to break these bonds of physical, psychic, and culture connections. However, it cannot be denied that an Africanist unconscious traveled with the diaspora and continues to live today. This joining at an unconscious level would include the necessity of looking to Africa and its foundational cultural philosophical roots for seeing and envisioning what can emerge on an egoic level through the Africanist dreamlife.

As I review the ideas expressed by various African philosophers, I consider the first major philosophical issue facing Africans to be one of identity, closely followed by intergenerational trauma that is also present in African Americans. I believe the issue of identity, and certainly trauma, is experienced by Africanist people who remained free from American slavery and even those who remained in Africa because Europeans came to Africa. First to

DOI: 10.4324/9781003219965-4

trade goods then to trade human bodies for goods. There are Africans who have the blessing of knowing their ancestors, their lineage, and their birth homes. Many African Americans are without this information. However, both Africans and African Americans share a loss of identity on some psychological level because of the nature of racial—and therefore all other types of relations, with Europeans. The identity that was created in America for newly arrived Africans was that of an "illiterate" slave. One contemporary effect of this label is the belief that African Americans are incapable of learning due to low intelligence. Is this concept radically different from that of the 18th century? Standards for intelligence and beauty as established by Europeans have always rated Africanist people at the lowest levels. Only in physical prowess were Europeans willing to grant superiority to Africans. This was for economic reasons in furthering the sale or auction of "healthy" slave bodies. Secondarily, it fit the European religious model that required an Other whose soul required salvation. Africans were likened to "beast," and creating an identity that promoted this belief was both spiritually and economically rewarding for Europeans. It is this history that Africans and African Americans continue to confront in contemporary life and that continues to make the question of identity such a powerful one for those of African ancestry.

In *The Idea of Africa* (1994), V. Y. Mudimbe conveyed to the reader an overview of various aspects of African thought inclusive of philosophy and art ("worked objects," as he defined them). He provided an in-depth discussion of the convergence of Greek and African histories, noting who followed whom in creation and imitation of philosophic thought as well as art. Mudimbe's approach was multi-faceted in reviewing Africa and what he considers to be the "idea" of Africa. His key premise was that most basic worldviews of outsiders regarding Africa and Africans were conceived and developed in the 18th century for economic gain by the Roman Papacy and the political rulers of Europe. Prior to this period, from the 14th to the 18th century, Africans, or *Aethiopians* as named by the Greeks, were treated semantically neutral without noted significance as to skin color (Aethiops, Vulcan's son, is the generic name for any dark-skinned person of intellectual status). "From the European 18th century springs a clear and strong connection between the African continent and the concept of primitiveness, and thus of savagery" (1994, p. 27).

Mudimbe (1994) identified "a static philosophical anthropology" wherein men such as Sir Walter Raleigh and Pierre Viret debated the question of the truth and validity of Genesis taken from the Bible. They believed and acknowledged that all humans derive from one man: Adam. But all men are not alike in appearance, manner of living, and other criteria established by 17th century Europe. How to reconcile such differences? Charles Darwin and the newly established historical anthropology provided the solution to what had been a moral philosophical question facing pre-18th-century thinkers.

Darwin and his followers ascertained that there was a natural order of "being" and all living things formed a link in this chain of existence. "Cultural anthropology, in its worst expressions, became then the mirror reflecting 'primitive' societies, focusing on their particular positions on the linear chain of civilizations, and, later on, as a service to colonial enterprises, analyzing the conditions for converting these societies" (1994, p. 29).

In the chapter "Symbols and the Interpretation of the African Past," Mudimbe (1994) completed a thorough and informative discussion of European philosophical and political history that was developed in the colonies of North and South America. The Roman Catholic Church held dictatorial power by the rule of confiscation and conversion through papal bulls such as *Romanus Pontifex*, laying a solid foundation for exploitation and enslavement of African peoples.

The central theme of these papacy doctrines was *terra nullius*: native peoples had no right to their land on which colonizers found them, and their "conversion" to Christianity was mandatory. This was the law of the European court and the Roman Church. Therefore, the men who sailed to "explore" non-European lands held, "from a Christian point of view, (that) to oppose the process of colonization or that of slavery could only be morally wrong" (p. 37).

In his exploration of what he terms African "worked objects" Mudimbe (1994) discussed the meaning of the word "art," especially when applied to African art. Mudimbe believed that African art had influenced well-known artists of the modern and post-modern periods without recognition of the source of inspiration for the art. "African worked objects impress upon their own society a silent discourse" (1994, p. 68). Much African art remains in ethnographic museums in foreign lands. Mudimbe recalled the initial purpose of these exportations: the enticement of European financiers to invest in the colonies, to further exploit native peoples.

Mudimbe questioned whether we can remove ourselves from the memory of this past as we view these objects, restrained, and immobilized forever behind glass. The process of *aestheticization* left the worked objects holding the values and associations of the current *owner*—the "civilized one"—rather than the *primitive*, who remained on display, captured for all time. What is the psychological influence of this on Africanist individuals and cultural groups? Is there a kind of repair happening now, is consciousness deepening as stolen art and artifacts are returned to their original, Indigenous people?

> African objects have thus had an irreplaceable role in the historical trajectory of Europe. They have not merely served as tokens of its chimerical (and often disastrous) quest for the unveiling and manifestation of truth in the world, or its desperate search for a compromise between spirit, the sensible, and matter. In almost spectral fashion, they have also served to remind Europe of the extent to which the appearance of spirit in matter (which is the proper question of art) always requires a language, another language, the language of the other, the other's arrival in language. Today, nearly everywhere in the

West, the question being asked is whether or not to restitute these objects to those entitled to them. Very few people, however, care to understand what originally justified their presence in Europe or to know what they signified in European consciousness .... After so many years with these objects present in its institutes, has Europe finally learned to come to terms with those who come from outside, and even from extremely remote places? (Achille Mbembe, *Out of the Dark Night: Essays on Decolonization* 2021, pp. 158–159).

It is through this capturing of the African in our mind's eye that Mudimbe (1994) brought us his review of the history, art, and literature of Africa. Our philosophical idea and belief of what and who Africa is has been affected and influenced by the intrusive force of European thought. The slave trade and period of colonialism had a profound effect on African culture. Though slavery had existed for centuries before, the slave system of Africans and later African Americans has resulted in one of the deeper and more paradoxical questions in philosophy. Questioning the existence of an African philosophy occurs throughout the writing of most African philosophers. An accompanying question is the appropriateness of applying European thought to the subject of African philosophy, but the broader question appears to be one of identity.

The question of identity is not only restricted to Africans. It is an existential question that confronts individuals as well as societal groups. However, the question becomes unique when asked by Africans. There is added significance because of past race relations between Africans and Europeans and the attempt by the latter to create and superimpose a European-designed identity on the former. Mudimbe (1994) reminded us that, whatever discussion African people may have regarding their philosophy or their art, European influence is present, affecting philosophical questions and the manner and form in which answers are created.

African Egyptian Philosophy

Richard Wright was the editor and author of *African Philosophy: An Introduction* (1979). The book is comprised of chapters written by African philosophers expressing various views on the merits, shortcomings, and character of African philosophy. In her essay "The Philosophical Tradition," Lanciney Keita divided African philosophy into three periods: classical, medieval, and modern. She proposed that Egypt was the birthplace of classical African philosophy and that because of this Europeans have been adamant in their claim that Egypt be considered separate and not a part of Africa. Keita wrote, "The belief that the ancient Egyptians were a non-African people is relatively recent and directly related to the period of European domination in Africa" (Wright, 1979, p. 37).

The decline of Egypt resulted from the occupation by Greece and Rome, and finally Arabs in the 7th century. The Arabic language was widely used because of trade and finance, but more important was the conveyance of Egyptian ideas, somewhat modified by Greeks, passed on to Europe and central Africa.

Keita states, "It would not be an exaggeration to argue that there is no systematic body of knowledge expounded by African thinkers today that could rightfully be labeled African philosophy" (Wright, 1979, p. 48). She claimed that the *negritude* school, a major force in African life, was a literary and poetic movement that reinforced the belief that Africa had no philosophical thought of its own. According to Keita, Africa was the first to reflect a philosophic attitude that other cultures have borrowed. The example she provided notes that English philosophers seek inspiration from the Greeks not directly from the Scandinavians, their ancestors. Although Keita believed there is no body of knowledge that is purely African philosophy, she said of African thought that it is "holistic and metaphysical." The "holistic" essence of Africa is an essential aspect of its philosophy and is the same key element found in the approach used by African healers in treating sickness, including psychological illness. Others may argue with Keita in her assertion that Africa lacks a philosophy. She did however see Egypt as a "classical" model for indicating an African philosophy that spread to other parts of the world. I believe it is relevant for Africans to lay claim to Egyptian philosophy as African philosophy. The metaphysical nature of African healing and medicine suggests a system that is alchemical. The alchemy of the Egyptians was known to have traveled to Europe in the Middle Ages and was developed there as an art form.

In *Stolen Legacy: Greek Philosophy is Stolen Egyptian Philosophy* (1992), author George. G.M. James offers a history of Egyptian philosophy, its development within the Egyptian Mysteries and its travels to others, including Greece. James says:

> Consequently, history makes it clear that the surrounding neighbours of Egypt had all become familiar with the teachings of Egyptian Mysteries many centuries before the Athenians, who in 399BC sentenced Socrates to death and subsequently caused Plato and Aristotle to flee for their lives from Athens, because philosophy was something foreign and unknown to them. For this same reason, we would expect either the Ionians or the Italians to exert their prior claim to philosophy, since it made contact with them long before it did with the Athenians, who were always its greatest enemies, until Alexander's conquest of Egypt, which provided Aristotle free access to the Library of Alexandria. (pp. 9–10)

Although Keita held that the *negritude school* reinforced the belief of a lack of an African thought system, I think it is more likely that the focus on literature and poetry deepened the African's sense of identity. When Africans were searching for a more acceptable collective cultural persona following the last period of colonialism in the 1940s, the literary movement of this period was very influential in helping Africans create among themselves another layer of self-identification. I believe it is perhaps the struggle for differentiation in this remarkable movement that is equally commendable, rather than a focus only on *negritude* actual writings. African political, economic, and psychological struggle has been a consistent fact for centuries. The struggle to survive takes precedent over all other group needs. Within the *negritude* movement was contained an essence of African thought—a search and struggle for identity.

Who Decides?

In *Foundations of African Philosophy: A Definitive Analysis of Conceptual Issues in African Thought* (1993), Gowin Sogolo began by discussing the dilemma of the African philosopher and the problem of choosing internal versus external standards on which to base African philosophical thought systems. He considered the philosopher's possible conflict, acknowledging the rules of his profession while remaining relevant to society. In deepening the discussion of his topic, Sogolo cited Hountondji and Wiredu as universalists—philosophers who practice with full awareness of the African life experience. In this, he considered that they are both following the rules of their profession. However, he noted that their style of professional philosophy might prove irrelevant to their fellow Africans.

Once again, it is the issue of using European philosophy to create an African philosophical identity. However, there is a hope developing in this area within the social sciences and beyond. Molefi Kete Asante in his essay "Telling an African Social Sciences Narrative: An Approach":

> Across the world, there is a general yearning today for these indigenous wisdoms-as if the promises of modern civilization-in contrast to the smallness and sacredness of these cultures-have been tested and found wanting. Thanks to shamanic arts and local voices from the fringes, trans-local communities are seeing a revitalization of the feminine, a reclamation of ancestral reciprocity, a valorisation of a new sense of holistic sacredness and a depathologization of profane, carnal, gooey traditions; they are seeing a recovery of our beautiful insignificance, a rejuvenation of our multidimensionality and astounding sacredness, a trouncing of boredom and a penetration of the politics of the normal .... In these shifts lie our collective hope for new landscapes-away from the messages of disciplinarity and the social sciences, into the unfettered, ever-dancing arenas of magical consciousness. (pp. 36–37)

Sogolo (1993) compared traditional versus contemporary philosophies. African societies are considered the former. Within this context, he highlighted the anthropological work of Levy-Bruhl for whom scientific objectivity was paramount. Sogolo contradicted Levy-Bruhl's theory that Africans possessed "prelogical mentality" as opposed to the superior reasoning ability of Europeans. The use of *alien* languages (English, French) used to inquire within and build African philosophy is faulty at best and may be an impossible task. In quoting Quine's theory of indeterminacy, he stated "in translating our language into an alien one or an alien language into ours we must not pretend that the original meanings are conveyed" (1993, p. 28). Sogolo reiterated that what is most essential is bilingual analysis by those fluent in both the native and alien languages. They must first translate the cultural meanings of words before a philosophical discussion may be initiated. In refuting Robin Horton's typology of traditional versus modern thought, Sogolo (1993) proposes that both African and Western cultures have a blend of magical thinking, scientific knowledge, and reflective thinking. According to Horton, in a traditional society, individuals have no "vision of alternative." They are confined to repeating past behaviors because their ideas are locked to a particular event that is very familiar.

Modern people, in this case Europeans, have a *nonmagical* attitude to words and are therefore better able to be flexible and reflective in their thinking. Sogolo questioned how value is or can be determined and by whom. For further clarification on this issue, he referred to the three ways of discriminating between traditional and modern as suggested by John Skorupski. Sogolo then proceeds to discount Skorupski's system of determination stating that all societies have both features of traditional and modern.

The categories used by anthropologists and sociologists do not reflect existing, contemporary societies. "For them [Levy-Bruhl and Durkheim] there is only one way of judging the intelligibility of any thought system and that is to see whether or not it conforms to the rules of formal logic" (1993, p. 70).

Sogolo (1993) considered Levy-Bruhl to be a very important influence in the present-day belief that Africans lack an intellectual capacity that Europeans possess. The latter promoted the idea that Africans from the beginning of life were prelogical, unscientific, and uncritical, there was/will never be a way for them to *think* themselves out of their illogical perceptions of life (and death). Sogolo made an excellent and convincing presentation of the similarities and differences between witchcraft and miracles as conceived by both Africans and Europeans in his chapter titled "Explanatory Models: The Scientific and the Non-Scientific." He noted that both miracles and *witchcraft* "violate" the laws of nature but whereas the former is considered positive and "good," the latter is always referenced as evil and "bad." He also noted that God is considered the unseen agent performing miracles. Evil forces or the devil are behind witchcraft. Sogolo suggested this is because of the strong influence of Christianity in falsely determining the value of African societal patterns and institutions. This influence has made traditional African cultural ways of healing, including dance, divination, medicine, dreamlife, aspects of "witchcraft" and evil. In spite of this circumstance, Africans and the African diaspora continued to *create*.

The suspended humanity of the slave was defined by the fact that he was condemned to reconstitute himself perpetually, to announce his radical, unsinkable desire, and to seek liberty or vengeance .... Although legally defined as movable property, slaves always remained human, despite the cruelty, degradation, and dehumanization directed at them. Through their labor in service of the master, they continued to create a world. Through gesture and speech, they wove relationships and a universe of meaning, inventing languages, religions, dances, and rituals and creating "community." Their destitution and the abjection to which they were subjected never entirely eliminated their capacity to create symbols.

By its very existence, the *community of the enslaved* constantly tore at the veil of hypocrisy and lies in which slave-owning societies clothes themselves .... To a large extent, the term "Black" is the sign of minoritization and confinement. It is an island of repose in the midst of racial oppression and objective dehumanization (*Critique of Black Reason*, p. 48).

The dreamlife happens on the individual as well as the social level, social dreaming. The philosophical beliefs that infuse the unconscious are relevant to the culture. As the discussions in this chapter would suggest, African philosophy can be divided within as well as without itself when referencing European theories. The most naturally organic underpinning of African thought evolves from the ethnophilosophy representing cultural history and present-day rituals within the society. Anything else that enters this arena, such as European ideas and ideals can only change the makeup of what is purely African. The question then becomes how to keep the purest of African cultural philosophy. It does appear to be possible because comparisons is one major interfering problem. The most pragmatic way to have an African philosophy is to have one that is/was developed by way of culture, something that did exist before the arrival of Europeans to the African continent.

In reviewing African philosophy, one notes the absence of what could be called a linear path in African philosophic thought. This is due not only to the differences that may exist between African countries but also to the overall impact of European colonialism. The philosophies that have developed are in part a reaction to the introduction of European thought and worldview in direct opposition to African traditional thought. There is, however, agreement that four separate strands of African philosophy currently exist in Africa.

Of these four philosophic strands, ethnophilosophy proposes a return to a traditional, precolonial status in recognition of a system that has merit and value. This philosophy embraces traditional African medicine, mythology, and a cultural way of being in the world that was dismissed by Europeans as illogical and without "reason." Ironically, one of the most historically recognized works of African ethnophilosophy, *Bantu Philosophy*, was written by Placide Temples, a Belgian Protestant minister. Temples' work has come under much criticism due to its obvious racial bias against the intellectual capacity of Africans. He writes,

We do not claim, of course, that the Bantu are capable of formulating a philosophical treatise, complete with an adequate vocabulary. It is our job to proceed to such a systematic development. It is we who will be able to tell them, in precise terms, what their innermost concept of being is. (1945, p. 36)

This European influence in African thought serves to add to the dissension among Africans themselves over what constitutes African philosophy and what does not. Ethnophilosophy, although it embraces all that is traditional in African life, comes under attack because many of its chief proponents are European, or Christian, or both and can support racist ideas about Africans. Ethnophilosophers are criticized for not requiring a sufficiently rigorous continuous dialog and investigation of philosophical thought. Instead, they are said to rely on history and the retelling of history through an adherence to what some view as an unchanging traditional past. Some African philosophers maintain that ethnic philosophy is the traditional philosophy that has been inherited by today's Africans through their oral tradition.

It appears that the validity of this point of view is being tested by the sagacity studies of Professor J. O. Sodipo and Dr. Barry Hallen at the University of Ife in Nigeria (Oruka, 1990). One of the arguments that persists regarding tradition is the lack of a written historical text. Oruka argues, however, that philosophic thought does not cease because it is not in a written form. He suggests that philosophical ideas and thoughts are present in the memories, stories, and oral traditions brought forward over the centuries. Within Oruka's argument, one finds a defense that is inclusive of traditional thought as well as sagacity—"serious rational discourse"—that is reflective and offers potential for deepening an Africanist consciousness as regards the interweaving of philosophy and culture.

Psychologist Peter Onyekwere Ebigbo writes of his early university studies in Europe in the essay "*Exploring Indigenous Healing Methods.*" One of his professors tells him that what he learns in his European schooling will be of little to no use for him in working with individuals of his own cultural group, and so he returns to his native Nigeria. After beginning his clinical work back at home, Ebigbo says, "The test I brought back with me such as Minnesota Multiphasic Personality Inventory, Freiburger Personality Inventory, Pauli Test of Concentration were not useful to me. I had to free myself of all tests and listened, observed and investigated with a view to learn the root of the basic problem of our people" (*We Will Tell Our Own Story*, 2017, p. 229).

Ebigbo writes of listening to his patients' voices—this becomes a return to his own cultural roots in formulating culturally sensitive psychological healing practices. This is "serious rational discourse" that is both philosophically, psychologically, and inherently organic to Africanist people.

Chapter 3

Re-Framing African Mythology

Dreaming Goddess and God

In his opening discussion of African mythology, author of *The Hero with an African Face: Mythic Wisdom of Traditional Africa* (2000), Clyde W. Ford says the following:

> But the literature on African mythology is not welcoming. Western mythologists, including the late Joseph Campbell, write sparsely and often derisively about African mythology, demoting African contributions to the level of folktales rather than including them in the ranks of the "higher mythologies" reserved for oriental and occidental cultures. Campbell, in particular, is enigmatic concerning Africa. During his lifetime, he did more than any single individual to promote popular interest in mythology, yet Africa is mentioned only rarely throughout the broad range of his scholarship. Admittedly, I have been influenced by his thoughts on mythology, even though he said little about Africa's important role. Indeed, here I have applied the universal themes he spoke of to the African myths he never bothered to explore. And I have found the results astounding and profound. (p. ix)

My writing of this book is an expression of interest in exploring the unconscious of African Americans by way of dreams, "making the unconscious conscious" in all ways that may be possible. This is particularly through a discussion of African mythology and also the archetypal, since I perceive them as being intertwined in consideration of an African unconscious. Traditional African belief is that the conscious and the unconscious are joined together in most areas of life. The dream folds and unfolds into daily life. The conscious and the unconscious affect and react upon each other. The dreams that come forward carry one to a deeper place and to deeper meanings in the wake state of life. The intent of my writing is to explore the realm of dreams of Africanist women, and through this exploration, open to dialog the images appearing in dreamlife.

DOI: 10.4324/9781003219965-5

Post-Jungian analytical psychologists have furthered the mythological work begun by Jung. This exploration of mythology serves as a foundational plank to envisioning the archetypal as a part of dreamwork.

James Hillman has expanded archetypal psychology beyond Jung's original confines of opposites into an image-dominated, polytheistic view of the psyche. The "heroic ego" no longer holds a superior place in the unconscious but is only one of many within the unconscious realm of archetypes. For some analysts, dreamwork has evolved from a one-to-one experience with a single analyst and analysand to the group setting. Though the foundation of Jung's dreamwork remains the same, contemporary practitioners may choose different means of working with dreams. Robert Bosnak uses the group as part of the therapeutic process in deepening dreamwork with participants. His work involves the use of active imagination, as did Jung's, but on a larger scale within a group context.

African dreamwork has been a structurally organic group process, especially within the context of psychological healing. Family members and community participants are expected to join in with hearing and contributing to understanding dream images, words, and locations.

This awareness too will hopefully expand our knowledge of what is known of Africanist dreamlife and free us to inquire further from a place of unbiased curiosity as we in America become more accustomed to group *social dreaming*.

Many Indigenous cultures have well-developed myths which describe the creation of their world through the dream. The opening paragraph of a book on dreams by David Coxhead and Susan Hiller (1990) begins with the myth of the Uitoto Indians of Colombia describing how the God, through dream, created the reality of earth. Later, in a discussion of "Ethnographic Traditions," the Senoi of Malaysia's dream psychology is explored. Within this community, dreams, and the understanding of dreamwork, the influence of this dreamwork on daily life and Senoi dream theory were interwoven into the structure of the lives of all community members, including children. Even though it was during the 1930s that Senoi dreamwork was first introduced to Europeans, its popularity evolved well into the 1970s with the establishment of a Jungian-Senoi Dream Institute in Berkeley, California, founded by Strephon Williams.

Artemidorus of Ephesus has been credited with being the first Greek to study and maintain an approach to dream interpretation based on his observations of 3,000 dreams. *The Oneirocritica* ("The Interpretation of Dreams," 2nd century) by Artemidorus described an analytical approach to understanding the dreams of Greek citizens. In establishing a systematic investigation of the study of dream, he created a lineage of dreamworkers who followed using his methods.

The study of the meaning of dreams has occurred in many cultures for as long as there have been dreams to study. In the earliest times as recorded in the Bible, dreams are spoken of as means to communicate with Jehovah. It appears that the study of dreams has generally been taken up by those equally interested in them because of the possible religious or spiritual experience. From the first dream myths of Indigenous people, there has been an attempt at connectedness with the Sacred through dreams. They have been explored as a means of direct contact with the Gods in Asclepian sanctuaries. Greek patients who attended the sanctuaries of Asclepius were taken through a ritual of healing which included dream incubation, ritual cleansing, and prayer. There was no dream interpretation per se, rather the actual dream of the supplicant was accepted as the answer to whatever illness or negative situation from which relief was being sought. It was left to the dreamer to understand the dream and finds its applicability to his or her situation.

Edward Tick in his text, *The Practice of Dream Healing* (2001) states,

> Epidauros was a sacred sanctuary, a place permeated by the spirit of the god. Patients were not 'treated' as in the modern sense, and physician-priests were not the principal characters in the drama of healing. Rather patients were immersed in a completed sacred ecology ... afflicted people healed themselves through their own hard-won meeting with the god. (p. 57)

A variety of Greek cultural attitudes influenced Christian life. Dreams were one of these influences. In Christian stories, it is the angel who delivers messages in dreams and appears in visions. The New Testament has many references to visions, angels, and Biblical characters responding to life's demands based on dreams. However, over time, the early influence of Greek over Christian dream acceptance deteriorated.

This change is attributed to Saint Jerome, a Christian hermit who wrote a Latin Bible from Greek and Hebrew languages. Ironically, it was reportedly due to a dream that Jerome determined that dreams were *anan*—witchcraft. Because of the power of his translated Bible and its selection as the most established and widely read Bible, it was the Christian Bible of choice through the 20th century. St. Thomas Aquinas, though he had dreams and visions, eventually followed in the steps of Saint Jerome. The Christian Reformation with its goal of eliminating beliefs in miracles and accompanying events—dreaming and visions, saw the end of the popularity of dreams and the studying of dreams.

The Purpose and Function of Mythology

Tales of Yoruba Gods and Heroes (Courlander, 1973) is a collection of stories about various Nigerian gods and goddesses. Courlander has written widely on the culture of Africans and those of African descent in the Americas. However, I will focus only on the Yoruba of Nigeria. The stories speak of the vulnerability, arrogance, and cleverness of the gods. The first god, Olorun, created the other gods who played various roles in the lives of humans. Obatala "formed" human life and was said to have given humans their bodily shape. One of the first myths presented in the text, "The Descent from the Sky," related how Obatala created people. "He dug clay from the ground, and out of the clay he shaped human figures which he then laid out to dry in the sun" (Courlander, 1973, p. 19). Growing tired and thirsty, Obatala decided to have a drink. He became drunk after a time from palm wine but returned to his task of making humans from clay. These humans were created "misshapen," but Obatala did not notice this situation at first. After creating the humans, Obatala spoke to Olorun, asking that he "give them the breath of life" (p. 20). Once sober, Obatala saw the humans who were made deformed. He committed to never drink again and to become the protector of those who were deformed. In this initial early story, we learn of Orunmila, Esu, and Agemo.

The second story, "The Orishas Acquire Their Powers" (Courlander, 1973), told of how some of the gods became resentful of having to speak to Orunmila, Olorun's spokesman, whenever they needed something. They felt that they should each have specific powers for creating whatever they desired without the intervention of Orunmila. The minds of the other orishas turned the same way. Esu, who already had the knowledge of language, went to Orunmila seeking more knowledge. Shango, Sonponno, Ilu-Igbo, and Osanyin went to Orunmila. And after them still more orishas went, all asking for a special gift of some part of Orunmila's understanding of the world and its forces (Courlander, 1973, p. 26).

In his unhappiness and distress over the dissatisfaction of the gods, Olorun sought the advice of Agemo.

> Perhaps it would be best to leave the distribution to chance. Return to the sky. Then send messengers to announce that on such and such a day you will pour the powers down on the earth. Let each orisha catch what he can or retrieve it from the place where it falls. Whatever powers an orisha collects in this way will be his. (p. 27)

Olorun considered this fair and thanked Agemo for his advice. Each myth reflects the characteristic of a god that is present in humans. In "The Quarrel between Oya and Oshun" (Courlander, 1973), jealousy is portrayed. Shango, husband of Oyo, had several wives, including Oya and Oshun. Oya was Shango's favorite because she was the best cook. As the festival cooking day approached, Oshun feeling insecure about her cooking abilities asked Oya to tell her the secret of how she prepared such meals that appealed to Shango. At first Oya felt sadness for Oshun, knowing her lack of ability, but then she thought more about it and decided against helping her. Oya told Oshun that she cut off tiny pieces of her own ear and added them to everything she cooked for Shango and that this was what made him pleased with her cooking. Taking this advice, Oshun went home to prepare Shango's soup, making certain to drop parts of her ear into it. Later, at the banquet, a guest found Oshun's ears in his soup.

Shango demanded how such a thing could have happened. Oya spoke first, saying that Oshun had put her ears in, hoping to "make it more palatable." Shango saw that Oshun lacked ears and found that Oya had ears in spite of Oshun claiming differently. Realizing that she was deceived, Oshun left Shango and traveled to the river, where she walked into the water. Oshun became the spirit of the river, and the Oshun River is named in her honor. She is the goddess of fertility for women seeking to have children.

The myths from Courlander's text (1973) convey the ways in which many of the more popular gods of Yoruba mythology came to exist, develop their powers, and interact with humans. Of significance is the dominance of myths about masculine gods as opposed to feminine goddess myths.

The 32 myths (Courlander, 1973) reveal not only the stories of Yoruba tradition, but also the teachings available to humans through the archetypal presence of the gods. I feel very similar to Eliade in my questions regarding mythology and contemporary life. How can we develop mythological thinking? Are we capable of doing this in today's world? Holloway believes it is through writing that we can remember. Eliade takes a similar position, viewing reading as that attempt to visit and live in liminal time. If the spiritual practices of our most recent ancestors are unfulfilling, how do we develop a deeper richness for them as we move further away in a linearly focused culture? How can we deepen our circular thinking of time? I believe that myths must be spoken, read, and lived in some manner to remain vital and to revitalize us. Courlander's myths appeared dry to me, lacking something. Perhaps it is the absence of the *griot* (bard). Perhaps it is the lack of descriptive richness in the author's telling. Perhaps it reflects the missing quality of the authentic mythologic. There is something that is not "lived" in my experience of these myths. Perhaps it is necessary to reflect on Holloway's concern regarding the historical text while accessing our own "lived experience." Maybe this is the most readily available solution to truly remembering the mythic and connecting with its spiritual essence.

Racial Mythological Theories

How Natives Think (1960), originally published in 1910, was written by anthropologist Lucien Levy-Bruhl. Ruth Benzel, also an anthropologist, provided the introduction to the fourth edition of the text. She wrote that she "values the substance but deplore(s) the language." She gave praise to the author's ideas about the thinking of Indigenous people.

Levy-Bruhl (1960) wrote *How Natives Think* in response to the rationalist movement of the late 19th century. Levy-Bruhl believed basic concepts and methodologies of the physical sciences applied to the study of societies.

Through his study, he sought confirmation of his belief that Indigenous people had a different way of life, which resulted from a different way of thinking, and that this way of thinking, compared to Europeans', was considered *prelogical*. The rationalist stance regarding the thinking of Indigenous people did not take this into account.

> The predominant mode of thinking in anthropology, as in the physical and biological sciences in the 19th century, was rationalistic; since primitive cultures are basically no different from us, they must think rationally as we do. If their perceptions of reality seem strange to us, it is because they are arguing from false premises and with inadequate information ... (Levy-Bruhl, 1960, p. xi)

Levy-Bruhl differed in his position. He rejected the above rationalist position statement because it emphasized only the intellectual, not the emotional aspects of Indigenous thinking. Secondly, he rejected it because it was his belief that Indigenous people were prelogical and mystical thinkers, and this was not due to faulty perceptions of reality. Levy-Bruhl did not state that Indigenous people are incapable of rational thought; rather, he said, "the totality of the experiences of primitives differs from our own; they perceive nothing in the same way we do" (Levy-Bruhl, 1960, p. xii).

The main thesis of Levy-Bruhl's theory (1960) was that Indigenous people formed a collective representation held together by a group experience of symbols.

These symbols were both internal and external. Levy-Bruhl (1960) proposed that these collective symbols included myths and rituals that determined how group members would behave.

According to Levy-Bruhl (1960), Indigenous people were controlled by their senses and emotions, not their ability to reason. Eventually, Levy-Bruhl replaced the term *prelogical* with "logic and mystical," though this in no way changed his basic belief about an African ability to reason. Levy-Bruhl is widely known within Jungian schools for his theory of *participation mystique*, which developed from his "observations" of Africans. According to Levy-Bruhl (1960), objects, beings, and phenomena can have mystic powers, virtues, and influence beyond those "normally" seen or thought. From this, he theorized that African individuals affected one another consciously as well as unconsciously in the same manner. "Myths are, in due proportion, the Biblical narrative of primitive peoples" (Levy-Bruhl, 1960, p. 332). This resulted in a continuous state of psychological and emotional merging without the possibility of individuation.

Levy-Bruhl's theories (1960) were criticized primarily on two grounds. The first was for his use and concept of the term prelogical—there was no hierarchy of thinking from prelogical to rational. Secondly, at that time in Europe, séances and spiritualism were very popular. These *mystical* practices, developed within European society, were a contradiction to his theory that Europeans were purely rational thinkers.

Levy-Bruhl (1960) believed that the myths of his time lacked vitality and that mystic elements had disappeared from his culture's myths. However, he noted that Indigenous people were still able to experience this mystic element in their myths. "In short, to the mind of the primitive, myths are both an expression of the solidarity of the social group with itself in its own epoch and in the past and with the groups of beings surrounding it and a means of maintaining and reviving this feeling of solidarity" (Levy-Bruhl, 1960, p. 332). In conclusion, Levy-Bruhl (1960) stated that due to a "primitive mentality" and the changes in myths over a period, it was impossible to interpret these myths. In a manner like Sigmund Freud's, Levy-Bruhl (1960) wrote in part to counter the influence of rationalism in European society. The latter's emphasis on finding a community of individuals whom Europeans could emulate for their "emotionalism" was readily welcomed in the early years of the 20th century. One of the most important points in Levy-Bruhl's writings was his idea of the inability of Africans to reason. This idea did not originate with Levy-Bruhl. However, it is from his work that others have developed similar or exact psychological theories. The idea that Africanist people are the primary carriers of emotions and instinct has been brought forward as a part of the *social racialized mythology* projected upon Africanist people. Levy-Bruhl found a formula for describing the thinking and feelings of Africans that was more acceptable for European society and unfortunately more destructive for Africanist people.

Levy-Bruhl's (1960) perspective on African myths primarily focused on myth as agent for "solidarity" within African communities. Partly because of this theory, Africanist individuals are considered unable to reason. I find the power and influence that this idea has had for almost a century very disturbingly powerful. Levy-Bruhl was no different than others of his time, as has been said of Jung, in formulating racial "theories" and applying them to Africanist people. However, I believe that his has been one of the most damaging in the creation of later sociological theories, especially in American society, pertaining to the humanity of Africanist people.

African Mythology Within a Diaspora Context

I believe there are several threads of spiritual practice operative among African Americans. In the last 50 years, many individuals have actively sought a closer identity and involvement with African-oriented spiritual practices. These include practitioners of Santeria, Voudou, and Yoruba. Others continue in the Protestant religion of their family and African American ancestors. Women such as Harriet Tubman and Sojourner Truth were converted to Protestantism but appeared to speak with the spirit of the Orisha.

Author Terrell Kyles in his essay "Yemonja and the Dark Waters of the Unconscious" (2021), says the following:

> The African worldview, like many indigenous worldviews, not only foregrounds the primary of spirit but also accepts the multidimensional nature of reality, not as an abstraction but as lived and experiential. In this world view the spiritual and the material are not separate, but are rather, interrelated aspects of divinity. Relatedly, the archetype of the Divine Feminine can in this way be approached as being as vast and complex as the earthly oceans we find on the material plane of existence. (*Recovering the African Feminine Divine in Literature, the Arts, and Practice*, p. 13)

Sometimes there is a questioning of unrest regarding traditional Protestantism among African Americans that is reflected in loss of membership in the traditional church by those seeking a more "charismatic," neo-Pentecostal interpretation of their faith, or Indigenous-oriented engagement. In *The Black Church in the African American Experience* (1990), Lincoln and Mamiya define this loss of membership in their chapter "Challenges to the Black Church." Factors influencing the decline include African American men who chose to become Muslim and follow the Islamic religion. A lack of church growth is attributed to the absence of young adults, primarily male, without church affiliation—the *unchurched*. A third factor is the current political and economic climate in America, which began providing support typically given within the African American church. As professional African Americans move more into the middle class, the church is viewed as less of an economic, social, and political necessity than in former times.

I have not seen studies that draw correlations between levels of discontent and a lack of connection based on specific spiritual lineages but am curious about this possibility.

Henry Louis Gates, Jr., in *The Signifying Monkey* (1988), explored Esu (or Legba), a mythological god from the Yoruba tradition. Gates defined mythology using Esu as a model. He stated that Africans did not arrive in America with a *tabula rasa* ("blank slate") but with the cultures of their heritage. Esu's survival in the New World is evidence of this transport of culture. Gates described Esu as messenger of the gods. Like Hermes, the Greek messenger god, Esu traveled between the gods and humans, living, as Gates said, with "one leg in each realm." In this way, Esu survived in countless mythologies, serving not only as messenger but also as trickster god, creating chaos and confusion. In his more spiritual function, Esu was able to "read the signs" of Ifa divination as taught to him by Ifa. Esu served as divine interpreter of the Ifa oracle, interpreting to humans for the gods.

Esu, who was sometimes known as Legba, acquired a monkey as companion when brought to the Americas during the time of slavery. This monkey appeared to have become the possessor of the "tricks" for which Esu was known in Africa. Gates (1988) noted that Esu was known for his duality. He was distinguished among the Yoruba gods for creating chaos and confusion, and for returning during the most passionate, embittered exchange to offer a rational, calming solution to a problem he himself had created. Esu was both male and female. He was an unknown factor, and always created uncertainty wherever he goes. One of his greatest powers was his ability to connect with and interpret life's events.

According to Yoruba tradition, just before birth we are given knowledge through our *ori* (head) of who we are to become. We choose the life we live. At birth we forget these choices, and Ifa divination serves to help remember one's destiny. Esu was the mythological god who served as mediator in this spiritual task. As one seeks understanding and interpretation of myth, Gates (1988) suggested that it is through Esu that one can expect to find human answers as well as divine knowledge.

Authors Allison Sellers and Joel E. Tishken say the following in their essay "The place of Esu in the Yoruba Pantheon" (2013):

> Together, Olorun, Ifa, and Esu form a divine triumvirate, assisting humans in pursuit of their destinies. In the Yoruba belief system, destinies are assigned to humans before they are born, in order to realize one's destiny, one's ancestral soul must be identified. Each person has not one but two souls, one of which is that of an ancestor that has been reincarnated within the person. Without the assistance of the Babalawo humans would not be able to discover their ancestral souls or their destinies, and therefore they could not hope to achieve them. Babalawos assist clients in discovering the proper sacrifices to make, both to the gods and one's ancestral guardian soul, and the appropriate taboos to follow. Properly adhering to sacrifice and taboo will provide one with divine blessings, grant wisdom such as which occupation to follow, and enable one to live out the full span of life that has been assigned. These three deities therefore work together to help humans achieve these ends: Olorun controls destiny, Ifa provides access to Olorun through divination, and Esu serves as the divine messenger for all the orisas, delivering the sacrifices humans have provided. (p. 47)

In further discussion of Yemonja's presence in the West, author Tyrell Kyles says: "Yemonja's breadth encompasses the western hemisphere because her enslaved worshippers bought her with them across the ocean into their new lives as chattel. In this study, the major premise is that Yemonja's divine power stayed with her children even when she had been blotted from their memories and replaced with other gods." (p. 71)

African Americans have a spiritual tradition that is strong, even though traditional African slave spiritual practices were forbidden by slaveholders. These culturally different practices were held to be demonic or heathen. In accommodating themselves to their new environment, these first American Africans incorporated the slaveholders' Christian religious beliefs into their own. Today in different parts of North America there exist communities of Ifa, a Yoruba religion of Nigeria. In Ifa, divination continues as a spiritual practice as it has for centuries. The *babalowe*, assisted by Esu and others of the Orisha, provide spiritual direction. This African religion has maintained the character of its African origin without much influence from European religion. Other religions of Africanist people such as Baptist, Pentecostal, and African Methodist Episcopal (AME) more clearly show this influence.

If it is true that we bring forward our ancestral/archetypal patterns, how might they show themselves in today's religious practices? Santeria is practiced mostly among South Americans and Cubans. What of the integrative spiritual practices of African Americans? What form do they take? How would they evolve? Where is Esu's place in contemporary Africanist spiritual practice?

Through the course of this book, reference will be made to various African myths and theories from a variety of sources. A major focus centers on the mythology of Nigeria. This selection is supported by the consistent presence of this heritage in the African diaspora residing in South America, New York, Cuba, and other islands of the Caribbean. The religions of Santeria and Voudon have a foundation based on the mythological structure of Yoruba gods and goddesses.

Much of analytical psychology has developed from the concept of archetypes. Though Jung and several of his followers made mention of Egyptian and Ethiopian mythology, there was no further exploration of African mythology. Perhaps, this is due to Jung's expressed belief that Africans had not developed sufficient "consciousness," having "one layer" less than Europeans, and were therefore necessarily excluded from his considerations. There is a contradiction, however, between Jung's negative point of view regarding Africanist consciousness, and his stated belief that race is not a factor in the realm of the archetypes.

When exploring African mythology one sees myths of creation, the origin of death, stories of the gods and the beginning of humankind. The mythology is rich with stories of human relationship with the deities. In *The Faces of the Gods* (Desmangles, 1992), the author stated, "To understand the function of the religious myths in a society, one must recognize that they are more than literary techniques for they possess a paradoxical capacity to express complex truths in everyday language, to use common words and familiar objects to reveal what is most sacred in life" (p. 61).

In *Powers of the Orishas*, Migene Gonzales-Wippler discussed the Santeria religion, noting that the Nigerian gods form a pantheon of worship. According to Karade, "Orisha is actually the combination of two Yoruba words 'ori' which is the reflective spark of human consciousness embedded in human essence and 'sha' which is the ultimate potentiality of that consciousness to enter into or assimilate itself into the divine consciousness"

(1989, p. 23). There is a great similarity between Karade's thoughts in *Handbook of Yoruba Religious Concepts* (1994) concerning the relationship between human and divine essence and Jung's belief that through, and because of psyche we are in fact able to move into a place of spiritual divinity.

Bynum, Malinowski, and Family

Edward Bruce Bynum has authored several books that discuss the Africanist experience of consciousness including dreaming. His writing takes a pioneering lead in helping develop ideas, philosophical thought that is both Africanist and universal. Bynum most often delves into discussions of connectedness within our individual bodies and always looks to extend this into showing how we are connected as a family. In his book *The Roots of Transcendence*, Bynum says, "The family's influence on health and illness is immense. Whether it be a physical illness or disease process, an emotional or behavioral problem, or that elusive somatizing or psychosomatic disorder, the reactivity of the family matrix is crucial to its outcome on many levels."

The discussions within Bynum's writing point to how what he has termed the "Family Unconscious" exists as "a matrix of shared imagery, ideation, and affect developed over time and enfolded in a holographic way into each individual member of the matrix. It is both a psychological and an energetic field capable of influence beyond the usual understanding of the constraints of space and time." This does remind one of *participation mystique* and without the negative implications of a lowered consciousness attributable to race.

The relevant importance of his writing cannot be overstated due to its uncompromising willingness to open discussions regarding Africanist thought, creating new descriptive language while including the human body and somatic psychology. Bynum's discussion of the *Family Unconscious Field* promotes an expansion of our thinking regarding how we are bound together as family over generations. It guides us to a better understanding of how our individual psychological identities are always engaged with our bodies and how this is possible with its own reality, within the family kinship circle and is not bound by chronological time.

As we look at Africanist cosmology and beliefs regards the interconnectedness of us as kin, we see how the basis for such beliefs adhere to the Africanist philosophical stance of being an aspect of Nature—as human beings.

Bronislaw Malinowski's text *Sex, Culture and Myth* (1963) was a discussion of marriage, family, and mythology within the comparative framework of European and non-European cultures. The opening section of the book deals with sex, family, and community. It reviews changes occurring in these areas since the end of World War II. Malinowski noted that the rules regarding marriage have remained consistent in most cultures. He stated that there is a "foundation" for marriage, and this determines how and why marriages occur. Included as a part of this foundation are the motives for marriage, consideration for the welfare of the children, and the expectation of community involvement in raising children. In his review of marital customs, Malinowski referred to Sigmund Freud's theory of repression and sexual taboos. Malinowski stated that he found no such repression resulting from a strong patriarchy in the societies that he himself studied. In addition, he found that unlike European society, the incest taboo was against brother and sister, not mother and son. In conclusion, Malinowski refuted Freud's libido theory but generally maintained a positive view regarding Freud's concepts of psychoanalysis and anthropology.

In Part 2 of the text, Malinowski (1963) stated that cultural anthropology must become the foundation of the social sciences. He argued for a withdrawal from the "sensationalism" of the "savage" and the exotic. He argued for what he believed to be a more scientific approach that recognizes that which is "universally human" in all societies. The focus of research must be on the economics, law, and social organizations of Indigenous people rather than on cannibalism and "primitive" marital rites. The universal approach that he sought included the domestic hearth, work in the community, and religious congregation that he said all societies create. Malinowski followed Hegel in his belief that each society has one primary dictum and that is for the survival of its culture.

Throughout the writing of this text, Malinowski (1963) supported Indigenous society and its culture. In reviewing the various areas of life in these communities, he explored and initially presented an alternative view to the dominant anthropological, psychological, and scientific beliefs of his day. Malinowski began his view of mythology from a multi-faceted approach. He provided the social context of mythology in African culture and addressed the universalities of myth that underlie African society. I appreciate this generalized view of mythology and how it affects the various levels of African culture. However, unlike Eliade, Malinowski did not see the *magic* or spiritual practices of Africans as religious, or as having significant indications for those in contemporary life. His view that mythology supported social customs and behaviors (ritual, order) is in agreement with my own. In our contemporary society, as gangs become prominent and violence more pronounced, I question the missing social order that in part is formed through participation in rituals of family life. If we require liminal time and space to connect with our "spiritual" selves and guides, how can these be found in such a technologically fast-paced culture? Malinowski's studies provided an in-depth perspective on the culture. Though I do not agree with all that he has theorized, I agree with what it allows for development of an understanding of African culture as viewed through his anthropological frame.

A key feature of the primary dictum is that there is a "genius" of a culture, a supreme idea that guides the society. Malinowski (1963) disagreed with this concept as proposed by Franz Boas and Ruth Benedict. Malinowski stated that even though he and Boas agreed regarding the need for classical anthropology, he disagreed with him that there was a hierarchical order in which European culture is civilized and at the top and non-European are considered abnormal. He believed that this concept is too close to the Nazism that had proven so destructive in the past. In a further critique, he stated that he was opposed to Benedict's theory of collectivism traits. Malinowski stated that this type of labeling makes what he calls "scientific analysis" impossible. He said that scientific study is the essence of anthropology—seeking the commonalities that exist, rather than the differences.

Malinowski (1963) applied his concepts of culture when investigating the Masai and the Eskimos. In his attempt not to seek out "strange, exotic material," he instead asked, "What are the main interests of the natives, the pivotal points of their tribal life" (1963, p. 170). His own answer was that the main interests were "food, sex, defense, and aggression." He stated that each culture was a servant for satisfying the most basic needs of the human organism. "Every culture must be analyzed in terms of economics, politics, laws/customs, education, magic and religion, recreation, traditional knowledge, technology and art" (p. 177). This analysis, according to Malinowski, must look at the structure—or architecture, as he defined it—of the family. He concluded that this family structure was the same everywhere; those cultures may appear different but actually function in very similar ways.

Malinowski (1963) said of magic in Indigenous cultures: "On the psychological side it leads to a mental integration to that optimism and confidence in the face of change which has won to man many a battle with nature or with his human foes" (p. 189). Furthermore, he saw magic as a political tool, giving power and leadership to an individual when the society was in crisis. Malinowski based his view of Indigenous peoples' "magic" not on a religious foundation but rather as part of his study of scientific anthropology whose foundation is biology and physiology working with the psychology and geography.

In the chapter "Myth as a Dramatic Development of Dogma," Malinowski (1963) stated that myth has a functional purpose: it provides a structure for determining behavior, beliefs, ritual, and social order. He did not believe that myths were for retelling the past or expressing the fantasies of the community. Malinowski reviewed previous theories of myth as put forth by Max Mueller, who stated that myth consisted of an "allegorical presentation of natural phenomena (solar mythology)"; by Andrew Lang, who believed that "savages" lacked attention and mythology was their science"; and by Robertson Smith, who in a differing opinion stated that "most dogmas have their foundation in myth." It was with this last theorist that Malinowski agreed.

Malinowski (1963) questioned the religions of Indigenous people. Did they have a religion? Did they have a science? What was their primitive religion? Giving the definitions provided by Taylor, Lang, and Frazier, Malinowski stated that religion is animism, totemism, nature worship, and ancestor cult worship. After relating a story showing the rituals performed at the death of an old man, Malinowski went on to say of animism: "the belief in the immortality of the soul, not a mere philosophic doctrine, it is the result of a deep emotional revelation.

In animism, religion standardizes the comforting, the saving belief and thus it solves the dilemma of life and death of survival and decomposition" (1963, p. 258).

Malinowski (1963) stated that Indigenous people use science and scientific thinking in daily life. He said that Europeans have "modern magic"—that is, theosophy, clairvoyance, and astrology—in the same way, that Indigenous people had rituals, taboo, and spells. However, he also stated, "Magic never undertakes to do that which primitive man can easily achieve by knowledge, manual skill, and bodily effort. The savage never digs the soil by magic, nor does he throw his spears by ritual or sail his canoes by magic" (1963, p. 261). Malinowski thought that the function of magic was to serve as an organizing force: "it brings order, rhythm and control into the practical activities" (p. 261).

Chapter 4

African Mythology and Changing Perspectives

Cultural Mythopoetic

In his discussion regarding the presence of mythological gods and goddesses in contemporary human life, Clyde Ford (2000) says:

> Most observers have applied Western standards in interpreting this unique aspect of African sacred wisdom; in other words, they see the gods and goddesses of the Yoruba pantheon as entities or forces, "beings of fact," capable of possessing those who address them through dance, song, drumming and other ritual means …. There is another approach, however, which is to view the orishas as one views all gods and goddesses in mythologically grounded cultures: as personifications of those archetypal energies that manifest in nature and within human life. Then the orishas are beheld not outside the individual but deep within; and the individual, through ritual address, possesses the gods and goddesses as a way of repossessing those essential, divine aspects of one's self. (p. 145)

In continuing his discussion of mythology, Ford offers the following comment by Jungian analyst Jean Shinoda Bolen: "And when you interpret a myth about a god (or goddess), or grasp its meaning intellectually or intuitively as bearing on your life, it can have the impact of a personal dream that illuminates a situation and your own character, or the character of someone you know." (p. 146)

As in my own readings, Ford also found that myths of the African goddess are not as frequent as one would suppose considering that Africa is the birthplace of the archetypal Mother (2000, p. 115). There is, however, a more recent move to return to the African goddesses—especially Yemonja, Oshun, and goddesses of the Yoruba pantheon. The archetypal is a most significant aspect of understanding psyche, psychology, and divinity within the human life. Today, as more individuals turn toward the interior spiritual space, writings by Africanist individuals add to our literature on the Black goddesses. In speaking of the presence of the African goddess archetypal energy

DOI: 10.4324/9781003219965-6

within a historical context, Ford refers to Victor Turner, an anthropologist, and his discussion of Ndembu initiation rites performed in the 1950s. Ford then writes of a "primordial image dwelling within us that finds expression in our feelings and actions, our beliefs and behaviors." (2000, p. 116)

Ford gives us the historical perspective on why there is an absence of writings on the African goddess:

> But the Goddess in African mythology is frequently hidden. One major reason lies in how myths of the Goddess in Africa were originally collected, recorded, and interpreted ... the earliest written accounts of orally transmitted African myths did not come from professional mythologists, anthropologists, or ethnographers; rather they were provided by missionaries, explorers, and adventurers. Almost all were men, almost all were Christian, and almost all had biases and motives through which their recording of African myths were filtered. Christian dogma predisposed them to find a Supreme Creator who was male, even when the local African account may have suggested otherwise." (2000, p. 116)

It is often with the poets where I found myself when seeking literary company. Where I can be welcomed once again, same as when I was a young child, sitting in what appeared to be a strange enormous classroom, on my first day of kindergarten. Learning how to form my first letters and to write my name. Through the tears of that first day, I must have fallen in love with writing. Of course, I did not know it that day—I only knew that I was in a strange place with women dressed in strange clothing—they were actually African American Roman Catholic nuns, who had traveled from their community in New York City to teach in my segregated Catholic grammar school. I am reminded of mythologist Christine Downing's story of her beginnings with writing and what it means to be a storyteller from a depth psychological perspective. I will share a quote here from her book *Mythopoetic Musings*:

> Ever since I discovered my writing voice in the process of working on my Goddess book, I have known how important it is to me to intertwine the person and the scholarly .... the essays on jealousy and on the feminine make explicit this conviction that a genuinely depth psychological approach—a genuinely deep engagement with any theme—will always include our very personal involvement with it. Our stories! I've been a teacher and writer but really what I have been is a storyteller. Always .... And I think I can safely tell myself I'll never stop being one. (2019)

Being a storyteller means sharing the personal and other essential pieces that touch the senses. I believe it means being alive to the phenomenological field in which you live—both culturally and collectively. I believe this is the essence of the mythopoetic and true mythmaking.

Recently, Luisah Teish, of African priestess lineage and the author of the classic book *Jambalaya* visited Pacifica Graduate Institute via Zoom, as a part of our first Diversity Day, joining with the United Nations in the celebration of our human diversity and inclusion. The words "serving in the house of the Mother" stirred something in me as I read from one of her narratives. These words meant so much to me. I believe that they touched that place in me that believes in the divinity of the Mother—not only my birth mother or grandmother but also all the mothers of my matriarchal line—going back to the very beginning.

Mother also means my archetypal mother. I have three archetypal mothers—because why not? It was on this journey of discovery of my archetypal mothers that I could truly learn to be more of service to my own biological mother. My service became an expression of the ego's need to learn how to love my mother in ways that I didn't even know existed before my analysis. My service could deepen to hold dear that which was mythological and go beyond the oftentimes limited vision of the ego in viewing my biological mother.

Jung speaks of the archetypal Mother as the first of many to follow. She is the one who welcomes us into the world even when we cannot see her presence—only feel the power of the passage of leaving the birth canal. Feeling the pain of leaving the protection and the womb of the birthing mother. Today, I can write about the myth of Mawu. When I consider my own development as a writer, a lover of mythology, I often begin with African myths first. I do this in service of my own Africanist heritage, my imagined and felt the sense belief that in the African village I *would* have been a griot, a storyteller, and a healer. I believe that my first day of school, learning to write my first letters and the trauma, *and* drama of that day—that I can now laugh about in reflection, imprinted me and guided my destiny. But the very first myths that came into my life were not those from Africa—they were from ancient Greece. I learned about Perseus before I knew Osisi, African Yoruba god of the forest. I learned of Medusa before I knew of Oshun, African goddess of beauty and love.

Those childhood days of segregation, even with Black nuns, did not often bring the teaching of what was African or Africanist within the literature. Those were the days when we had to learn that everyone in Africa was poor, and that we had to pray for them. We did not learn the political and sociological reasons for this poverty and that the need for great prayer was due to colonization and thief of African treasures in all ways possible—spirit, mind, and diamonds. However, I wish to say that what was brought forward into consciousness in those childhood days of the first learning how to read and write letters was the transmission from these early nuns/mothers that learning about everything was possible. This was the most important part of that education—that I could have an appreciation for all learning. Everything was possible. All learning was possible. This became the foundation of my childhood experiences in those first days in a segregated school in a kinder-garten class.

My life as a storyteller, someone who seeks to carry forward an Africanist lineage, gives me the freedom to read and re-tell the African myths. I can feel empowered to tell the stories that my Southern plantation great-great-great-great grandparents were forbidden to share, even with one another. However, I cannot speak of mythopoetic and the imaginal possibility and futuristic potential of an Africanist mythopoetic without remembering its transformation within the African American psyche. There are those today who wish to exclude the stories of the lived history of the African diaspora. We are not there yet. I don't know that we ever should have a time when the holocaustic event of a people should be forgotten. It is this suffering that really has brought us to today—with the survival, and the stories of those who did survive. The African Holocaust is a story that weaves together our passage, our strength, and our survival. I foresee that this 21st century will encourage the development of storytellers, mythologists in the form of film makers and writers who take the power of the myth born of Africa and create myth-making. We can see this already happening in the creation of films such as the Black Panther and just recently released *The Woman King*.

I recently read a review of this film. The review writer, an African American man was disappointed in the film because it showed the engage-ment of Africans in the slave trade.

He felt that it glorified the taking of Africans from the motherland and put them into bondage in the same way that whites had done in those days of slavery. There is power in his side of the story as there is in the fantastic, myth-making story of a black woman warrior. Nowadays, when we tell the story, when we create the story, we are going to include some of the sufferings—maybe both personal and collective. The historical suffering of slavery includes the fact that Blacks sold Blacks into slavery. This is not the whole story, *and* it is a part of the story of Africanist people. As Africanist people are we allowed to make up our own stories to include and/or exclude what we wish? Is this not a part of mythmaking? When our stories are developed 500 years from now, a thousand years from now, will we be better able to bear parts of our history that were so very painful, that showed our deep suffering? Will others?

Another recent story from the news has engaged the Mermaid myth. Another new film, a re-make of the Mermaid tale has been released. Apparently, there are many who do not like it that the main character in this film, in this mythopoetic work of art, is clearly an Africanist animated figure. I speak about these things because this is the world that I live in. My cultural lineage, my mythopoetic lineage calls me to share words. These words are not always the words that speak to the beauty of poetry or the wonderfulness of Black beauty. It can oftentimes be the words that recognize that there is the exterior self—the world that my ego endures, one influenced by identity *and* the inner landscape of the imaginal. The two are not separate but share Psyche's space.

It has been written that the African chiefs who sold "othered" kinsmen from different tribes, did not realize the suffering aboard the slave ships or the lifetime of slavery that their tribal enemies would endure generation after generation on the slave plantations. American slavery was a form that did not exist anywhere else before or since then.

I will share a poem from my manuscript: *Journey: The Door of No Return.*

The poetry from this manuscript tells the story of a young man, caught, enslaved, and brought from the African rainforest to the coast. The poems create a mixture of myth and poetry that sees into the history of the African Holocaust, the mythological and the poetic form. Ogun is the Yoruba god of war, iron, mechanics. Osisi is the god of the forest, like the mythological Green Man.

Ogun a da jo
Ogun will be the judge

In the forest
the trees stop echoing the drum
silence sits on our ears
our tongues
four days we listen
our children fuss
our wives prepare more food for Ososi
ask more of our ancestors
increase their prayers to Ogun

does he still listen?

fallen forest leaves lay in silence
prepare for the footsteps
of strangers we know will come
the elders have also fallen silent
those who choose prepare to leave
to abandon this forest land of our fathers

we move as branches
swayed by the breath of approaching death
the red sky lowers herself
trees bend
their tops touch the forest floor.

How do we make stories that speak to and for us, as African diaspora? What do *we* need?

The mythmaking that develops from our consciousness, I believe comes from the archetypal, from our mythological lineages. We create because we must. The stories that emerge from our being come forth and enter the world out of necessity. We were born to tell stories, to repeat the myths of the gods and goddesses, to let their archetypal energies flow through us. We are still on the threshold of the 21st century. When I look at the sky and see the light of stars that have long since died, I consider my own miniscule existence. Yet, with this tiny bit of humanity, I want to make an imprint as I have been imprinted by my ancestors and my known elders. What are the stories that have spoken to me, that I am archetypally pressed to tell? What have these stories given me that I needed for the deepening of my own consciousness and what am I required to share and leave for others? I believe that these are questions that emerge from the consciousness of Africanist writers of mythopoesis. These writers, such as author Gwendolyn Brooks the first Black woman author to receive the Pulitzer Prize for poetry, wrote extensively about the African American experience. I do not believe that in mythopoesis we can separate our culture from our writing. Brooks' incredible creative and imaginal poetic lineage is evidenced by all of the women writers of the Black Arts Movement that were birthed through her pioneering work. In her poem entitled "The Mother" you see the starkness of her words, the bold beginning of the very first line, makes us think about where we find ourselves today in our collective. When I say that the mythopoetic must include our culture and those artifacts, I think it must also reflect the historical as well as that which is becoming history as we live it. The first line by Gwendolyn Brooks in her poem *The Mother* speaks to how abortions never allow the woman, the future mother to forget.

Brooks ends the poem with words of how much love she has for the child (ren) she has not been able to birth into the world. The opening and ending words of this iconic poem address not only the contemporary but also the ancestral lineage of the meaning of motherhood.

What does our future hold in terms of the 21st-century mythos and poetic Mother? How can I, and others to come, best serve in the house of the Mother as Africanist writers of the mythopoetic, following in her footsteps? When I ask this question I think about our current lives and the recent decision of the Supreme Court. Serving in the house of the Mother allows me to honor women writers like Gwendolyn Brooks—hopefully both in consciousness and through my own writing. Her poem, "The Mother" was published in 1942, decades ago. Can you imagine the boldness, the vision, the mythopoetic historical foresight to be able to write such a poem in the 1940s? Who can write such a poem? I like to think that within the mythopoetic cultural frame of being an African American woman, Gwendolyn Brooks could imagine and create such a poem. I believe that her voice represents many women of those times and women born before her time. I believe her voice also is the voice of women right now.

Collectively, we are in the midst of feeling the tenderness, the vibrations of the Feminine striving to gain a stronger foothold in a collective environment that can discard that which belongs to the Mother, to the archetypal as well as the biological. Poet Brooks wrote this poem for me, for her children that she did not "get" to have, and for all the women today who struggle with the issue of abortion. This struggle as we can see is not only an internal, deeply personal one but has become a lightning rod for politics. As it always has been. Politics, religion, and mythology. Intertwined. Will it be forever? I was with someone the other day and we began to speak of what we eventually came to call the entanglement.

Are we destined to always have such a thing when we bring into our personal stories the politics of power, and the demands of a patriarchal focused on control? What is the future of our mythopoetic Feminine voice, how will it continue in its struggle against ways of attempted repression? We can look to Iran and see the burning of the hijab as women continue to free themselves from the oppression of patriarchal dominance. I have heard women's voices speaking out today that say they never thought they would have seen the repeal of *Roe versus Wade*. I guess I haven't had that much faith in the American political narrative that can *still* influence and define our collective lives. I do believe this has to do with culture of both the Feminine and my Africanist group.

When I think about the American psyche and the pseudo-myths that have risen from this place, I have learned that the mythopoetic of Africanist people and our writers must always hold onto the aspect of our story that relishes truth and understands the constant need of engagement for survival. This is an aspect of our mythological story that has merged with the cultural poesis of our existence. For now, it cannot be told any other way. Our imaginings hold forth flights of fantasy even when harkening back to the African mythological landscape. It is wonderfully represented in the story *The People Could Fly*.

This story is mythopoetic to me. It has the qualities of mythmaking: cultural aspects of Africa, the fanciful tale of magical realism—taking flight—like the gods, a historical context that reflects part of the African American life. This story is a beautiful one that embodies all the best of that which is mythopoetic, which looks to an Africanist perspective.

The Spiritual Ground upon which We Stand and Build

What happens to the writerly imagination of a black author who is at some level *always* conscious of representing one's own race, or in spite of, a race of readers that understands itself to be "universal" or race-free, color blind? How do embedded assumptions of racial (not racist) language work in the literary enterprise that hopes and sometimes claims to be "humanistic"? When in a race-conscious culture, is that lofty goal actually approximated?

These are questions posed by Toni Morrison in her book *Playing in the Dark: Whiteness and the Literary Imagination*. I find that in my own work as a Jungian analyst, I must use what Jung termed ego awareness to really look at and lean into, push against, the idea of depth psychology being that universal world where all is possible. I had to explore and find that place on the "collective unconscious" theoretical landscape that could conceive of an Africanist depth psychology. Here I could breathe and say, yes, to Jung and some of his teachings.

Because my imaginal self could find those African creation myths, imagine a Black goddess and write from the voice of an enslaved 20-year-old stolen from Africa, I could then trust somewhat in the universality of Jung's theory. When Jung came to America on one of his trips, he came to Washington, DC, to visit African American men at St. Elizabeth's Hospital, he came to prove his theory of the non-raciality of the collective unconscious. In his monthlong visit, one of the men had a dream about Xion and Jung interpreted the dream to mean that because the African American dreamer could not possibly know about the Greek myth of Xion, he *could* have a membership in the collective unconscious. What Jung did not take into consideration was the cultural lineage of the dreamer.

This was a dreamer who would have known about torture techniques and of the wheel as a physical punishment device that had been used since the Middle Ages. My point—while seeing the universality of his theory, Jung negated the cultural identity of the dreamer and his dream associations.

As I look at the writing of Africanist diaspora women poets, I include the cultural lineage from which they have passed. Some recent Jungian depth psychologists can say that culture does not matter—Jung's work is for everyone and is universal. We only have to read sections of the *Collected Works* to know that this is not *all* of what he had to say about Africanist people. It is fine to say that culture does not matter when the culture is all about one's *own* culture. It is a form of color blindness in its most ultimate existence. An aspect of sitting within the frame of Africanist writing is being able to note elements like *literary color blindness*. Culture does in fact matter. Africanist writers cannot afford to leave out segments of our experiences because this is how the stories have oftentimes been told.

The quote from Toni Morrison is referencing this fact. When Christine Downing speaks about bringing the personal and the scholarly within her writing, this is what she is referring to. Claiming ownership of one's lineage and tradition is significant for writers of any cultural group. The social history of Black writers must be included just as the mythology of African must find a space more frequently for the continuance and re-creation of a mythopoetic tradition that tells the stories and honors evolution. This remains a challenge of an Africanist mythopoetic. Referring once again to film. The Black Panther was a critical success. The Africanist mythopoetic on film. We have moved away from the 20th-century films of Tarzan where

Africans were made into "mythological" beings without the power to fly—only carry luggage on their heads on safari. This was the white man's imaginal and historical literary mythopoetic vision that became the psychological burden of Africanist people. They were the empowered published storytellers and we had to listen and see their stories about Africanist people.

Honoring the mythological foundations of your people means bringing forward the myths that have survived through the ages. Therefore I enjoy the traditional myths of the Yoruba. When I researched my own African roots, more than a third of my bloodline comes from Nigeria. This would not be surprising to me due to the movement of slaves and my ancestor's arrival at Charleston, South Carolina. Most of the slaves during those early years came from the west African coast. Following the spiritual roots of Africanist people, Voudon, Santeria, and many African American spiritual practices were enlivened and transformed amongst the African diaspora. Caribbean author Dereck Walcott says the following: "I have never separated the writing of poetry from prayer." This tells me of the power of the written word with the spiritual underpinnings that drives the consciousness of the Africanist writer. African Indigenous Spirituality was formed from the myths of the gods and goddesses.

These myths show the beliefs that inspired the philosophy of African culture. In Yoruba tradition, the Ode tells the stories of these beliefs. When one goes to the Babalawo for guidance, he looks at the destiny based on the first spiritual imprint from the ori—the head. It is from this place that the future life can be predicted and lived out in a meaningful way. The following myth shows the foundation of mythological spirituality that flows into the African oral tradition and eventually into the written work of both African and African American women writers. This poem entitled *Esu's Vision* from my manuscript *Blue Pearl Incantation* shows the joining of the spiritual with the mythological:

Esu's Vision

Crows with iridescent rich feathers
swoop in layers in front of my windshield.
Their chatter hales down like hard pellets
fallen from an August rain cloud in this October month.
I drive into furious black wings, expecting they can be swept aside,
made invisible, that they have not chosen me, only like me, are weary after
night flight across a sleeping continent.

But their black pea eyes refuse to blink.
Instead, wings push roughly against air forcing,
startling me to breathe deeper like the first time, out of the birth waters,
trying to catch that first breath of air,

On this umbilical highway each exhalation releases:
wings rise and fall to earth,
these messengers of Esu, bring divination, falling like rain,
blurring my vision in embryonic air.

Finished, they fly east to the ocean.
Sunrise reflects like water and oil on wings of charcoal.
The space behind my heart darkens, while nigredo feathers fallen to earth,
predict my mother's death.

The spiritual practices of African Americans have been documented through the generations and have taken a solid literary footing in the publications of Diaspora women. In my own journey, I have turned to writing as a form of spiritual psychological, healing, within myself and through my work with others.

Moorings

Karla Holloway's *Moorings and Metaphors* (1992) addressed African American women's literature, focusing on mythology from an Africanist perspective. In her introduction, the author defined moorings as "where behavior, art, philosophy and language unite as a cultural expression within an African-American literary tradition" (p. 1). Holloway's primary thrust was identifying the common ways of knowing and the resultant framing of language that exist in the writings of Africanist women. The author described "metaphor" as soul and as gender and goddess or ancestor. She saw a bridge between African spirituality and African American writers' call to the goddess in their writings. Holloway's stated purpose was to extend the "frames of traditional methodologies."

Three contextual perspectives of mythology include revision, remembrance, and recursion. The author discussed each perspective, noting the difference between "recovery" and "retrieval." Black women have been able to recover the soul or self-loss through colonization by writing and taking the "word" as their own. However, she said, "All that was buried in colonial Africa—language, religion, political independence, economic policy—was lost by enslaved Africans. Retrieval for Africans means an overthrow of power and a reinvestment in self-determination. For the African American, retrieval is not possible. Instead, recovery means an act of spiritual memory rather than physical possession" (Holloway, 1992, p. 20).

This appears to be the case in the traditional Yoruba yam festivals as described by authors Awolalu in *Yoruba Beliefs and Sacrificial Rites* and Velma E. Love (2012):

Awolalu cites the annual yam festival, in which farmers gather yams from the first new crop and ceremonially present them to the divinities, spirits, and ancestors as an expression of thanks for fertile soil and sustenance. This elaborate festival includes much singing, dancing and praying as all members join the oba and the chief priests in offering prayers for blessings in the coming year. (Divining *the Self: A Study in Yoruba Myth and Human Consciousness,* p. 30)

Holloway observed that Black women writers have the goddess or mother spirit at the center of most of their writings. In agreement with Holloway, I believe that African Americans can recover and hope to recover the psychological identity and resources lost through enslavement, not the physical possession to which Africans have access. The spiritual memory of which Holloway speaks reminds me of the archetypal possibilities that we all have through the spiritual memory of the unconscious. Remembering through stories and myths becomes a method of psychological renewal where a re-framing of life and identity occurs in a spontaneous way, at the will of psyche. Holloway, by using Black women writers, provided another avenue for looking at mythology, recognizing the legacy of the African oral tradition while accepting the phenomenological experiences of contemporary life. A blending of the mythic old with the new is essential not only for creating a dialectic but for moving the mythic story forward and giving it new life rituals. The act of writing and reframing of traditional stories allows for participation in an ancient African ritual.

In her essay "Yemonja/Yemoja/Yemaya Rising" (2021), author Sheila Smith McKoy, in her discussion of Black writers and music says: "Hurston's work celebrated the multiple journeys, appearances, and syncretic manifestations of the energy of the African Divine that shape Santeria, Candomblé, Lucumi, and Voodoo cultures. These belief systems are intimately tied to the adherents of Ifa whom the Orisha protected on their journeys to the new world. They are contextualized by the recognition of the spiritual realm, the calling of ancestors, and the importance of ritual process that .... are recognizable components of African-based epistemologies" (p. 59).

Holloway (1992) began her initial exploration of myth by investigating and developing her concept of remembrance. She believed that "memory is culturally inscribed .... This kind of inscription is assigned to the genre of myth" (1992, p. 24). Holloway said of myth that it is a dynamic entity that "(re)members community, connects it to the voices from which it has been severed and forces it out of the silence prescribed by a scriptocentric historicism" (p. 25). It was this mythic remembering that the author described in the writings of Gloria Naylor, Alice Walker, and Toni Morrison. Holloway stated that these writers "nurture the spoken word within their texts" (p. 26). According to Holloway, myth is a cultural memory, belonging to both the spiritual and physical worlds and is "a collective linked by story and traditions" (p. 31).

The novel *Sula* (2002) by Toni Morrison is an example of the mythic tradition as continued and remembered in the literature of the African Diaspora.

Holloway (1992) disagreed with Levi-Strauss's notion that poetry was an opposite of mythology. She perceived his stance as a traditional Western one in which mythology is separated from other linguistic forms. Clarifying her position, Holloway cited a scene from Alice Walker's story "Everyday Use" (Walker, *In Love and Trouble*, 1973) in which a quilt is both hung on the wall and used by the family. This quilt represents a merger of the past and the present, creating what Holloway defined as an "authentic life." The author found the elements of myth—metaphor, spirituality, and memory—in the systems of literature of African American women. She did not find them in individual myths of West Africa. "Myth is a linguistic mediator between spirit (the objective or perceived world) and self (the subjective or experiential world)" (p. 90).

Holloway (1992) noted that Levi-Strauss's theory of opposites differed from her own with its central reference to memory.

She stated that myths must extend beyond the limited number of actual African myths that do exist because the translations of these myths have been "bastardized." In addition, Holloway believed that Western literature has generally preserved those stories or myths that "match their own frameworks about myths" (p. 93).

Holloway (1992) argued for a careful selection of the historical filter chosen for viewing mythology, a filter that comes from within the text. Discussing author Zora Neale Hurston, Holloway said that Thurston's writings have a cyclic vision, with a circular view of time; they provide the reader with an Africanist perspective of time and its continuity before birth, through life, and after death, encouraging memory used to recollect myth.

Holloway emphasized that we cannot, because of Western biases, accept without question any historical reading or interpretation of a mythological text. Black women writers, she believed, are not biased by the majority culture. She further described mythology as "a moment when a metaphysical disturbance substantiates the physical" (1992, p. 88). The writings of Africanist women serve as both container and transformer of stories that affect spirit and matter.

"My argument is that the mythologies in Black women writers' texts are self-reflexive, and their history is the history of orator—the primary mythic source" (Holloway, 1992, p. 100). Holloway believed it was possible to bring forward to present time the myths of one's ancestral community. As far as mythologies are concerned, it is the "re-memory" that is important, not the "textual prehistory." Holloway concluded that theories of mythologies create a frame that keeps the spirit mindfully alive in a regenerative community.

Bemba Mythology

An African community that appears to have the regenerative spirit of which Holloway spoke was discussed in Kevin Maxwell's *Bemba Myth and Ritual:*

The Impact of Literacy on an Oral Culture (1983). Maxwell traced the development of oral traditions controlled by Africans to written language controlled by missionaries and colonial administrators. In an oral-aural culture such as Bemba, where so much emphasis is placed on sound, there is equal emphasis on sound-producing activities such as drumming, singing, and storytelling.

In the Bemba creation myth, black and white races initially lived together, but the whites eventually leave. Mumbi Mukasa falls from the sky and marries, producing three sons and one daughter. In his analysis of this myth, Maxwell (1983) states that the myth describes the "origins of the basic features of Bemba culture." It contains tribal geography, genealogy, and central African "mythological clichés such as incest, white magic, seeds in the hair." Through their religion, members of the society express respect for the hierarchy of its crocodile clan, observe sacred territory, and reenact "archetypal" values of the ancestors through ritual. Mumbi Mukasa, the mythological hero, joins earth and heaven and lives comfortably with animals—both the elephant (land+water) and the crocodile (land+water). He creates marriage, sex, and procreation, establishing the divinity of the matrilineage.

Maxwell (1983), in his analysis of Bemba mythology, referenced the theories of Luc De Heusch. The towers' collapse is a sign of dysfunction between heaven and earth—cosmic discontinuity. In the myth, East is cosmological and analogous to heaven, to which the Divine withdraws. Maxwell stated that the journey motif of the myth is "authentically Bemba" and that the myth discloses the destructive consequences of adultery. In this regard, it is possible to observe clearly the influence of Levi-Strauss in Maxwell's analysis of Bemba myths.

Maxwell (1983) saw a connection between ritual and myth. Both are narratives that develop an elaborate symbolic system. He quoted Eliade in stating his own position regarding ritual, which Eliade identified as the "dramatic re-enactment of myth." Symbols carry tradition and authority. Each ritual defines some element of the creation myth and in this way continuously reinforces the power of cultural or mythological symbology. Maxwell noted that there are hermeneutical differences between written description of myths and rites and their performances. In a detailed description of a female puberty rite, *cisungu*, the mythic comes alive through ritual.

The first element of the *cisungu* ritual is one of transformation. A specific pattern of time suggests preliminal separation, liminal transition, and post-liminal reincorporation, all as a part of the transformation taking place during the rite. Themes of the ritual itself include sacredness of female sexuality, centrality of matrilineal descent, honoring the traditional duty of wife and mother, and veneration of the spirits. Maxwell (1983) explored the symbols of the rite, noting that the sun signifies immortality, as does the snake.

The rites of the young women directly connect with the actions of Mukulumpe—at the sign of their first menstruation, the women run into the forest and, as Mukulumpe imprisoned his daughter, the initiates are locked in huts. In describing the oral features of *cisungu*, Maxwell identified *mbusa*, sacred pots and the sacred emblems that are hand-painted on the pots. Each initiate has a specific poem and dance that the initiate is given to memorize and recite at selected times. The tradition of honoring the elder is shown when senior women from the community take an active leadership role in the initiation rites of the young women. The word *mbusa* itself means "things handed down." During the ceremony, the sacred pots are handed down from seniors to initiates, who receive them on their heads. Each pot is decorated with seeds representing wisdom. In the ritual, the initiates' mothers sow seeds in the garden, and the girls lie down and place their heads against the seeded mounds.

In the final section, Maxwell offered his own thoughts and ideas regarding these rituals from his personal observations and implementation of the guidelines established by Levi-Strauss and earlier mythologists. According to Maxwell's research, literacy has not displaced the dominance of the oral tradition. The strength and longevity of mythology combined with religion has created a powerful force in community life surpassing the effects of written language.

Two Historical Views of Mythology: Levi-Strauss and Eliade

In a series of lectures given from 1951 to 1982, published as *Anthropology and Myth* (1987), Claude Levi-Strauss discussed his fieldwork findings, his philosophy of mythology, and a working frame for his theory of structural analysis. Levi-Strauss saw no connection between myths and dreams: "the dreams cannot be used directly to explain the myths" (1987, p. 20).

In Chapter 1, he pondered the possible continued existence of anthropology, questioning if it would continue to exist as "primitives" disappeared and cultural diversity increased.

He did not appear to anticipate this possibility with objectivity but seemed to regret this future event. In Chapter 2, Levi-Strauss reviewed totemism and stated that it was a "universal mode of thought" understood by no anthropologists. Because anthropologists bring to their subjects a different way of thinking, it is not possible for them to understand on a first-hand basis the thinking patterns of Indigenous people, which is totemism.

Levi-Strauss' expressed regret over the disappearance of the "primitive"— and therefore of anthropology—highlights Eliade's objection to Indigenous people being the subject of anthropological studies. Cultural diversity allows for claiming and exploring within one's own culture without the added biases of others attaching their own values. Levi-Strauss (1987) assumed that anthropologists were better equipped than others to understand Indigenous peoples' thinking totemism. His belief that dreams and myths have no relationship was faulty, as viewed by many Africans, for whom dreams are valued and explored with respect as an aspect of spirituality. Dreams are often considered to have a pattern recognizable as mythic and are told and discussed as ancestral stories. Levi-Strauss displayed a racial arrogance in his desire that Indigenous people remain "primitive" for the sake of his continued anthropological research, "subjects" for European investigation. In Part II, Levi-Strauss (1987) covered a variety of topics having to do with the study of mythology. He spent a great deal of time exploring and discussing parallel myths. He also discussed the idea of transformation from Nature (meat) to Culture (honey and tobacco)—his theory of "the Raw and the Cooked." He noted that through the study of these myths, one can determine a structure that is indicative of the movement within the society, and its transformation from one intimately involved with nature to one more steeped in "civilized" culture.

In the lectures, Levi-Strauss (1987) showed the geographical movement of parallel myths, and their transformation and diffusion from Canada to the Gulf of Mexico. He stated the details of the myths that remained constant, and those that changed. Astronomical codes that appeared in both North and South American myths strongly suggested to Levi-Strauss that the myths on both continents, although having minor differences, were basically the same. The consistency of numbers as determinants of calendar, character, and marital rites was also closely aligned in both North and South American myths.

In Chapter 6, Levi-Strauss (1987) indicated that through his study of myths, he was attempting to show the rules of transformation of myth, how each myth can be identified by its cultural marking, and finally that mythical fields do exist. He identified significant patterns in these parallel myths, most notably those of the *stranger* or the *other*, and the existence of *opposites*. In the final lecture and chapter of the text, Levi-Strauss reviewed previous topics of discussion and debate from the preceding 9-year period.

In the development of his theories, Carl Jung relied on the studies and ideas of men such as Levy-Bruhl and Levi-Strauss. The former's theory of participation mystique and the latter's theory of Opposites became part of Jung's theoretical foundations. In the same way that Levi-Strauss validated the existence of mythical fields, Jung asserted the same for dreams. Jung found within dreams themes of opposites, collectivism, and patterns that he labeled "archetypal."

The Structural Study of Myth and Totems (1967) by Michael Baton is a compilation of various studies of mythology by noted anthropologists and mythologists. Levi-Strauss has been selected as the only author for this discussion to provide a more detailed description of his work. Levi-Strauss's study concerned a myth of the Tsimshian Indians of British Columbia, Canada. The purpose of the study was to research various aspects of their myth—geographic, economic, sociological, and cosmological characteristics—and to compare the different versions of the myth, checking discrepancies between them. Franz Boas had collected four versions of this myth, and Levi-Strauss referred to these as he reworked the story within the frame of structural analysis.

The summary of the myth was recorded by Franz Boas in 1912. In reviewing the myth, Levi-Strauss (in Baton, 1967) stated that the essential points include the physical: the actual places named in the myth do exist and famines are usual for the area; although there is a system of matriarchy, the residence of natives is considered patriarchal; and finally, as in the myth, the natives are divided by class.

Looking at the patterns in mythology, Levi-Strauss considered the above elements significant, especially as they related to matching myths from different localities.

The myth opened with the major female character being freed through widowhood from her marital "paternal kin." Levy-Strauss (in Baton, 1967) found it significant that the story concluded with the reunion of a father and son, freed from "maternal kin." This was the first of the opposites throughout the myth that were indicated by Levy-Strauss. He saw parallel opposites in the cosmology between heaven (Asdiwal's trip to sun) and earth (when he visits with the wounded sea lion). The marriage of Asdiwal and Doe was the joining of these opposites.

Levi-Strauss (in Baton, 1967) provided his interpretation of the myth showing different figures as representative of various states. The ravine represented hunger, and the two women at the beginning of the myth were in fact hungry. Hunger is typical in the lives of the villagers, and a great deal of time is spent collecting, preparing, and storing food. However, Levi-Stares suggests that this hunger experienced by the women is also a "cosmic" hunger. He pointed out opposites in the story: the mother and daughter, the older and younger, upstream, and downstream movement, and north-south/east-west directional at the story's beginning.

Asdiwal, the myth's hero, was not following the socially acceptable path. He had been deserted by his brothers-in-law because of his behavior with their sister. They ridicule him and leave him on a reef (his name means "Crosser of Mountains"). An additional mockery occurs when he, the ruler of wild animals, is rescued from his reef by a mouse. The hero was unable to mediate the relationships with his in-laws and thus found himself in opposition to them. It is the hero's father, Hatsenas, who possesses the power to mediate for Asdiwal when the latter fails in his talk with the Sun.

Levi-Strauss (in Baton, 1967) described two major aspects of the myth: the sequence of events (chronology) and the myth's schemata. These two aspects interplay with the geographic schema of the hero's travels from east to west and south to north; the cosmological schema of below and above, which the hero cannot resolve; the sociological schema in the movement from patrilocal to maternal and the final return to patrilocal. Finally, there were the economics of famine and the successful hunt, indicating a life cycle. Levi-Strauss believed that these schemas revealed the integration of all aspects of the myth. He indicated that the structure has been sufficiently analyzed and the remaining task was to "decipher" the myth's meaning.

Levi-Strauss (in Baton, 1967) compared the Nass River and Sheena River versions of the myth. He noted that the Nass River version is "very poor." He felt that in this version the opposites, on which he put great emphasis, were weakened in the storytelling. "When a mythical schema is transmitted from one population to another and there exist differences of language, social organization or way of life, when the myth is difficult to communicate, it begins to become impoverished and confused" (p. 42).

In the movement of African mythology to the Americas, it is possible to observe the weakening of the myths that Levi-Strauss describes above. With the disruption of African cultural ways by slavery, African myths and storytelling suffered, as did other aspects of African culture that were transplanted to America. In this respect, I agree with Levi-Strauss, and in this agreement recognize Holloway's claim regarding the impossibility of reclaiming the myths in their original forms. Levi-Strauss ended his discussion of this myth by stressing the dialectical relationship that exists between myth and society.

Fifty-three Bantu myths were analyzed in Luc De Heusch's *The Drunken King or the Origin of the State* (1982). In the introduction, De Heusch stated that he was a "faithful" follower of Levi-Strauss. He applied Levi-Strauss's structural analysis of myths to the study of these African myths. "It was Levi-Strauss," he explained, "who discovered and demonstrated ... that the structure of myths, like those of mathematical groups, consists of systems of transformation ... they possess the properties of wholeness, transformation and self-regulation" (p. viii).

In the introduction, De Heusch (1982) stated that the purpose of the text was to increase understanding of African symbolic thought. Quoting Levi-Strauss, the author stated," a myth consists of the sum of its variant versions" (De Heusch, 1982, p. 4).

Indicating that it is important that there be several versions of the myth to allow for an in-depth analysis, Levi-Strauss defined *mytheme* as a "constituent element in the structure of a single myth." De Heusch defined mytheme as a theme occurring in many myths from various areas of culture.

The first chapter (1982) addressed the relationship between myth and history. It was the author's contention that through the careful study of the foundation myth of African kingdoms, one can determine the history of these kingdoms. De Heusch stated that the overt meaning of the myth is directly related to the origin of divine kingship. This myth has 12 versions, the oldest version dating from 1913.

There are two main characters in the myth of the divine king (De Heusch, 1982). Upon their relationship rests the structural framework of Levi-Strauss's interpretive model. Nkongolo is portrayed as an incestuous, cruel, and drunken king. Mbidi, the hero of the myth, is his opposite. He is handsome, has a gift for hunting, and differentiates himself by marrying outside of his kinship collective. The logic of forms, Levi-Strauss's technique, indicates that the opening and closing of a mouth is the symbol of the nature of the mythic relationship. Nkongolo's mother was killed and placed in a ditch (an opening) due to her inappropriate laughter. The author suggested that Nkongolo's opening of his mouth and laughing at Mbidi at their dinner table indicates an abandonment of nature, impending death (spiritual and physical), softness, and sterility. The name Nkongolo means "a world of holes." The opposite, indicated by Mbidi, is one of closure. The elements of this position are refinement, procreation and life, sacred power, and hardness.

Nkongolo's praise name is "master of the clans, peaceful lord of the sky." His name also means "rainbow." Nkongolo is identified with terrestrial waters and celestial fire. He embodies opposites and contradictions, including wetness and dryness, fire and water, high and low, and male and female.

The way he dies, buried halfway up to his waist in soft dirt, is indicative of failure, mid-way between heaven and earth, failing to unite the two. Geographically, Mbidi's and Nkongolo's kingdoms feature opposites: east and west, earth and sky, dry season, and wet season.

The text contains descriptive examples of the myth from the Kuba, Luba, and Lunda communities—De Heusch (1982) adhered to Levy-Strauss's requirement that there be a variety of myths for examination.

In *Myths, Dreams and Mysteries* (1967), Mircea Eliade addressed the recent recognition given to non-Western symbology and mythology that previously had been left out of what he termed the "orbit of history."

He stated that the Western world could no longer be the maker of history, with all others simply functioning as subjects. He suggested that depth psychology, which has always referenced the unconscious, must also look at psychological attitudes that may seem "strange and inferior." He also stated that depth psychology had derived meaning from giving mythic figures an "explanation." He said, "The myth defines itself ... by its own mode of being. It can only be grasped as a myth in so far as it reveals something as having been fully manifested and this manifestation is at the same time creative and exemplary, since it is the foundation of a structure of reality as well as a kind of human behaviour" (p. 14).

I find it important to understand the value of Eliade's structural view of mythology to those who lived in the past as well as to current lineage holders. His ability to see the connection between myth and ritual recognizes the purpose of these two aspects of human life.

In this recognition, Eliade makes possible the applicability of mythic rules to any ethnic group. I believe his willingness to claim the noble savage of the European psyche brings something of the projected "primitive" shadow back to its owners. Through his definition of mythology, Eliade proposed its spirituality and universality. I disagree with him that myths completely reveal our humanity and that dreams do not. I believe that both myths and dreams provide partial views of who we are in both our human and spiritual selves.

Eliade (1967) suggested a solution to man's isolation and sense of being lost in time, through reading (in which one loses time) and "remembrance of the primordial deed." I find this is not unlike Holloway's proposal of re-membering through reading. Eliade's belief that the practices of Christianity and those of the shaman and his community exist in the same lineage may be partially true.

His suggestion that revisited childhood trauma returns one to a psychologically liminal place offers possibilities for how one conceives of that space. It reminds me of the necessary rituals for entering, remembering, and emerging, knowing that one has contacted a god of healing. I believe Eliade's theoretical work reflected on present-day realities of African life and customs, and reformulated applicability to contemporary life.

Eliade (1967) listed the five key features of myth: (1) theophany—myth is a divine creation, (2) myths are neither private nor personal, but universal, (3) myths reveal mysteries, (4) myths are exemplary—the gods do, man also does, and (5) myths unveil the nature of reality. Eliade did not believe that dreams and myth are identical though they often may share the same symbols and figures. It is his belief that myths reveal the whole man, and dreams cannot.

He noted that religion also fulfills this function, bringing individuals into present reality through spiritual and personal crisis. In the section entitled "The Myths of the Modern World" (1967), Eliade asked the question, "What exactly is a myth?" His answer was that anything that opposes reality is a myth. He stated that according to "primitive man," the myth is real+sacred +repeatable and because of this is true history. Eliade asked another question: "If the myth is not just an infantile or aberrant creation of primitive humanity but is the expression of a mode of being in the world, what has become of myths in the modern world?" (p. 13). His response was that modern culture in general lacks myths. However, he noted a possible example of a modern myth in the political confrontation between Nazism and Communism. He labeled it a "pessimistic tale" that has replaced Marx's Judea-Christian tale of good versus evil.

Individuals in search of a return to primordial times have sought escape in visual entertainment and reading. It is through the latter that mythical archetypes have survived.

"Every great poet is re-making the world ... [there is] no time, no history" (Eliade, 1967, p. 20). Eliade believed that poetics and linguistic creations abolish time. Modern man, because of his ability to read books, uses this as a replacement for the oral tradition. Reading causes a break in time, allowing man to escape from the present. Eliade noted that in Indigenous societies, time and actions were sacred; there were no "leisure" activities per se. All activities were "sacraments." Eliade observed that in modern times, mythical behavior has been repressed in the psyche of the individual.

Chapter 2 was a discussion of the myth of the Noble Savage, which Eliade (1967) stated is an invention of the 16th and 17th centuries. "The myth of the

Noble Savage was but a renewal and continuation of the myth of the Golden Age; that is, of the perfection of the beginning of things" (1967, p. 41). Eliade stated that the literature regarding the Noble Savage showed a longing for Paradise. Native peoples' belief, said Eliade, was that perfection existed at the beginning of time but was now lost. Their essential task was to remember the "fall."

The next section of Eliade's text (1967) was a discussion of yogic, traditional, and psychoanalytic traditions. In comparing the three, Eliade (1967) saw a connection between the cosmological myth of the "good savage," the karmic return to the past of the Hindu, and the return to the psychological traumatic past of a childhood event that occurred in *illud tempus* ("that time"). Eliade identified within those traditions the belief that man became who he was through what occurred in *illo tempre*. Quoting Plato and the Greeks, Eliade showed through example the necessity for an *impersonal memory*. "The cure ... the solution of the problems of existence becomes possible by the remembrance of the primordial deed, of that which came to pass at the beginning" (1967, p. 51).

The final section of Eliade's text (1967) is a discussion of Paradise and how modern individuals strive for and succeed in reentering Paradise.

In the Paradise myth, humans and the gods were able to communicate directly. Heaven and earth were physically close via a central axis point. Humans were immortal, free, and had an easy rapport with animals. Relationships with the gods were positive and friendly. But since spiritual separation from the gods, humans must seek an emissary to re-establish this contact. Traditionally, this has been the shaman. In ritual, the shaman leaves the body, climbing the tree that returns to the heavens, and flies to the "Center of the World," where communication takes place with the gods. Through mystical experience, the shaman can once again experience Paradise. Eliade stated, "There is no break in continuity between the ideology of primitive mystical experience and Judeo-Christian mysticism" (1967, p. 70). Therefore, modern individuals, in the religious practice of Christianity, reenact the myth of Paradise in a manner identical to that of the Noble Savage. It is through reenactments that modern men and women attempt to live a mythological life.

Though Eliade did not appear to believe that dreams held the same possible experiences for humans as did mythology, there has historically been a connection between the two. The study of dreams has shown that there are universal patterns significantly related to mythological imagery in different cultures. Jung's work regarding universality of the collective unconscious bears truth for seeing into and having the most practical understanding of our unconscious selves. This aspect of our humanity joins with the archetypal—with the universal of patterns that exist across cultures and is supported by mythology. It is often through our dreams that we can become the heroine, the one who can see into psychic darkness and move into the egoic light of better understanding.

This in turn provides us with a greater experience of enjoying and being present for our everyday life. We cannot live as goddesses except through the human, bodily experience. We need our egos as we also require visitation from the gods—from the mythological.

The five features that Elide includes for defining a myth resonates with my idea regarding the features of dreaming: (1) theophany—myth is a divine creation, (2) myths are neither private nor personal, but universal, (3) myths reveal mysteries, (4) myths are exemplary—the gods do, man also does, and (5) myths unveil the nature of reality.

I do think that dreams have a divine element that supports developing an inner strength when the ego feels powerless and with less energy to accomplish necessary life tasks. Dreams reveal mysteries as well as the nature of reality that might go unseen by the ego's eye.

The dream has its own reality, and this can be joined by that of mythic imagery appearing in the dream. Myths are personal as well as universal as are dreams. Within an African context, the myths that exist and many times the dreams are for entire families, traditionally for the village.

The use of racially pejorative language (savage, primitive, etc.), remains a factor in reviewing and discussing the work of even those writers like Eliade who are attempting to add to the positive deepening of consciousness towards Africanist people. Still, we must continue to evolve in our thinking, writing, and considerations of raciality in language as applied to Africans and the African Diaspora offering deconstruction as often as possible.

Part II

Dreamwork Practice

Chapter 5

Analytical Psychology and Dreamwork

The Tavistock Lectures

Analytical Psychology: Its Theory and Practice (Jung, 1968) consists of five lectures given in 1936 by Carl Jung in London to an audience of medical doctors and psychotherapists. The lectures are generally known as the Tavistock Lectures. The subject matter comprises the major components of Jung's work up to that time: dream analysis, transference, and the nature of the psyche. Each lecture was followed by discussion with participants. The foundation of analytical psychology, the name Jung chose for his form of depth psychology, was the study and exploration of the collective unconscious and personal consciousness. Dreams of the unconscious are explored with a view to archetypal energies, which are often interpreted by James Hillman and archetypal psychologists in almost exclusively Greek mythological terms. The relationship of the analyst and analysand is believed to be held by the analytic framework as though it were a private world.

Jung was reluctant to put forth a theory of the unconscious and addressed this in his first lecture. His stated reason was that "whatever we have to say about the unconscious is what the unconscious mind says about it" (1968, p. 6). Jung believed that life was complicated by the fact that what is under observation (psyche) also creates the condition (means) of observation. According to Jung, one could never completely know the nature of the unconscious and that conclusions about the unconscious were to be held in an "as if" state. In comparing the conscious state with that of the unconscious, he found the former to be narrow and discontinuous whereas the latter was wide and continuous. He believed the unconscious came first in man and the reflection of the unconscious created consciousness. He further held that consciousness requires an ego to which it can refer.

I do not agree with Jung's view that indigenous people lived from a constant state of consciousness layers "below" that of Europeans. This type of racially biased perspective is like that of Levy-Bruhl, appears borrowed from him. In his attempt to prompt Europeans to see their own lack of "instinct" and to promote and gain acceptance for his idea of the archetypal, Jung used

DOI: 10.4324/9781003219965-8

the strategy of other European men of his time. He placed his theory on a continuum using Africans and other indigenous peoples as models of the lesser, undeveloped, "primitive" end of human consciousness. Jung could have used members from his own ethnic group for development of his theory. As Gyekye and others have pointed out, Europeans have their own "primitive" history to draw upon. However, as was popular during the times, Jung chose to use indigenous people for his theories. He made his position clear with this statement:

> In the collective unconscious you are the same as a man of another race, you have the same archetypes ... It does not matter that his skin is black. It matters to a certain extent, sure enough—he has probably a whole historical layer less than you. (1968, p. 51)

Jung used Africanist people to indicate the "primitive" or archaic mind showing the *lower* level of the hierarchy in terms of the "evolution of consciousness." Jung's "historical level" is equal to Levy-Bruhl's pejorative theory of "prelogical" thinking of Africans. They are words indicating intellectual and social lack and a lower stage of development of consciousness in African people.

In the second lecture, Jung discussed what he considered to be "by-products" of the unconscious. These include the personal unconscious and what he later called the "collective unconscious." At first, Jung believed that dreams were a result of heredity. He traveled to the United States and studied the dreams of fifteen African American men. One man dreamt of a figure being turned on a large wheel. Jung recognized this dream figure as that of Ixion from Greek mythology and stated that the African American dreamer would have no possible way of knowing this myth. Jung thought his belief in the collective or universal nature of dreaming was confirmed. From these and other dreams, he determined that some dreams are "collective," neither personal nor racial. This collective pattern in dreams he called archetypal. Jung, in this second lecture, defined an archetype as "archaic character containing in form as well as in meaning mythological motifs" (1968, p. 41).

The material of the collective was uncontrollable, and according to Jung, could be seen in others as projections and, when constellated in large groups, could become war.

Although Jung (1968) believed that collective material (shadow) gets projected onto individuals as well as groups, he seemed unable to see his own shadow projections onto indigenous people. He said that it is in war that the collective material becomes activated. The experience of African and, later, African American slaves, and the existence of the slavery system, indicate to me that it is not only through war that collective material is projected. The Jewish Holocaust is often used as an example of massive shadow projection.

It is my belief that the slavery system affecting Africans and African Americans is a shadow projection of the same magnitude and was an African Holocaust. Discussing complexes, Jung (1968) stated that our complexes are made up of various powerful associations. He related the dream of a 40-year-old man who came to him complaining of a feeling of mountain sickness even though he had not been climbing mountains. Jung determined that the man is ambitious and had "climbed" high in his career and life circumstance. However, the dreamer has refused to recognize how high in life he has traveled and the facts (complexes) of his youth that continued to hold him back. Jung identified the dream as one of compensation, to remind the dreamer of his former "lowly position" in life as he sought an even higher position of power and authority.

Jung (1968) stressed that his aim in dream analysis was to determine what the dream says about the complexes, not to identify what the complexes are. Quoting from the Talmud he said, "The dream is its own interpretation." The mountain dreamer, said Jung, was inferior in his feeling function; he was a thinking type. His mother was a peasant woman, uneducated. His dream indicated a need to bring the mother or anima figure into his conscious life in the decisions made about his profession. According to Jung, this would allow for more of his feelings to emerge and would help decrease the dreamer's attempted use of reason alone to resolve his problems.

In the last lecture, Jung addressed the importance of raising the personal to the impersonal (archetypal) level. "The myth or legend rises from the archetypal material which is constellated by the disease and the psychological effect consists in connecting the patient with the general human meaning of his particular situation" (1968, p. 115). Jung related the story of the Egyptian bitten by a snake who was brought to the priest for healing. The priest told the patient the story of Ra being bitten by a poisonous snake. Jung drew a parallel between this story and our need to tie our personal stories to those of the gods (myths). He noted the compensatory function in describing the dreams of Gilgamesh and Nebuchadnezzar. He stressed the importance of asking the dreamer about associations to the dream. Jung believed that dreams serve a self-regulatory function of the psyche and are unpredictable. He stated: "it is impossible to formulate a general theory of dreams" (p. 123).

During the development of dreamwork practices by Jungians, we can observe that dreams can be both personal as an aspect of the personal unconscious, as well as collective.

The selected part of dreaming Jung did not address in his writing regarding the African American dreamer was his associations. I think this shows how dreams can be "racial" in terms of culture. I do believe Jung was thinking of racial as determined only by one's ethnicity.

Since he was attempting to prove his theory of the collective, universality of unconscious patterns, it makes sense that his focus would be on that as most relevant. This too can happen as he determined by the dreamwork that he did with his patients since their dream symbols would have probably reflected their ethnicity and culture. As we have learned more about dreams and the dreamlife, we are able to draw even wider the expansive perspective that Jung first proposed regarding dreams. They can show raciality, the mythological, the archetypal, ego consciousness as well as complexes. These and more appear in the dreams during dream analysis.

Early Greek Dreamwork Practice

Healing Dream and Ritual: Ancient Incubation and Modern Psychotherapy (1967) by C. A. Meier was a study of the *incubation* motif as a means of ancient healing of body and soul and as an indication for today's psychotherapy in an analytical psychology context. According to Meier, the effectiveness of incubation is directly correlated with the importance given to the dream. The soul is allowed to speak directly and to divinate because of the incubation process.

Meier viewed religion as an ancient prototype of modern psychology. In ancient Greece, sickness was viewed as a divine condition and as a visit from the gods. "The divine affliction then contains its own diagnosis, therapy and prognosis" (1967, p. 13). The divine physician was sickness as well as remedy. Psyche both wounded and healed herself with Cupid's arrow. Said Meier, "classical man saw sickness as the effect of a divine action, which could be cured only by a god or another divine action" (p. 2).

According to Meier, Greek scientific medicine was developed along with theurgic medicine. "The inner connection between the divine sickness and the divine physician formed the core of the art of healing in the ancient world" (1967, p. 7). Hippocrates and Galen, the founders of scientific medicine, were also participants in the Cult of Asclepius. Galen was influenced by his father's dream to become a doctor; he used dreams for making patient diagnoses and most often worked under the direction of dream images.

In Meier's discussion of Epidaurus, he referred to a patient's dream (Dream I) of which he said, "The best thing he created is Epidaurus" (1967, p. 1). Meier amplified the word Epidaurus within an objective context since no subjective associations were available.

He believed that the amplification of this word would clearly show the lineage between the Greek healing cult and its focus on psyche and today's psychosomatic medicine as practiced in psychotherapy. Epidauros Hiera ("Epidaurus the Holy") dates to the 6th century BC and is a sacred enclosure. Asclepius was the major deity of worship at Epidaurus. Meier looked at the movement and development of the Asclepius cult at various cities over a period. In 291 BC, a Roman temple was established on Tiber Island that, according to Ovid, resulted from the travel of Asclepius in the form of a serpent from Epidaurus to Tiber. There are a total of 410 Asklepion Sanctuaries, almost all of which are linked in some way with Epidaurus.

Asclepius was a pre-Greek god, previously considered a demon. He was said to have both mantic and chthonic qualities. His father was Apollo, hunter, and lover of dogs. Meier reminded the reader of dogs as guides in the underworld and their association in Egypt with birth and death. The serpent with which Asclepius is identified was known for its regenerative power, keeping it free from sickness. Meier (1967) said of the genealogy of Asclepius that he appeared as part of Greek mythology, but was first a mortal physician with oracular powers, worshipped as a demon or hero. Coronis, Asclepius' mother, was pregnant with him when Apollo killed her in a rage, saving his son by Cesarean section. Chiron the centaur was assigned the task of raising Asclepius and it was from Chiron that Asclepius learned to be a healer. The prototype of healing by touch can be seen in Chiron's healing and teaching work.

Because he healed Hercules and Philoctetes, Asclepius was punished by Zeus.

Even after Hades complained that Asclepius was healing too many dead men, the latter continued to create healing miracles.

Meier (1968) believed it was important that although Asclepius went to Olympus to sit among the gods, and that he performed healing from a "higher level," Asclepius remained chthonic by curing at the local sanctuaries. Meier said that Asclepius united man and god, chthonic and Olympian, boy and man, and sun and moon. The Asclepion Sanctuaries were in remote places. Pregnant patients or those near death were kept outside the sanctuary. A rite of purification occurred before the rite of incubation and sacrifices were made during the visit to the sanctuary. The rules were strict concerning dream interpretation, and this was disallowed in the sanctuary. Everyone there was sent for by the gods. Isis sent for those she desired with a dream. It was believed that if one dreamt of Asclepius, there would always be a cure. Anyone cured was required to record the curative dream. The offering of thanks was typically a fowl.

In the epilogue of the text, Meier traced the history of dream in Greece, from the ancients as a religious experience, through Aristotle to the Stoics who were the first to classify dreams according to sources: god, demon, or soul's activity. Heraclitus believed that dreaming moved one into a mythological world with cosmological happenings. Writing in the 5th century, Hippocrates "thinks the soul can perceive the causes of illness in images during sleep" (1967, p. 116). Meier wrote that Hippocrates believed the health of the dreamer is reflected in his dreams.

Classical Jungian Dreamwork Practice

The text of *Way of the Dream: Conversations on Jungian Dream Interpretation* (Boas, 1994) is from a film of the same title.

It has a question-and-answer format, in which Dr. Marie-Louise von Franz responds to questions from Fraser Boas about dreaming and dream theory. The book included the dreams of several individuals that were interpreted by von Franz.

In the opening introduction to the text, von Franz (Boas, 1994) stated that it is a Godhead—Nature—"who makes up the dream" or creates dreaming. It is because of the psyche giving direction to ego consciousness that the latter is supported in its conscious development. Von Franz said that a "superior intelligence" inside us gives us guidance via dreams. However, she also noted that there should be a balance between the dreamworld and one's "actual life."

Part 3 of the text (Boas, 1994) provided descriptions and definitions of Jungian psychology. Von Franz said that Jung drew a map of the human psyche. In defining the unconscious, she said that Jung used that word because it means "nothing"—"a mystery" (Boas, 1994, p. 21). Of the complexes she said that they are motors of the psyche; she also called them energy centers of the psyche. In her discussion of the shadow, she used Don Quixote (ego) and Sancho Panza (shadow) to illustrate what she describes as the inferior side of oneself. She further described the anima, animus, and the self. Of the self she said it was the "divine center of the psyche which we have to explore all our lifetime." She further added, "The dreams are the letters which the Self writes to us every night" (Boas, 1994, p. 27). The neurotic symptoms that one experiences, according to von Franz, come from being disconnected from the unconscious, thereby creating anxiety. Dreams show behavioral, emotional, and psychological patterns in life. She stated that in the first half of life, the dreams are about adaptation to life, and in the second half they are about the development of wisdom and insight.

The structure of the dream requires that the approach to understanding them be what von Franz referred to as scientific and an art form (Boas, 1994). It is through experience, feelings, and intuition that one can learn what dreams are saying. The dream is a dramatic structure consisting of introduction, peripeteia, and lysis.

According to von Franz, 85% of all dream motifs are subjective, and so she recommended interpreting the dreams from this approach, always with the associations of the patient. She added that when dreams are interpreted correctly, the patient agrees. She said, "Analysis is educating people to be able to hear their inner voices and follow it with the help of dreams" (1994, p. 41).

Part 3 of the text, "Dreams of our Culture," reviewed the Judeo-Christian perspective on the history of dreams. Von Franz (Boas, 1994) used the biblical dream of Jacob's ladder for illustration. She spoke of the sacredness of certain locations, such as mountain tops for upper deities and underground for lower deities. The stone upon which Jacob rested his head to sleep was said by von Franz to be considered sacred. When questioned by Boa regarding the appearance of angels in Joseph's dream, von Franz said that they personified "intelligent help from beyond." She said that Jacob's dream predicted his destiny as a leader and showed his own lack of concern regarding his social importance. Dreams show what is possible, and what may be necessary for life activities.

Von Franz (Boas, 1994) discussed masculine psychology in Part 4 of the text. Included in this section is a rather detailed analysis of the shadow. She related the dream of a 13-year-old boy who dreamed of himself as an eagle who defecates on the head of his friend. This is a friend of whom he is very envious. Von Franz gave the literary example of Dr. Jekyll and Mr. Hyde, noting that in that story the positive is exposed and the negative is hidden.

Von Franz said that we are most likely to see our shadow when we are tired or under pressure. She cited ways in which the shadow may appear. The shadow is likely to be present in the case of police and criminals, for example, where the former is fighting their own shadow projected onto the latter. Anger at another's defects may be shadow material.

In her discussion of female psychology, von Franz (Boas, 1994) referenced the good mother as well as the devouring, dragon mother. She gave an example of this bad mother: a man dreams of meeting a Brazilian female vampire who desires to have sex with him. The dreamer fears that having sex with her will cause his death. Von Franz interpreted the dream as the man's failure to integrate his own sexuality.

This was illustrated by his anima figure attacking him and attempting to suck his blood, indicating that he is dead to his own life force. Von Franz said this nightmare was a call for the dreamer to awaken to what she considered to be "an urgent problem." Masculine fantasies of women as either virgins or "whores" reveal a split that keeps men from experiencing their own authentic selves. It was fairly common in early Jungian dreamwork to have any dream Black or Africanist figure be representative of some aspect of the Shadow.

Von Franz said that women wrongly accuse men of stealing their identities. She said this is projection because "We have no goddess to worship" (Boas, 1994, p. 36). In the "Hanged Man" chapter, she showed the development of the animus via three different dreams. In a dream, a negative animus separated the woman from her femininity. When this happened, she became a trapped victim. Von Franz added that the relationship with the father greatly influences a woman's relationship with men in later life.

In the final section of the text, Part 7, von Franz looked at the self and the changing nature of dreams that move in accordance with one's life transitions. "Now all dreams point out to the individual the unique meaning of his or her unique life. That is perhaps the most important feature of dream life" (Boas, 1994, p. 211). I believe this is the important uniqueness of Von Franz's information regarding dreams. In many African cultures, dreams are held to be signposts for direction in life. In analytical psychology, the analysand shares and obtains interpretation from the analyst. In Africa, the patient receives guidance regarding dreams from the diviner or traditional healer. The significance lies with a particular individual and his or her particular dream. Although there are, as in every culture, standard meanings (signs) for dreams, in Africa dreams are also interpreted specifically to the dreamer.

James Hall's text, *Jungian Dream Interpretation: A Handbook of Theory and Practice* (1983), consisted of 11 short chapters with a detailed discussion of dreams. In Chapter 1, he presented the basic concepts of Jungian psychology.

He wrote that there is a topographical division between the conscious and the unconscious. According to Hall, the unconscious contains both the personal unconscious and the objective psyche. The four levels of consciousness included are personal conscious (ordinary awareness), personal unconscious, objective psyche (collective unconscious), and collective consciousness (cultural world of shared values). Hall listed the parts of the psyche: ego, persona, shadow, anima, and animus.

In defining complexes Hall said, "Complexes are groupings of related images held together by a common emotional tone" (1983, p. 7). He added, "Complexes are the basic contents of the personal unconscious" (p. 9). Hall described how Jung developed his theory of complexes using the Word Association Test. Discussing the archetype, Hall said it can create certain images but are not the images themselves. He said that the principles are the archetypes, and the form is the archetypal image.

Archetypes are believed to have a more "universal" meaning than complexes; complexes tended to be personal, developing out of personal life experiences. "Archetypal images that are meaningful to a large number of persons over an extended period of time tend to be embedded culturally in collective consciousness" (Hall, 1983, p. 11). Examples that Hall gave included the Virgin Mary, Buddha, and Jesus Christ.

Hall (1983) stated that the Self is the regulating center of the psyche. It is the Self that is the archetypal basis for ego. He said that at times the ego might experience numinosity when having an experience of the Self. Hall equated the Self with God. He added that the deeper levels of the psyche were experienced in dreaming and psychotic episodes. It was through active imagination that one was able to connect with deeper levels while in the awakened state.

Hall believed that through analysis and deepening this therapeutic process, one can reach the underlying archetypal layers. "It is often only in analysis, in dreams, or in very moving emotional experiences that the developed ego can experience the true archetypal foundations of the complexes" (1983, p. 13). There should be a healing connection between the personal and objective psyche. The psychological structures and relationships that help bridge this healing are the ego or shadow and persona or anima-animus.

Hall said of the shadow: "The tendencies and impulses which are rejected by the family are not simply lost, they tend to cluster as an alter ego image just below the surface of the personal unconscious" (p. 15). This shadow is usually projected upon someone we dislike.

Hall said that a healthy ego can adapt the persona to meet a variety of social needs. This persona (derived from the Greek word meaning "mask") enables one to interact with others in a social manner.

When the persona is overdeveloped or underdeveloped, the individuation process suffers. A balanced persona accommodates a process that allows for a realization of the "deeper potentialities" of psyche.

In Chapter 2, Hall discussed the nature of dreaming. "In the Jungian view, dreams are continually functioning to compensate and complement (a milder form of compensation) the ego's waking view of reality" (1983, p. 25). Hall likened dreaming to a psychic function that also serves a regulatory need. The dream is never exhausted in terms of being examined for meaning and applicability. Hall stated that the purpose of clinical dreamwork is to lend support to the ego as it develops and moves in a process of individuation.

I am in partial agreement with Hall's statement regarding the purpose of dreamwork. I do, however, believe that there is an imaginal place in psyche that is not only about the work of ego development but is also about other life functioning. These include creativity, pleasure, and so forth, and provide other avenues for exploration in conscious life.

Hall outlined the key features of his approach to Jungian dreamwork and the use of what he terms a "peeling" process to working with the three layers of the complex. The first level of peeling is seeing the associations and images of the dream. The second level contains cultural and transpersonal images, and the third peeling reveals the archetypal level. It is important to recall throughout this process that "the dream must be read against the context of the dreamer's current life" (1983, p. 36).

Dreams are used in diagnostic and prognostic ways, especially the initial dreams that occur at the beginning of analysis. Early dreams often show the outcome of the therapy. Hall said that dreams are also able to help in the case of a differential diagnosis. Hall provided an example of an individual who is depressed and unable to express his anger. In the patient's dream, the dream ego experienced aggression directed at it by another dream figure. This indicated the need for the dreamer to develop a stronger, more assertive ego in his awake state.

In his chapter on transference and countertransference, Hall stated that the main responsibility of the analyst is to "maintain a transformative field" (1983, p. 54). Occasions when stress may occur in the field include the patient identifying the analyst with a dream figure or when the patient appears in the analyst's dream. Hall said that the *temenos* must be secure and safe for dreamwork to be effective for the analyst and the patient.

Further dream areas explored by Hall (1983) included common dream motifs, symbolism in alchemy as related to dreams, and dreams as part of the individuation process. Throughout the text, he continuously reminded the reader that the dream must always be held within the context of the dreamer's life associations. He stressed that the strength of the ego is always relative to the development of the individuation process and that dreams are in service of the ego. He concluded his text by stating the two tensions he considered present in dreamwork: (1) the objective versus subjective interpretation of dreams, and (2) the personal versus the archetypal meanings of dreams.

Dreams: A Portal to the Source (1991) is written primarily for psychotherapy trainees working in dreamwork analysis. The authors, Sylvia Perera and Christopher Whitmont, believed it was important to have a "multifaceted approach" to the analysis of dreams that included many different perspectives beyond those of simple opposites. The authors suggested the need for an "integrative consciousness." The approach of "integrative consciousness" that these authors suggest parallels my own belief regarding the structural frame of dreamwork. The movement away from a theory of opposites as an anchoring point in dreamwork allows for varying possibilities of meaning from dream imagery. The movement from opposites decreases the conscious need to create an Other for purposes of projection. The theme of dreamwork as both art and craft is from the lineage of Von Franz. I believe that both are essential in doing work that is of value to the patient. Hall's stance on dreams being mostly in service of the ego can work with the potentially artistic quality of dreamwork. Dreams come as complementary material, emphasizing situations that are going well or show more creative ways to enhance life's activities. I believe that Perera and Whitmont's suggestion of creative play in amplifying dreamwork mirrors a creative, open approach to understanding and implementing dream messages.

Throughout the text (1991), the authors reminded the reader that dreamwork requires both art and skill. The same characteristics present in understanding and creating art are present in the dream: sensitivity to content, character development, rhythms of events, and emotional tone. Rational thought is secondary, compared with the above characteristics, according to Perera and Whitmont.

"Thus in clinical practice each dream offers diagnoses, prognosis and appropriate material and timing to address the dreamer's current psychological reality and compensate the dreamer's and/or analyst's blind spots of consciousness," concluded Perera and Whitmont (1991, p. 7). The authors believed that it is essential for the analyst to work with the patient in interpreting her dreams. This work means that the analyst must have sufficient insight to allow for assimilation of dream material at the appropriate time.

The authors stated that when there is resistance on the patient's part, then the analyst has chosen an approach that is incorrect or inappropriate at the time. When the patient is unable to work with symbolic images, the authors suggested the use of creative play—art, sandplay, and so forth. The dream reflects the unconscious in its true state.

The authors' believed that it also was possible to trace the dream ego's position and draw parallel lines of development in terms of understanding the direction of the psychological work that will follow. The language of the dream is given in images that may be visual, auditory, kinesthetic, or proprioceptive. The images can be either symbolic or allegoric. To see the symbology of the dream, one must have a feeling-intuitive sense.

"The meanings and implications of the various dream motifs are never fixed," said Perera and Whitmont (1991, p. 34). It is necessary, according to the authors, to have the patient relate any associative material before interpretations are attempted. These subjective associations help to establish the accuracy of any interpretation; they "ground" the image in "current psychological reality." The authors stated the effect of targeting the correct associations: "only when an affect is touched may we assume that the essential core of psychological reality including ... complex ... has been reached experientially" (p. 37). Through a patient's bodily response in the session and in the dream, the analyst can gain insight for validating a particular interpretation. In attempting to amplify dream motifs, the authors cautioned that there must be a match between the generally mythological material and the dreamer's "life problems and patterns."

James Hall was a practitioner of classical Jungian theory of dream compensation. Perera and Whitmont further developed the classical approach of compensation theory. They believed dreams are not for the sole purpose of completing the ego's failures or desires. Compensation highlights opposites. When dream images are viewed as a complement rather than compensation, it is more possible to accept the wide variety of dreams that appear. Prospective, oracular, and parallel are a few possible complementary perspectives mentioned by Perera and Whitmont (1991).

Perera and Whitmont provided a detailed description of the significance of dreams by patients and analysts discussing transference issues that may occur. Examples were given of different dreams and how these dreams reflected and affected the therapeutic process through dream figures or through archetypal or complex material.

Chapter 6

Traditional African Healing Practice

Dreamwork

Traditional African Healing

Author Peter Onyekwere Ebigo has documented his Nigerian clinical practice work in the article "Exploring Indigenous Healing Methods: A Personal Account" (2017). After his initial training in Europe, he returned to his homeland to begin as a clinical psychologist with individuals of his own cultural group. He found many elements of his practice that he felt were culture-bound in terms of patient care. He also noticed that the geographical location of his patients supported their philosophical beliefs regarding their physical health and well-being. In his comments regarding those patients who have grown up in villages but have left them to live a city existence, Ebigo notes their beliefs regarding the connection between the traditional healer methods that acknowledged "gods, spirits and human beings" (p. 233).

Egibo notes the relationship between hypnosis and his work with patients: "Psychoanalysis or behavior therapy is foreign to Nigerians. Because however, most people can easily be influenced and they already know about dream interpretation from traditional healers, the experienced clinical psychologist will try hypnosis at the first meeting. If he succeeds in hypnotizing the patient, the patient will be ready to believe in him and give up tablets and injections. I made the experience that one has to speak with the patient before and after hypnosis to clear doubts and questions. Some will otherwise call the hypnotist a magician" (p. 235).

The writing that Ebigo shares with us speaks to his incorporation of traditional healing with a Eurocentric training in psychoanalysis. He uses writing within the practice, giving patients an avenue for self-expression in their psychological healing. Ebigo says:

> I let my patients also to write essays. The topics are the persons' autobiography, "the story of my life" or "my present situation", or "the story of my mental illness." I use them to try to awaken consciousness of their own problems. Later the essays are read back to the patients in katathymic state for the purpose of re-experience. We exploit therapeutically the

DOI: 10.4324/9781003219965-9

ability for fantasy and imagination of Nigerians, as well as their readiness to subjugate themselves to inexplicable things, to accept interpretations of symbols and images. After reading the written topics we animate the patients to bring forward remembrances, experiences, fears and hopes, real and unreal possibilities of solving the problems. The therapist understands and interprets the produced materials. (p. 237)

The patients' experiences also centered on dreamwork within Ebigo's clinical practice. He describes two dream studies that he completed with patients at the Neuropsychiatric Hospital. The author says that his study found basically two types of dreams—"fearful dreams and dreams of a sexual nature" amongst the dreamers. In the second dream study, students from the University of Nigeria Enugu Campus had their dream content collected and interpreted. Regarding the results: "The 74 dreams reveal that the Nigerians in this study are very much preoccupied with family and natural phenomenon. Many of them believe that dreams can forecast events" (p. 246).

John Janzen stated that his text, *Ngoma: Discourses in Healing in Central and Southern Africa* (1992), was an attempt to create a more popularly acceptable concept and view of the healing communities, or *ngoma* rituals, that existed in southern and central Africa. These communities, named "cults of affliction" by anthropologist Victor Turner, were distinguished in African communities not only for their therapeutic effect but also as socializing elements. They provided support and emotional comfort in times of physical and psychological difficulty. *Ngoma*, defined as "drum," signified the presence of drumming and dancing in the ritualistic ceremonies conducted under the direction of a traditional healer.

Janzen provided a detailed and rich written report of the nuances of the ngoma. In doing so, he pointed to the historical and contemporary nature of the ngoma. Reviewing the status of medicine in Africa, he strongly suggested recognition of the ngoma as an established institution. He believed this would greatly support the development of social agencies for the care of sick individuals. He noted that ngomas thrive in African communities and should be supported in a broad manner for the social, psychological, and physical well-being of Africans.

In his opening chapter, Janzen (1992) takes the reader to the four geographical areas he selected for his research on the ngoma communities. These were comprised Kinshasa (Zaire), Dar es Salaam (Tanzania), Mbabane-Manzini (Swaziland), and Cape Town, South Africa. These areas were chosen because they differ from each other in language and in general social custom. Janzen detailed his meetings with healers. He described their work with patients and his own personal experience of ngoma work with several of these healers. For example, in the city of Kinshasa, he met with a healer who was of the *nkita* lineage. Nkita defined not only the lineage, but also the name of the illness, the spirit behind the illness, and the therapeutic rite to be performed for healing. Janzen spoke of the signs of illness particular to the patients seeing this healer: psychological distress, disturbing dreams, fever, childhood disease, and female infertility. The patients' illnesses became areas of specialty for the healer. The initial healing ceremony took place at a river.

An important element of the ngoma is that in many respects it serves as an initiation to become novices and eventually healers within a healing community. The sickness or illness experienced by individuals is often considered to be a spiritual calling to become a healer. However, it can also be a sickness brought on by magic or due to disrespect for the ancestors. The nature of the illness and its origin is determined by the healer, who provides guidance about the healing solution.

Another important feature of ngoma is that this tradition, which began in the rural areas of Africa, is now common in urban life. Janzen (1992) noted that the negative side of this is the dominance of charlatans preying on lonely, sick people who have moved to urban areas due to poverty and stressful circumstances in their homelands. However, he said that the more positive side is the considerable exchange of healing therapies and remedies from a variety of communities whose members have met in urban areas.

In reviewing ngoma on the Swahili coast, Janzen (1992) recalled the work of Hans Cory, an ethnologist from the early 20th century, who recorded the ngoma communities and their make-up. Cory observed that they were communities not only for ancestor reverence and divination, but also served as guilds for professional and artistic development.

Janzen (1992) interviewed Botoli Laie, a healer from this area. Laie noted the spirits that afflict and describe the accompanying sicknesses. Omari, the second healer interviewed, stated that he learned ngoma from his father and was not himself a "sufferer-novice." Omari was viewed by the author as more of a medical doctor with a clinical practice. However, Omari did work with patients who had *sheitani* (spirit) sickness and stated that he referred patients with "ordinary sickness" to the hospital.

In South Africa, Janzen (1992) described a different ngoma that he believed was influenced by the hostile and potentially volatile atmosphere of the townships. Within this atmosphere, the ngoma offered a much-needed place of solace and support. The author noted that one of every four households belonged to a ngoma. He described in a case study the initiation of Ntete, a Cape Town man. Janzen compared the differences and similarities in ceremonies between Cape Town and other ngoma locations. The basic nature of the rituals remained the same as those conducted in the rural countryside: calling the ancestors, smearing medicine on the initiate's body, sacrifice of a goat, and dancing and singing. All activities were completed over a three-day period. Janzen observed that this ngoma of Cape Town had several of the main features of the broader ngoma institution. These included entry of a sick person into ngoma training under the supervision of a healer, novices working together to learn and study dreams, and songs and divination practices. Individuals celebrated rites of passages through sacrifice and sharing of meals.

Janzen stressed the importance of lexicon in determining the nature of ngoma.

He described in detail the origin of ngoma and how this aspect of African life spread from one location to another. He determined that by tracing the linguistic features of the Bantu languages through selected African regions, he could observe the history and development of ngoma. He discussed ngoma musical instruments and how they promoted development of ngoma as an institution. Janzen stated that the methodology of genetic classification has been the key factor in determining the historical development of ngoma through shared features. He provided a list of cognate terms that "reveals symptoms, etiologies, healer roles, medicines and ritual activities with end-goal of health of cognate reconstructions based on a comparison of modern semantic variations" (1992, p. 63). For example, the Bantu proto-cognate word for *dog* suggests that which causes sickness also heals.

Janzen (1992) described the core features of ngoma therapy, from the initial sickness and identification by an established healer through the ceremonial rituals of whitening the body, purification ceremonies, and dream and divination training. Again, referring to Turner, Janzen (1992) noted the rites of passage in the separation of sacred and profane space and time in the healing rituals.

Divination, a diagnostic tool, is always a part of the work of the ngoma. It assists the healer in determining the cause of the sickness and the direction of the healing. Spirits are a major feature of ngoma therapy and must be communicated with, either through channeling or through requests for assistance in healing. Often spirits are identified as the source of the sickness. Someone following this *sign*, indicated by sickness or dreams, will become a healer in the spiritual community or ngoma of this identified spirit. It is believed that a society should remain stable and without *misfortune*. The sacrifices made by the ngoma assure its members of good fortune. Janzen stated that the animal sacrifice "purifies the universe in that it restores or regenerates the human community to its ideals" (1992, p. 104).

In my opinion Janzen's recommendation of the ngoma as a recognized institution would be most beneficial to Africans. A social institution that has remained as consistent as this one should be supported. Additionally, the ngoma is a purely African institution that has survived and provided much for the spiritual and financial well-being of Africans. Its ability to withstand the pressures and influences of colonialism proves its viability. Based on Janzen's research, it appears that there are correlations between ngoma healing practices and those of modern medicine.

Bantu Folklore by Matthew Hewat (1970) was originally published in 1906. It has been chosen for inclusion because of the author's apparent familiarity with the social customs of the Bantu people. According to Hewat (1970), when death came suddenly, it was believed to be caused by family members, and they were the first to be held under suspicion. Within Bantu cosmological belief, a spirit world existed. Sacrifices by "medicine men" were offered to appease the "offended spirits" and were also made when someone dreamed of the ancestors. Hewat described in detail the specific rituals for offering sacrifices. He also reported that amulets were worn by most Bantus as a form of protection against sickness and evil.

Hewat (1970) noted that there were several different kinds of *amagqira* (doctors), including herbalists, witch doctors, and surgeons. They could be either men or women. The doctors could attain this position through lineage or choose the path of medicine on their own. Individuals who became doctors or healers went through a training period. This training began after the initiate was identified as having a calling through a dream, a spirit river calling, and visions. Once these events occurred, then training with a teacher began. Hewat stated, "Taking a herb doctor all-round he is often a clever fellow, good at the cure of some diseases, and his methods and principles compare favorably with those ascribed to Aesculapius and Galen in the early history of medicine" (p. 28).

In Chapter 4, Hewat (1970) provided the reader with a list of diseases, causes, and prescribed traditional cures. Chapter 5 continued in the same manner but also included instances where surgery was performed, and stated the medicines for diseases where surgery was necessary.

Hewat (1970) also wrote about the Bantu rituals related to midwifery and children. Of note was the ten-day rite following birth: placing children in a hole in the earth to protect them and keep them healthy. Related and of equal significance was the burial of small children in the earth when they appeared to be getting sick. In his summary, Hewat allowed that native healers or doctors were knowledgeable and adequately prepared to provide healthcare services to their patients.

Harriet Ngubane lived among the Zulu people, conducting anthropological fieldwork. The text *South African Zulu Medicine* (1977) was a result of her investigative studies.

In opening, she said that her book grew out of "a desire to look into social behaviour that was considered traditional" (p. 2). In this introductory section, Ngubane discussed the advantages and disadvantages of being Zulu to completing her research study.

Chapter 1 began with a historical review of the Nyuswa people. The Nyuswa, according to Ngubane, had resided on their land for 130 years. They were a clan people with strong lineage lines. She said of them, "I would argue that in spite of Christianity the permeating influence in the Nyuswa reserve is based more on Zulu culture than any foreign culture" (Ngubane, 1977, p. 20).

In Chapter 2, Ngubane (1977) discussed the causes of sickness and related facts and defined various terms. *Umuthi* (medicine) is a tree or shrub both poisonous and curative. *Isifo* is defined as somatic symptoms, misfortune, or disease. In Zulu culture, illness has two major causes. One is biological (natural forces), which occur as part of the life process—i.e., aging, childhood illnesses, seasonal sickness, and family genealogical sickness. This type of illness is termed *umkhuhlane*. Medicines used for umkhuhlane are not part of a ritual but are considered sufficiently potent to help with sickness. Africans believe that non-Africans are capable of understanding these kinds of illnesses but not those" based on Zulu cosmology" (p. 2). *Ukufa kwaban* was defined as a disease of the African people. "This name is used mainly because the philosophy of causality is based on African culture" (p. 24).

The second major cause of illness was directly related to an imbalance in the psychic and physical environment of an individual. "Pollution" existed through sorcery or the negative actions of one person or animal upon another. This "pollution" could be reversed by a balancing between order and disorder. "For a Zulu conceives good health not only as consisting of a healthy body, but as a healthy situation of everything that concerns him ... Good health means the harmonious working and coordination of his universe" (Ngubane, 1977, p. 27).

There were some who were considered more vulnerable to environmental pollution; those included infants, strangers, and individuals who had been sick for long periods of time without treatment. In the chapter discussing sorcery, Ngubane said that it resulted from intentional pollution of the environment that left something behind that caused illness. According to the author, everyone had the right and was expected to protect himself or herself against sorcery. She listed three types of sorcerers: night sorcerers, day sorcerers, and lineage sorcerers.

Another chapter of Ngubane's text (1977) was devoted to a discussion of ancestors and sickness. Zulu belief is that ancestors are a major factor in health and sickness; the living have a responsibility to respect and acknowledge their ancestors. When this does not occur, it is more likely that an individual or close family member with "Pollution" was a mystical force. There were two situations in which it usually dominated. The first was the birth of a child, and the second was death. Other circumstances considered to be polluted (but less so) were menstruation and the day after sexual intercourse. Someone who murdered another was in a polluted state. To rid oneself of pollution, it was necessary to seek treatment. This treatment was typically sought from three different sources. Classified by group, these included the diviner, the bone thrower, and whistling great ancestors. Herbal medicine was considered a part of treatment and was classified according to the colors red, black, and white. "Colour plays an important and dominant role in symbolism related to therapy of mystical illness," reported Ngubane (p. 113).

The colors black, red, and white were always used in strict observance of sequence. Black and red were considered equal, both good and bad. White was held to be good. Black and red medicine was always followed by white medicine. The former two were used in treatment to rid the body of what was bad:

the sickness. White was then given to restore the individual to good health. The colors were related to the "cosmic order of day and night." It was believed that danger existed at night in the form of night sorcerers, sick people, and ancestral spirits. Black medicine was necessary to help restore health and provide a time for resting. "Herein lies the relevance of the equivocal power of black medicines. While they are dangerous, they are nevertheless necessary to make a person strong and powerful" (Ngubane, 1977, p. 115).

Sunrise and sunset that had a reddish color represented the state between something dark and something light.

In discussing red medicines, Ngubane said, "Red compared with black represents less danger and more good" (1977, p. 116). Going further, she added, "Daylight represents life and good health. To be (mystically) ill is likened to moving away from the daylight into the dimness of the sunset and on into the night." In sorcery, it is black medicine that is used, which signifies the darkness, the night. In order for one to become healthy, one must move from night to day. Ngubane also stated that "illness is associated with heat." Black and red medicines were always heated before application. In contrast, white medicines were usually not heated before application. Although the author refers to the theory of color evolution by Berlin and Kay, where colors evolve from stage one (black and white) to stage seven (purple, pink, orange, or gray), she stated that she did not find it relevant in her study of Zulu society. Once the illness was removed it was usually placed in one of two locations: either cast onto an animal (a goat or black bull) or at the crossroads and highways. It was hoped that in this secondary way a passing stranger would absorb and carry the evil away with him. Ngubane wrote,

> the symbolic therapy is fixed and standardized for each mystical illness. It is not abandoned if good results are not realized, but is repeated all over again, because such rites are rites of transformation, rites of process, of passage from a mystical state of darkness to one of mystical light. Treatment in this sense is a religious act. (1977, p. 132)

Ngubane (1977) carefully outlined in the succeeding chapters the Zulu view of the nature of spirit possession. In the summary conclusion, she discussed spirit possession, anthropology, and its relationship to Zulu beliefs. Referencing Gluckman, Levi-Strauss, and Turner, Ngubane concluded that women were not witches, and that sorcery was masculine, pollution feminine. She referenced Turner's symbology of colors: red for transition, white for life, and black as an indication of death. She applied Levi-Strauss' raw-cooked symbology to the Zulu concepts of good and evil opposites.

Ngubane's research (1977) and discussion of Zulu healing practices touched on several topics by other authors. The fact that black medicine was found to be so necessary to the healing process is reminiscent of Hillman's insistence on darkness and the journey to the underworld. The *umuthi* (medicine) is both a poison and a curative. Meier (1967) noted the Greek acceptance of this healing concept in his text. Like Ngubane, Meier said it was someone from another world—a god (or ancestor)—who brought sickness. I note the strong similarities between Ngubane's findings related to healing practices and those of others. The longevity of African healing practices suggests a capacity for healing that goes beyond the body-only orientation of modern medicine. It inherently relates directly to that which is spiritual.

Xhosa Healers

M. Vera Buhrmann, author of *Living in Two Worlds: Communication between a White Healer and Her Black Counterparts* (1986), was a Jungian analyst who spent nine years studying and working with Xhosa healers in South Africa. Her text described her initiation into this community of healers. In the introduction, Buhrmann stated that the primary objective in writing her book "is to show that much of what is called magic in the healing systems of the *amagqira* is not 'magical' … but is based on sound principles of depth psychology, especially as formulated by Carl Gustav Jung and his followers" (p. 14).

I think that Buhrmann's writing is very informative, giving us an insider's view of African healing practices. Her text is one of only two that I know of that provides a cross-cultural perspective of analytical psychology and traditional African medicine. Buhrmann stated (1986) that Xhosa healing practices were based on the principles of analytical psychology. From everything I have read, and given the factor of time, the reverse is true: depth psychology, as developed by Jung, was based in large part on the social and spiritual concepts of indigenous people. Jung generally used indigenous people as evidence of the "original" state, the archetypal or collective unconscious. My differences with some of his writing are not only with the negative racialized opinions of some of his writings, but also with the lack of credit he gave to indigenous people in using their cultural beliefs and practices. Reminding us that as researchers we see as we are trained to see, Buhrmann stated that "pure objectivity is a myth" (1986, p. 14). According to Buhrmann, the Tiso School—named after psychotherapist Mongezi Tiso, with whom she studied—relied heavily on the unconscious processes of patients in resolving psychological problems. Her experimental research included travel with the community, participation in rituals, and journaling her experiences. She said, "I try to link my own inner experience to what I am learning about the Xhosa and their methods and then to my knowledge of psychotherapeutic practices, both modern and ancient" (p. 11).

In Chapter 1, Buhrmann (1986) reviewed concepts of Jungian psychology. She defined the cultural unconscious as a communal unconscious, considering it to be a cultural layer containing both the conscious and the unconscious. Projections would arise from contents of the unconscious. She stated that archetypes were models of the unconscious and added, "It must be stressed that those original patterns of psychic perception are universal, but that the images by which their activated presence can be observed are colored by cultural factors" (p. 12). She noted that symbols and images were the language of the unconscious, and it was through these those archetypes speak.

In chapter 2, Buhrmann (1986) reviewed Xhosa cosmology, stating that one must know the history and worldview of a people to increase understanding. Like Malinowski, she stated that the main goal of culture is group survival, and as a result a high level of social functioning is required. There is a great deal of importance placed on group service, not individual achievement. Psychotherapy, then, was for the entire family, not only the individual.

A second major belief of the Xhosa is that there was no distinction between the *soma* (body) and psyche. As Buhrmann described it: "When part of me is ill, the whole of me is ill" (1986, p. 26). In a further development of the Xhosa concept of health, Buhrmann reported, "In illness and in the art of healing the pivotal concept is the ancestors" (p. 27).

Rituals for the ancestors were performed to learn their wishes and to have communication with them. To stop dreaming was an indication that the ancestors were not present to offer protection. Buhrmann (1986) explained that there were two kinds of ancestors: those of the river and those of the forest. The former was more numinous. However, the ancestors of the forest, though more distant, were more powerful. Xhosa belief was that the ancestors communicated through dreams. This created great respect for dreams and understanding the nature of dreaming. Burhmann said that dreams were "treated like fragments of reality." It was the relationship between the *igqira* (healer), the patient, and the latter's ancestors that determined the healing. Furthermore, the thoughts and methods of a healer depended on her worldview, relationship to the ancestors and the patient's ancestors' roles.

In the third chapter, Buhrmann (1986) discussed the various categories of Xhosa illnesses. Included in this discussion were the key customs related to healing: (1) patients never came alone but always with friends and family, (2) money for the healing was placed on the floor, (3) the *igqira* invoked the assistance of ancestors, (4) the *igqira* identified the nature of the sickness and its cause, and (5) a discussion of remedial steps. The categories of illness included *pambana* (insanity), *isiphoso*, and *thwasa*. The most important of these, *thwasa*, was defined as the "emergence of something new." It was described as an emotional disturbance with physical symptoms. Characteristics of *thwasa* included excessive dreaming, hearing voices, disappearing for days, being restless, and eating poorly. Buhrmann said, "The diagnosis of *thwasa* is often resisted" (1986, p. 37). This is primarily because the training is difficult, expensive, and family members must participate. The final decision of whether or not to undergo therapy and training is usually based on dreams. General aspects of *thwasa* treatment were discussed in Chapter 4.

These aspects included purification, inclusion in the family life of the trainee healer, a daily reporting of dreams to the healer, and the eventual change of status from patient to *umkwetha* (novice).

The novice was given herbal mixtures said "to open the mind to the dreams, to clarify their meaning and to call the ancestors" (p. 44).

In Chapter 5, Buhrmann (1986) discussed dreaming among the Xhosa, and provided a cross-cultural perspective with the cult of Asclepius, the Enlightenment and Romantic periods, and a comparison to Freudian and Jungian views on dreaming. It was a Xhosa belief that illness is caused so that one will become aware of something that is being neglected. It is through guidance given in dreams, via the ancestors, that one is helped. Dreams over a period provide an indication of progress, appropriate times for rituals, and readiness to begin practice as a healer.

The dreams of both the healer and initiate are of paramount importance in the decision-making process. Buhrmann (1986) concluded the text with a discussion of the rituals and ceremonies held in conjunction with the novice's movement from patient to healer. Buhrmann's text (1986) is insightful for its rendering of the healing practices of the Xhosa. Buhrmann noted in her epilogue that there was a need for both the conscious and unconscious applied to an interracial understanding of dreams.

Traditional Healers and Modern Medicine

Murray Last and Gordon Chavunduka's edited volume, *Professionalisation of African Medicine* (1986), was composed of seminar papers presented at the University of Botswana in 1983. The articles were written by individuals who were primarily sociologists and anthropologists. The text was divided into two broad areas, the first entitled "Professional Association and Government" and the second "Professional Knowledge and Its Control." In the introduction, the editors addressed the issue of ambiguity regarding the terminology used by the authors.

The most significant terms requiring definition were traditional in African medicine and law. The editors speculated how these terms would be defined in relationship to Africans and their past, present, and future health care system.

In the history provided by Last and Chavunduka (1986), it was noted that the first non-African doctors in Africa were usually employees of the colonial government and worked without a professional organization. Indigenous healers had their own associations and guilds prior to colonialism. It was in the 1950s that medical doctors began developing private practices and university hospitals were established. "The process of professionalism became part of decolonization ... . It accompanied the establishment of a middle class whose legitimacy was based on educational attainments, a meritocracy to be open to all" (Last & Chavunduka, 1986, p. 10). However, because the rules determining advancement and measurement were Eurocentric, traditional medicine "was viewed initially with some suspicion" (p. 10). The first non-African doctors were supportive of traditional medicine. However, this eventually changed as they became more affluent and assumed a more biased

European stance. There then came a "second generation" of traditional healers who moved toward reclaiming this lost power and again positioning themselves among Africans as their primary healers.

The first article of anthology, by Chavunduka, was entitled "Zinatha: The Organization of Traditional Medicine in Zimbabwe" (1986). The author began by stating that traditional medicine had a lengthy history in Zimbabwe prior to the arrival of Western medicine. Traditional healers were once called incorrectly labeled witch doctors. Although their work included delving into the spirit world, their work also involved finding solutions to health problems caused by bacteria and germs. The Christian colonial government tried to eliminate traditional African practices. A dominant reason for this was the belief that traditional medication was fake. Ancestor reverence impeded the establishment of Christianity. Eurocentric politics were devoted to their own ends and a desire to keep Africa dependent upon European pharmaceutical companies.

Although there was a concentrated and focused effort to destroy traditional medicine practices via Christian education, missionary hospitals, and legal acts outlawing divination, Chavunduka (Last & Chavunduka, 1986) found that traditional medical practice survived. There were eight categories of traditional healers, indicating not only survival but also expansion of traditional healing. In 1981, traditional healers were officially recognized by the Zimbabwean government.

The essay "Traditional Healthcare in Botswana" by Frank Staugard (Last & Chavunduka, 1986) stressed the theme of the traditional healer as "a religious consultant, a legal and political adviser, a political detective, a marriage counselor and a social worker" (p. 51). Staugard was in support of the integration of Western and traditional medicine. Religious belief in Botswana was very much integrated with the concept of healthcare. However, the author noted that Christianity caused changes in the society. As a result of its presence, the power of the healer decreased. The Catholic Church had its own sacred location and rites, seeking to eliminate those in African society. In addition, if the chief became Christian, the missionary became his advisor, thereby decreasing the need for a traditional diviner or healer.

Among the six types of herbalist healers in Zimbabwe was the *sangoma*, who was called to his profession through a dream. "The dream in which the individual is 'called' includes a multitude of scenarios and events but invariably involves a snake" (Last & Chavunduka, 1986, p. 57). The initiate trained with elders, learning divination, herbalism, and exorcism. Faith healers, another large segment of healing practitioners, were usually associated with the independent African church. "In the function as a health care facility rather than religious institute, the Zionist movement has gradually adopted almost all of the conceptions and treatments used for centuries by the traditional healers in the Botswana cultures," noted Staugard (p. 59). The people live within two cultures, Western and tribal. The author noted that the former had a curative medicinal focus and the latter a preventive focus. Diviners continued to be unwelcome but herbalists and body-oriented healers were treated with respect by the community at large.

The essay "Traditional Healers" by Pamela Reynolds (Last & Chavunduka, 1986) discussed the training of traditional healers in Mashonaland. Reynolds stated, "This paper is concerned with the privileged possession of knowledge by traditional healers and the potential power that this possession offers" (p. 175). The author believed that through a deeper understanding of the training of healers, there could be more acceptance of the work that they performed. For the study, 47 healers were chosen from three different areas of Mashonaland.

Of this number, 28 were men and 19 were women; 49% were between 40 and 60 years of age. Key characteristics of the healers were as follows: (1) all of the healers but eight were possessed by spirits; (2) all used plants and animal parts in their medicine except one; (3) divination included possession, *hakata*, dreams, and use of the Koran; (4) 68% had been in practice for over ten years; and (5) all had one or more healers in their families.

Reynolds cautioned against the use of superficial norms to determine ability of the healers. However, she noted, "Undoubtedly, Zezuru traditional healers do acquire a significant body of knowledge about their culture's symbolic systems (its myths, patterns of dream interpretation, use of colours) and the classification of flora and fauna" (Last and Chavunduka, 1986, p. 173). The chosen norm was established through observation of healers at work and the success or failure of their treatments. These healers appeared to have a broad knowledge of *materia medica*.

Healers were chosen because they possessed *hana*, defined as heartbeat or conscience. They were expected to have purity of heart. Said Reynolds, "*Hana* reveals itself in one who is strong-willed, well-behaved, and stone-hearted. Bad dreams are frequently interpreted as trials set by the spirits to test one's will-power, calmness and strength in the face of adversity" (Last & Chavunduka, 1986, p. 177). Healers were expected to follow principles that included never hitting another and abstaining from sexual relations during healing ceremonies and rituals, when acting as an advisor to those seeking help, and when angry.

Reynolds concluded by stating, "The curative strength of a medicine is believed to originate in a combination of the herbs' intrinsic qualities and the healer's spiritual power" (Last & Chavunduka, 1986, p. 183). Reynolds believed it was a time of transformation for the healing profession in her country. However, she recommended that traditional healers must be kept as a "vital" part of the community.

Chapter 7

Dreaming as a Creative Process

Reflective Mirrors of Creativity

In *A Different Existence*, Van Den Berg (1972), says that the past speaks to us in the present. Within the therapy room, both client and analyst bring the ghosts of their past. "The past that is significant is the past as it appears now. The past that is significant is a present past" (p. 80). In his description of the young man who visits him, Van Den Berg refrains from labeling him with a diagnostic term. Instead, he listens to the patient's story. "A tale is being told and the task of the therapist is to listen for the figure who tells the tale, for the figure who is spinning the story" (Romanyshyn, 1988). It is an approach which speaks to the naiveté and not—knowingness that must be present if the analyst is to bring trust to the relationship. It is a trust that knows: "That which touches us shows itself in the appearance of objects" (1972, p. 80).

> It is only through the moment to moment experience of being with the other that we are able to allow for "something"—the spirit of something to comfort in the space "between". To allow the past to be the present. " ... we are led and even forced by the evidence of experience itself to affirm the paradox that the past is something given in order to be made. Re—membering the past is a matter of making a real past real ... . fictionalizing the factual." (Romanyshyn, 1988)

In Swahili, there are two words which identify time, Sasa and Zamani. The first identifies events "about to occur, or in the process of realization, or recently experienced" (Mbiti, 1967, p. 23). Zamani is the past but also contains the present and future. When the physical body of an African dies he remains in the Sasa and becomes one of the "living dead." He remains thusly until there is no longer a family member alive who remembers him and says his name. Death is followed by ceremonies that acknowledge that the dead person is still a part of the community, living and dependent upon it to keep his name alive through ritual.

DOI: 10.4324/9781003219965-10

Death rituals may continue for up to a year past the physical death. "They are still part of their human families, and people have personal memories of them. The groups are bound together by their common Sasa which for the living—dead is however, fast disappearing into the Zaman" (1967, p. 82).

Dream

I arrive home. As I walk up the steps I see a child sitting on a man's lap. The man's chest and face is hidden from my view. He is well—dressed in a suit and brown leather shoes. I recognize the child as mine. My feeling is that the child belongs to me.

This is the first dream I have after my mother's death. It speaks to my feeling of vulnerability, my child—like a feeling of being held by an unknown, unseen stranger—the ability to finally hold myself in an unknown way which only her death permits. But it also speaks to my claiming myself. After her death, I live all the childhood experiences of pain and abandonment that I could not face during her life. I am a child again at my mother's death. There is a joyous freedom and release from having to keep her safe—something I was unaware I was psychically doing until her death. I begin to grow and become initiated into life as an adult.

In many African societies, a person is not considered a full human being until he has gone through the whole process of physical birth, naming ceremonies, puberty and initiation rites, and finally marriage (or even procreation). Then he is fully 'born', he is a complete person. (Mbiti, 1969, p. 24)

We miss something of value in our American culture by not having rites of passage that served our ancestors. It is as if all the pain of leave—taking which occurs at death has been stored and saved over the years rather than expressed through ceremonial rituals. In those moments of being with the death of loved ones, we suffer for all the deaths of missed rituals which would have prepared us for and held us at this final physical separation.

Dream

I am walking on a city sidewalk. Across the street I look and see my mother. She is dressed in a familiar checked suit that she had years ago. I'm excited to see her. She sees me and begins to cross the street towards me. I become apprehensive. I realize that she is dead. But she looks rested and happy. She smiles softly and kindly at me. She stands on the sidewalk in front of me but I cannot touch her. I feel as if someone is standing between us. I feel that she is removed from me. It looks like a shadow between us. I sense that I am to let go.

With the death of my mother, came a re-awakening of many things in my life, especially my creative self-expression—my creativity as a writer. In releasing her spirit, I have been able to release from within more of my own spirit. The poetry that I have written within the last few years speaks in part to that place of release that I have come to feel.

Dreaming Writers

In her introduction to *Writers Dreaming* (1994), Naomi Epel stated that her book developed from her work as a literary escort. During her encounters with authors, she asked them about their dreams. Their responses became the basis of conversation and later, of the book. Epel herself had a dream of standing by a door watching an artist at work in a basement room. The writing of this text resulted from that dream. *Writers Dreaming* was an interweaving of the author's thoughts regarding dreaming and the stories of published authors. The text examined at the creative process from the point of view of dreams and dreaming.

Epel composed an insightful text showing the interplay between these two different aspects of the unconscious: writing and dreaming. Each of the published authors she interviewed revealed something of the dream and his or her dream process that can be understood within a Jungian dream analysis context. Isabel Allende, one of the authors, spoke of her dream giving her the *tone* she required for the completion of her book. Jung often used the word *tone* in describing the dynamic quality present in dreams that help with clarification and interpretation. Allende's reference reminded me of this feature of Jung's dreamwork.

The first author interviewed was Allende, who said of her writing style, "I write in a very organic way. Books don't happen in my mind, they happen somewhere in my belly" (Epel, 1994, p. 8). Allende said that when she is writing, she "lives in the landscape of the book." She does not socialize nor travel. Living in this landscape of the imagination is like being in a dream landscape. She reported having difficulty finding the "tone" for the ending of *The House of the Spirits* (1985). She recalled waking up from a dream in which she was speaking to her dead grandfather about the book. This dream gave her the "tone" she was seeking for her book.

Relating to a second incident regarding her writing, Allende said that she was feeling unproductive, unable to develop her character past the point of a recurrent nightmare. In this nightmare, he is engaged in a gun battle and bullets fail to kill his pursuers. Later, while watching a film, Allende's partner commented on not seeing the movie characters' faces. Allende then said of her book's character, "But when he forces himself to look, he realizes that all those shadows have his own face ... The enemy is within himself" (Epel, 1994, p. 11). Her partner's comments helped to clarify her character's nightmare.

Allende's own nightmare was as follows: "I dream of a very disorganized and messy house" (Epel, 1994, p. 12). She believed that the house in the dream represented her, and that writing helped relieve the pain of the "mess" in her life. She woke up with a headache following this dream. There was something being postponed that needed solving. "So finally I am forced, organically forced, to face it and talk about it and solve it," Allende continued. Allende believed that the dream was a storage room of smells, colors, and textures that one can only access through dreaming.

Maya Angelou said of her own dreaming: "There is a dream which I delight in and long for when I'm writing. It means to me that the work is going well" (Epel, 1994, p. 26). In this dream, she is climbing a tall building "with alacrity and joy and laughter." In speaking of her creative process, Angelou said that when she writes she rents a hotel room in her hometown. In this room, she plays solitaire, which she considers "like dreaming." From this place, she is able to focus on her writing and create the work that is meaningful to her.

Of the authors interviewed, Bharati Mukherjee spoke explicitly about the intimacy of her dreaming and writing.

She said, "I have come to trust very much the unconscious within the creative process and the efficacy, the value of dreams" (Epel, 1994, p. 162). Mukherjee reported that as a child, she pulled the tail of a viper.

Since then, she has been afraid of snakes. Snakes are frequently in the hallucinations and nightmares of the characters in her stories. Of dreams she said, "I let a dream work underground" (p. 164). Describing the type of characters she creates, Mukherjee stated that they wake up to the unconscious, to their *dreamselves.*

Interviewed author Anne Rice said, "Dreams have not so much changed my work as deepened it … that's the same as writing … sometimes dreams show me that my writing should go deeper" (Epel, 1994, p. 215). Rice, who has written extensively about vampires, said in her own dreams she is Lestat of *Interview with the Vampire* (1976). Rice also told of a dream in which she sees her daughter sick and turning blue with a blood disease. Her daughter later died after being diagnosed with acute granulocytic leukemia.

Two more recent dreams have been included in her writing that deal with flying. Rice (1976) said that six years after *Interview with the Vampire* was published she had a dream in which the typewriter flew off the table and out of the window. All the while it kept typing. The typewriter landed on the street with Claudia, the young girl from *Interview with the Vampire* whose physical maturation stopped at an early age due to becoming a vampire. Rice said she felt the dream was telling her, "Go where the pain and the intensity and the fear is." She believes that she alone can interpret her dreams.

I believe that, through their writing practices, several of the authors reflected the theory and practice of Jungian dreamwork. Angelou's taking a reclusive space, a hotel room, brings to my mind the creation of a sacred or liminal space.

She said of playing solitaire that it was like dreaming. This practice appears very similar to active imagination, the conscious working with the unconscious in a creative process. For Angelou, the result is characters and stories.

Rice had a dream in which her daughter is sick from a particular disease, and the daughter later died from this same disease. Rice believes these two events are highly significant. She values dreams and insists that individuals must do their own self-interpretation. I disagree with Rice on this point. Perhaps in her case, she can interpret sufficiently for her individual needs. But I believe, as does Perera, that we require support in this area. I think it is impossible consistently to do successful dream interpretation for oneself because of unconscious blind spots.

Part III

Africanist Dreaming

Chapter 8

Embodiment and Dreaming

Post-Jungian Somatic Dreamwork

Edward Bruce Bynum (2017) notes the following in his discussion of Native Americans and cross-cultural dreams:

> The belief held by the Iroquois is that a wish in a dream must be acted out in some way, by oneself or others, in the waking state .... The Native Americans of the plains, eastern woodlands, lower Colorado River, central California, and the northwest coast all believed and acted on the basis of their belief in guardian spirits who could and frequently would speak, sing, grant wishes, and even dance with them in their dreams. In this way, the dream's process was felt, heard, and identified with on a very intimate level and even acted out behaviorally in the waking sate, often to enormous therapeutic benefit. (*The Dreamlife of Families* p. 27)

As Bynum details the connections amongst various cultural groups, he also addresses the connection between the living and those who have transitioned:

> In Africa, the importance of dreams, and family dreams in particular, also has a long cultural, clinical, and psychospiritual history. It is a given in many religious societies that family members, both living deceased, and also the gods themselves, can and do communicate with the dreamer in the dream. This belief greatly expands the personal matrix of experience, causality, and time flows since this extended family unconscious system enfolds not only the generation to be born and the currently living but also up to five generations of the departed. (p. 29)

In his text, *Working with the Dreambody* (1985), Arnold Mindell presented 50 case studies. He discussed the relationship between dreams and physical illness. His belief was that body symptoms are mirrored in dreams and vice-versa, and that these symptoms intensify as the body seeks health. Mindell related his story of becoming sick and the effect this had on his perspective as

DOI: 10.4324/9781003219965-12

he viewed his body's attempts to heal itself. In an example from a patient's life, he tells of a patient dying from a tumor. The author worked on increasing the level of psychic pain in the stomach, pushing for something to "break through." The patient had never been able to communicate with others in a manner he found satisfactory. Mindell believed that because of their work together, the patient reached a point where he was able to successfully express himself. The patient was relieved of his painful stomach symptoms and survived longer than expected.

I believe that Mindell's approach to dreamwork, with its emphasis on body healing, mirrors the African system of healing's inclusiveness of body and mind in the process. In Jung's theory there is recognition of the place of consciousness working with the unconscious.

I interpret his use of the word "conscious" within this context as an awareness that is inclusive of the body as part of ego functioning.

Amplification is the process Mindell used in his work with patients to discover the "channel" through which the body was attempting to manifest symptoms. He amplified both the dream experience and the body or proprioceptive experience. Mindell (1985) described his work as process work, stating that it is a "natural science ... I simply look to see what exactly is happening in the other person and what happens to me while he is reacting" (p. 9). He did not credit himself or the therapist with any special skill but rather stated, "The therapist's only tool is his ability to observe processes. He has no preestablished tricks or routines." It is through this process that the next actions can be predicted.

Mindell (1985) proceeded further to define process. He noted that the term is not viewed from a psychological perspective but rather from that of a physicist. He said of process that the primary feature is being close to awareness of all that is transpiring. Additional features include identifying "unconscious" body symptoms, working without judgment, and the use of neutral language in exchange with patients.

Mindell said, "I don't believe the person actually creates disease, but that his soul is expressing an important message to him through the disease" (1985, p. 13). He supported this statement by relating how many of his patients—most of whom were dying—moved from just being sick to a life-affirming process of inner development. He stated that often these patients were initially not interested in analysis, only in physical healing. An example he provided was of a woman, Frau Herman, who had cancer. In what Mindell considered a dream related to her physical condition, she took a trip to the gym. Later, she dreamed of a woman with milk in her breast. Mindell believed this dream opened her consciousness to being cured of cancer. Through the dream series of this patient, Mindell was able to follow the path of physical healing from beginning to end.

Mindell said, "The body has many centers and points of awareness. Your body uses projections and psychological problems to stimulate discovery of its different parts" (1985, p. 31). He said that shamans knew and understood about projection as a cause of illness by the placing of "black magic" on another. He believed that projections could make one sick. He told of a man with goiter, a throat problem, who had a very difficult and controlling father. As the patient was able to become physical, punching and hitting and screaming his hate for his father, he was physically released from negative father projections. Mindell maintained that the withdrawing of the negative projection from the father and the acceptance of his feelings of hatred enabled the patient to heal. He stated that successful bodywork depends entirely on the patient.

Mindell (1985) believed that the dreambody is a multi-channeled personality. He noted the process of healing changes "channels" and goes from hearing to feeling, feeling to visualizing, and from seeing to moving.

He indicated that it is through the experience of feeling pain that one is awakened to consciousness. When the pain becomes too intense, one changes channels and moves towards health. Mindell said the dreambody signals to the physical body identifying a symptom. The ability to be able to switch from one channel to another in the process, Mindell believed, is often a matter of life and death. If one cannot move in the direction of healing, then one dies, remaining, in effect, stuck in one channel.

Mindell (1985) reviewed the dreambody in fairy tales, couple relationships, and as a part of the world collective. He believed that understanding oneself makes for a better understanding of the world collective dreambody. Mindell stated that at an early age one might discover illnesses that would be chronic because they usually appeared in childhood dreams.

He outlined a plan for working alone without an analyst with the dreambody, using increased awareness, amplification, and channel changing as phases in the process. Mindell concluded his text by indicating that dying individuals beginning dreambody work often feel that they are getting better and report feeling less sick. Mindell summarized that this is because the dreambody is containing and healing the physical body even as it approaches death.

Author Marian Dunlea (2019) says the following in her book *Bodydreaming in the Treatment of Developmental Trauma* when discussing the human body and the stress of our current lives:

The organic process of self-regulation is fundamental to the survival of human life on the planet. Nature is adaptive and strives continually to return the organism from a state of chaos and dissonance to one of greater cohesion and flow. Our contemporary world with its culture of globalization, may well be out of sync with our intrinsic capacity for self-healing and self-regulation, leaving our nervous systems more often than not in a state of dysregulation. However, if we can *learn* how to reset our Autonomic Nervous Systems we may find that our stressed and traumatized systems are able to realign with the inherent organic capacity for self-regulation.

Jung argued repeatedly that the body and psyche are two aspects of one and the same thing: The separation of psychology from the basic assumptions of biology is purely artificial, because the human psyche lives in indissoluble union with the body" (1937, par. 232). (p. 13)

In seeking to better understand how we are in our dream bodies we must also be present for all that has occurred with our human bodies. What appears as a separation is only appearance. A respect for psyche and how it contributes to our dream as well as eventually our wake state supports us in achieving a psychological homeostasis. It is possible to see how stress from the parent carrying a fetus would influence the psychological condition of the child, past, present as well as future. The need for a state of centeredness and calmness within the mind of the mother during pregnancy has been shown to be a major influential factor in the mental state of the child. In consideration of the transmission of the archetypal trauma passed on to descendants—how much of this type of trauma can we deny or question, especially in the lives of the African diaspora. It is not only biological but also archetypal and must have elements of the unconscious.

Oftentimes, the dream images that appear to us are constellated by our psychological complexes. These complexes that engage us at the most basic level of our emotional bodies require that our bodies have a physical reaction. This connection between psyche and our emotions is present with us in both sleep and when awake. An on-going aspect of the clinical work is being able to revisit the complexes that can become activated and learn how to address the trauma and emotions that can appear. The body gives us the container for the necessary consciousness that is required to understand what is happening on a psychic level and a way to move towards healing the interconnected world of body-mind-spirit.

Dunlea says the following in speaking of her own initial training with Marion Woodman and her work: "BodySoul Rhythms uses movement, relaxation, breath work, voice and art to bring to consciousness the shadow material held unconsciously in the body and that presents in our dreams; most importantly, it encourages creative expression .... Where traditional psychoanalysis and psychoanalytical psychology value the transference relationship as the primary container, BodySoul Rhythms sees a loving relationship with the body itself as equally vital" (p. 20).

Trauma lives in the body and can appear in our dreams. Perhaps, the archetypal dreams of decades, centuries before, can put us in states of terror and demand that we work through our bodies to support deep healing. Dunlea recalls Jung's concept of the Transcendent Function and its emergence upon holding the tension of the opposites. Dunlea says:

In BodyDreaming, by bringing the opposites into dynamic flow— sympathetic and parasympathetic systems, psyche and body—we experience how our biology and psyche interact to produce a new position and possibility: a living third presents itself .... In a BodyDreaming session a client may present a dream that can, at first seem unconnected to the issue with which we are consciously concerned, its possible relevance a puzzle. Yet, in working with the emotion of the dream image and the felt sense resonance of the dream in the body through the process of inner attunement, we may discover that the image parallels (of images) our physiology and biological processes, and holds the key to new possibilities. (p. 101)

In 1974, Donald Johanson and his team of paleontologists made the discovery of an early pre-homo sapiens skeleton fossil. These bones, found in Ethiopia, were said to have been the skeletal remains of a female more than 3 million years old. The scientists who made the discovery of this first ancestor named her *Lucy*. The eventual examinations and tests that began on Lucy showed that she was indeed the oldest representation of early human existence. She was found in Africa.

The respect given to ancestors by Africanist people lives deep within the psyche and the body. Africans saw no separation between the mind and the body. When Jung references *participation mystique* in his discussion of the consciousness of Africans he is not mistaken in his recognition of such a possible state of consciousness. His error is in applying only a negative theory related to a lack of potential intellectual growth and individuation for Africanist individuals. He does not see them as capable of being individuals—only joined in a lower level of consciousness noted as *participation mystique*. Jung both accepted this state of consciousness as something Europeans had lost and had value while at the same time criticizing Africans for having a lower level of consciousness due to it. There can be no mistake. This was a racial commentary made in a sociological frame useful to building a theory of consciousness.

The philosophical beliefs of Africanist people are that there is no separation of mind and body. The body remembers long after the mind may forget what it has seen or heard. The body tells a story. This is a position that has become more evident in recent times as we see the development of Somatic Psychology as an area of professional interests and study among psychologists.

The African diaspora female body tells her own story. It is one characterized by centuries-long trauma, pre- and post-slavery. As Lucy appeared into our 20th-century life, as we considered the existence of the *first* female humanoid, the undercurrent of that time had existed for centuries. An almost parallel circumstance that continued as a part of the racial undercurrent was the persecution of African diaspora women in many forms. One of these forms included the prosecution of these women. Dorothy Roberts states the following in her preface to *Killing the Black Body: Race, Reproduction and the Meaning of Liberty*:

In the late 1980s, I began to notice news stories about prosecutions of women for using drugs while pregnant. District attorneys across the country concocted an assortment of charges to punish them for fetal crimes—child neglect, distribution of drugs to a minor, assault with a deadly weapon, and attempted murder. How did a public health problem become a criminal justice matter to be solved by locking up women instead of providing them with better health care? I was sure of three things about the prosecutions: they primarily targeted Black women, they punished these women for having babies, and they were a form of both race and gender oppression.

(p. xi)

As we consider the history of Africanist women bodies, there is an awareness of tension—an anxious gaze that anticipates a negative, life-threatening social event that will occur. We might say that this is the post-traumatic effects of slavery—Post Traumatic Slave Syndrome. It could be the constellation of a racial complex, or it might just be living in a daily conscious state of anticipatory fear in service to human survival or perhaps, all of these. By whatever name or description, we know that they survive in our racialized American psyche. Since leaving the African continent enslaved, the status of African diaspora women has been marked with horror, a profound lack of compassion, and a racist orientation that continues until today into the 21st century. In her book, *Sister Citizen: Shame, Stereotypes, and Black Women in America*, Melissa V. Harris Perry states:

Welfare policy is intimately linked in the American imagination with black women's sexuality. Political scientist Martin Gilens shows that white American opposition to welfare results from whites' fixed beliefs that the system supports unworthy black people who lack a suitable work ethic. Central to this opposition is a belief that black women do no appropriately control their fertility, that they have sex with multiple partners, producing children who must be cared or through tax-supported social welfare programs .... The depiction of black women as sexually insatiable breeders suits a slaveholding society that profits from black women's fertility. *But for a shrinking postmodern state, black women's assumed lasciviousness and rampant reproduction are threatening.* Therefore throughout the 20th century the state employed involuntary sterilization, pressure to submit to long-term birth control, and restriction of state benefits for large families as a way to control black women's reproduction. The myth of a plantation Jezebel can be deployed to limit today's welfare-dependent mother.

It is not just a matter of distorted perceptions; these misrecognitions can be used to punish African American women through policy.

(pp. 67–68, author's italics)

The black racial complex and therefore anxieties of white Americans can create any variation of imaginative roles for African American women. We have witnessed the development of these stereotypes over the years.

Some change form—like the creation of the Mammy—always available nurse and housekeeper, created in the post-slavery era now to the 21st-century angry, aggressive, over-sexed welfare mother of contemporary times. However, we may look at these images and fantasized African Diaspora women, those of this lineage carry not only the slavery-time DNA of survival but also the pre-colonial energy and empowerment of Africanist women. In the oppositional effort to make us forget ourselves and add to our own invisibility, we must always engage in the affirmative effort to remember and bring into consciousness the nature of survival—the necessity of remembering what our bodies tell us. To harness the survivalist energy of our ancestors who lived through slavery and beyond. For African Diaspora women the true work is recalling the Africanist's body story that developed from African queens and stories of beauty from the goddess Oshun. This story is not the racially-inspired false one which makes the Black body over-sexed and in need of sterilization, over-productive, and in need of oppression or overly-exotic, and in need of a white sanitization. Memory recall can be engaged to support the body heal through a re-collection of what the body already knows. If archetypally we are able to bring forth the grief of slavery's intergenerational trauma, our work is to bring forth the storied memory of who we were before the colonization.

Now there is no economic use for African American women's bodies in the reproduction plantation system of slave-breeding. Within the American racial psyche is the changed story of how Africanist women use their bodies to steal from the welfare system. There is a gross irony in this turn of events, in this thinking that *blames* the female victim.

There is no forgetting because the body does not forget. The archetypal energy of the ancestors and the archetypes themselves all join in pushing recollection when the ego desires only restful peace. But for those who made the passage across the waters and their descendants who survived centuries of slavery, the spirit of recall does not disappear. There can only be a profound archetypal recollection and prayers that turns the egregious into true grief that permits healing of mind and body.

Christopher's Dream: Dreaming and Living with AIDS (Bosnak, 1997) is the story of the analytical relationship between Robert Bosnak and his patient Christopher. It detailed their relationship from their initial telephone conversation through the death of the patient. The story was told from the point of view of the analyst, with dream journal entries contributed by the patient. The book was published after the patient's death.

I am appreciative of Bosnak's work because of the openness and vulnerability with which he shared his personal experiences of the psychological work with his patient. There are very few texts by Jungian analysts that review the inner thoughts and transferential elements of the analysts. I view this text as a model in the further development of understanding the transference and counter-transference nature of patient-analyst relationship.

The text, provided mainly through numbered dreams, showed the psychic processes of both patient and analyst through their dreams and the transference and counter-transference relationship. One example of this was Bosnak's resistance to beginning analytic work with Christopher, which Bosnak felt immediately after their first telephone conversation. The text opened with the arrival of the patient for his first session, looking "like the epitome of health" (Bosnak, 1997, p. 5).

The patient said that he was anxious to see what dreams would say about his future. However, because of his sickness, a year passed before the patient was able to begin working with Bosnak.

Christopher's initial dream in the analysis showed him visiting his Aunt Lib, who was dead. He said of the dream, "I cross to the other side." While discussing his associations, the patient told of his early childhood, living with this aunt in a religious fundamentalist community. When the religious college Christopher attended found out that he was gay, he was expelled from the school. Bosnak described his own feelings at hearing the dream associations: "I'm most aware of a fury rising within myself. I am furious with the college ... I begin to imagine shooting and killing people" (1997, p. 8). The counter-transference issue is brought to the forefront. Bosnak said of Christopher, "I feel certain that he is repressing feelings." The session ends with the analyst indicating to the patient a lack of understanding regarding the meaning of the initial dream.

Therapy sessions were described through the recollected memories of the author and through Christopher's dream journal entries (Bosnak, 1997). The memories were juxtaposed to the dreams and provided a continuous picture or narrative of the development of the relationship between the patient and the analyst. For example, when Christopher brought a dream containing a "weasel" character, Bosnak revealed his own discomfort around the fees that he was charging for the analytical work. Throughout the text, Bosnak referred to the alchemical qualities present in Christopher's dreams. For example, in his second dream, Christopher referred to the whiteness of a speedboat, the marriage of a king and queen, and related combinations of gold and silver. The alchemical elements of the dreams provided a further context for understanding the development of the therapeutic relationship.

Bosnak related receiving a call from Christopher informing him that he had AIDS. At that moment, Bosnak said that he recalled the patient's previously stated desire to leave the gay world. Only now was he able to understand the patient's initial dream.

The author described his own feelings, his determination to fight for the patient, refusing to accept the possibility of death for Christopher. He said of himself, "I feel some manic giddiness as well, singing songs of the Great Healer" (Bosnak, 1997, p. 32).

The following sections, which described the therapy sessions, provided a clear picture of the contrast between the feelings and physical appearance of the patient's and those of the analyst. The latter related his shame at being physically fit and agile, able to move without discomfort, in the face of his patient's obvious lack of vitality and strength.

Bosnak's book allows the reader to move between analyst and patient, gathering the threads of their experiences together. The author expressed his personal thoughts and feelings regarding the initial period of the analytical work. One can observe this happening with more frequency by the end of the text. The patient became better able to offer his own insights regarding his dreams. Bosnak used Christopher's dreams in countering with his own transferential experiences. When Christopher was hospitalized for the final time, Bosnak said, "Each day I push myself over to the hospital, not wanting to go" (1997, p. 163). But later he accepted his "longing for him [Christopher]."

Bosnak (1997) recognized and worked through his own rage at Christopher's roommate's decision to leave. As he explored this rage he understood that it was because he now felt fully responsible for Christopher. He was reminded of his initial resistance to Christopher when he first heard Christopher's voice on the phone.

Bosnak described, in a most intimate way, the dying of his patient, showing all of his accompanying fear, anger, and sadness at this death. He retold Christopher his dreams as Christopher lay dying in the hospital. Bosnak likened the use of dreams to bedtime stories. Hearing the dreams appeared to soothe and comfort Christopher.

The text continued in the second part with a transcript of a men's AIDS dreamwork group. However, it is the first part of the text that provides a depthful perspective into the nature of the analytical process as it relates to transference and countertransference, dream analysis, and the psychological issues around death and dying.

Archetypal Psychology Dreaming

In *The Dream and the Underworld* (1979), James Hillman stated that he perceived "dreams as phenomena that emerge from a specific archetypal place ... with a distant, mythic geography ... to reflect this underworld in psychological theory" (p. 3). He noted the difference from his own approach and view of the dream from those of Jung and Freud. He defined his as movement "into the dark." He said he will "till" the earth (the psyche of Western man) from their gardens, he will go deeper into and remain in psyche's darkness rather than seeking relief in the light of the self. His dream theory was based on mythology and the requirement to always keep the images of the dream as the primary focus. "The image has been my starting point for the archetypal re-vision of psychology" (p. 5). According to Hillman, the images of the soul are created in the darkness of night, and the workings of the soul participate in this darkness of death and the underworld.

I think Hillman is the most radical in his theoretical approach, compared to Jung's original work. Hillman has been the most critical depth psychologist in his review of Jung's theories, especially as they relate to dreamwork and the influence of the dream ego in psychological work. I find Hillman's concepts forward-thinking and freeing, as he pushes for more freedom for the soul and less emphasis on what he defines as the heroic ego.

I am reminded of Oruka's study with African sages, in Hillman's sacrifice of ego (the god Hillman uses for example is Hercules) and the African sacrifice, in which the word itself means god. There seems to me to be a parallel between these two culturally different circumstances—both emphasize the same psychological need. I am also reminded of Jung's killing of Siegfried in *The Red Book*.

Hillman (1979) reminded us that the dream viewed historically, held meaning on a personal level, with personal messages for the dreamer. In addition, the dream had been equated with temporary insanity. Previously, it was thought that daytime memories served to build the nighttime energy of the dream. The Romantics found beauty and power in the dream and the mythos of dreamlife. However, with the rise of rationalism, the dream was brought into the light of day, back to reason. Hillman saw this conflict in Freud's position. The dream which Freud felt "belonged wholly to sleep" now had to be saved from the madness of the underworld. The desire to interpret the dream, to save it, meant a translation "into the language of waking life." Hillman did not agree with Jung that the unconscious is to be made conscious and that dreams exist for the sole purpose of individuation.

Hillman stated that a "fundamental tenet of archetypal psychology ... [is] the interchange of mythology and psychology. Mythology and psychology both together create an action of deepening, rather than tearing apart" (1979, p. 24).

Soul, said Hillman, was not a location but the activity of being in process, a process of a specific movement that deepened as it searched. "There is no end to depth, and all things become soul" (1979, p. 26). For Hillman, soul-making equated with psychologizing.

Hades, the god of the depths had no temples or alters in the upperworld. He was invisible in the light of day. The hiddenness of Hades signifies the way in which dreams are hidden in the night, enveloped in sleep and death. In the underworld, only shades and shadows exist.

Said Hillman, "Shadow is the very stuff of the soul, the interior darkness that pulls downward out of life and keeps one in relentless connection with the underworld" (1979, p. 56). Addressing Jung's concept of objective versus subjective interpretation for dream figures, Hillman stated, "The persons I engage are neither representations of their living selves nor non-parts of myself. They are shadow images that fill archetypal roles" (p. 60). He said that it is through finding the etymon of the name that we can find the meaning to the mythic figure of the dream.

Hillman (1979) provided descriptions of what he considered to be three major barriers to accepting the underworld as a psychic realm, a place for deepening psychological work: materialism, oppositionalism, and Christianity. The first is related to the desire to live on the earth and to be of the earth—an Epicurean stance. Oppositionalism, as Jung expressed it, is created out of a Christian dualism that itself is monotheistic and seeks to eliminate any polytheism seen to be a threat. Hillman stated that when the psyche dreams, there are no opposites. "Each dream has its own fulcrum and balance, compensates itself, is complete as it is" (1979, p. 80). It is only through the image that one can gain an understanding of the dream, through developing a kinship for and with the image.

According to Hillman (1979), the third barrier to descent is the Christian perspective of Christ's victory over descent and death through resurrection. With so powerful a symbol of eternity through resurrection and ascension, death is "vanquished." He said that Lazarus instead was the paradigm of eternal life for humanity. Hillman (1979) noted that there are only three dreams related in the New Testament, indicating that dreams were now considered anti-Christian and therefore forbidden. He said of Jung that he was caught between a defense of Christianity and a defense of soul-deepening.

Hillman (1979) saw the ego as needing to become more imaginal. As he traced the history of the ego, he recognized the heroic ego of Hercules with which we continue to view the dream and how it views itself. It is important for the ego to become less heroic and more of a "free soul," willing to die in the underworld. Hillman noted that it was Hercules who had blood on his hands and an inclination to violence. Hercules, the hero of the myth, had never been initiated into the Eleusinian mysteries, and therefore had no "change in consciousness from dayworld's life to nightworld's death" (1979, p. 112). The heroic ego did not understand the dream and attempted to literalize it, thereby missing the connection with the experience of soul-deepening. Because it refused to die, but continued to fight aggressively, Hillman said that the "villain in the underworld is the heroic ego, not Hades" (p. 113).

In the final section of the text, Hillman looked at dreamwork, describing its meaning. He found that Freud's wish-fulfillment theory had meaning because "the images made in dreams fulfill the desire of instinct" (1979, p. 120). Dreaming is narcissistic because the images themselves are reflectively satisfying to the psyche. He said that even though Freud's theory of wish-fulfillment appeared biological, it was in fact romantic—images feed the soul. As an example, Hillman spoke of the cults of Asclepius, where there were no direct interpretations, only dreaming and healing. "Through dreamwork we shift perspective from the heroic basis of consciousness to the poetic basis of consciousness recognizing that every reality of whatever sort is first of all a fantasy image of the psyche" (p. 137). In conclusion, Hillman said that ultimately his goal "is to keep the depth of the dream intact" (p. 140).

Chapter 9

African American Dreamer Portrait Dialogues

Liz

Dreamer Portrait

Liz is a 32-year-old woman living with her boyfriend in Brooklyn, New York. She has resided in New York since arriving here with her family from Guyana 21 years ago. Currently, she is employed as an administrative assistant for an accounting firm in Manhattan. She has been in this position for a little over a year. Prior to this, she worked as an "office temp." Liz has completed 3-1/2 years of college and is one semester away from receiving a degree in Early Childhood Education from a local university.

Liz is one of five siblings, fourth born of four sisters and one brother. She and all family members arrived in New York together as a family. Both parents live in Queens, the home they moved to shortly after their arrival in New York. Liz says that when growing up, relations with her siblings were "average." However, as she began speaking more explicitly about their relationships, she described herself as the black sheep of the family. She notes that this is how family members conceive of her though this is not how she perceives of herself. Liz thinks that her family is "dysfunctional," saying of herself, "I try to see, not ignore, what's wrong."

Liz notes difficulties in relationship with her father. She says of him that he always demanded that she do whatever he asked of her without consideration for her wishes. In speaking of him, she recalls that when she was a child, "He always put others in front of me—cousins, family associates." She says of their present relationship that she "doesn't feel fatherly love ... not that close."

As a child, Liz describes herself as "outspoken." She says that this characteristic influenced how her father related to her. Because of her openly expressed opinions, Liz's father at times physically hit her. She remembers these experiences as humiliating.

Liz continues to view her father as judgmental and highly critical. Liz states that she is close to her mother. However, she says in speaking of her

DOI: 10.4324/9781003219965-13

father that he was oftentimes "critical of me via my mother as medium." Liz's mother would frequently say, "The important question is, will it make your father upset."

Liz describes herself as the "scapegoat" in the family. She believes that her father puts her on a "pedestal" because of her education; however, he still does not see her and the things that she does in an "open way." Liz considers herself to be deprived of a father's love. She does not feel loved for herself but is seen as a failure as a daughter by her father.

In speaking of her relationship with her mother Liz notes that their relationship "has grown." Liz describes her mother as an "abused wife." Although she views her mother as "strong," she remembers her mother crying and complaining about the frequent absence of Liz's father from the home. According to Liz, the "emotional absence" of her father caused her mother suffering.

I asked Liz what held the greatest importance in life. She responded, "It is relationship—honest, true love."

Liz has lived with Harold for three years. He is employed as a New York City Corrections Officer. Liz considers this her third most "serious" romantic relationship of her life. Previous to this relationship when she was in her 20s, she was involved and lived with another man, David. That relationship lasted one year.

Liz reports that David tended to be jealous and would get into rages about other men's attractiveness to her. At the time Liz was a model. One night she came home and found "all of my beautiful clothes in rags." David had cut them up and thrown paint on them. Liz, afraid, left the apartment and telephoned the police. That event brought the relationship to an end.

Liz's next relationship, with Earl, was never consummated sexually. They continue to be friends and she hopes that they may come together again in a more intimate relationship.

Liz has attempted to end her present relationship for the last 1-1/2 years. She is in a relationship with Harold who has told her that if she leaves he doesn't know what he will do because of his depression. Liz says that this is not what's keeping her in the relationship but is a factor. "I know he gets depressed. I don't want to hurt him. Now I think I'm hurting myself more."

Harold has never hit Liz or been physically threatening with her. However, she indicates an understanding of her mother's sadness as it relates to Liz's own inability to have a "peaceful, calm place" to live. Harold's mother died a little more than a year ago. She died unexpectedly of a heart attack. Though he drank before her death, his level of alcohol consumption increased with her death. Harold has tried psychotherapy twice but reports these attempts as failures on the part of the therapists to "understand" him. In moments of extreme anxiety, Liz has sought out psychotherapy as a means of emotional support. They have not sought out ongoing couple's counseling.

Liz became a participant in our dream study because of an expressed interest in learning more about herself through her dreams. At our initial meeting, while speaking of her dreams, Liz stated, "Sometimes my dreams are so powerful. I don't always understand them. If I can learn more about them then I would know more about myself."

Liz was an honest and willing participant in the project. She agreed to all the requirements of the research at our first meeting. One of these requirements was the maintenance of a dream journal. Though she did not keep a physical journal, Liz was conscientious in making a record of 90% of her dreams for a one year period of time. Her ability to provide dream associations was limited. Because of this, there were a decreased number of dreams available for selection and analysis.

When Liz gave me her initial dream for review, I wondered at the similarities between the dream and her present life circumstance. She has spoken of Harold as taking her life from her because of his depression. She has to spend a fair amount of time "inflating" him so that he will have life for the relationship. She carries him in the relationship, as the child in her dream is being carried and nourished by the woman. This is but a first impression of possible relations existing in the dream that perhaps mirror Liz's most pressing psychological circumstance. Of the dreams Liz gave me, I selected 12 for inclusion, analysis, and discussion.

Following is the initial dream Liz reported at the start of our interviews:

There was a young woman—pasty skin, muddy complexion and hair, mousy blond and greasy. Maybe 20 years old—seated on a child's wagon or baby carriage or perhaps a reclining bicycle. She was being wheeled past me through a high school cafeteria-like place. She was moving through no impetus of her own, but there was no apparent mover either. The other people who were there were acquainted with her. She was holding a little 4-year-old boy. Was she his mother? His sister? Why didn't she set him down? Then it was revealed that he was growing out of her body—a kind of Siamese twin. If she were his mother, she would have had to have had him when she was very young. The boy is robust and fresh. He has somehow sucked all the life out of her.

Liz stated that what is most important to her is love—true love. The image of the boy sucking all the life from the woman is perhaps not one of a nourishing love but rather a parasitic relationship.

Liz

Dreamer Dialogue

Each dream participant and I engaged in a dialogue regarding their dreams and cultural attributes. The purpose of the interview was to obtain dream details, associations, and beliefs regarding dreaming. The results of the interview questionnaire, based on participant responses, are given below. This portion of the questionnaire was completed at the start and throughout the duration of our work together.

Liz

Dreamer Dialogue

Question 6: What are dominant themes in your personal life? Do you believe they are reflected in your dreams?

The dominant themes in Liz's response were: (1) relationship with boyfriend; (2) relationship with family members; and (3) work and career. Liz indicated that these themes were sometimes reflected in her dreamlife. However, she stated that this occurred less than 50% of the time. She noted that the dominant themes in her dreams were typically about traveling somewhere.

Question 7: Do you rely on your dreams in making life decisions? If so, how frequently?

Yes. If a dream comes when I have an important decision to make then I try to take information from the dream as pointing the way for what I should do.

Question 8: Do you find your dreams predictive of future life events? If so, how often do you see a connection between dream events and wake-state event?

Yes, definitely. At least 20% of the time.

Question 9: Do you have dreams regarding slavery? If so, describe these dreams.

No.

Question 10: Have you ever had dreams where race or racism is an element of the dream?

Yes. The dreams are always a result of something seen or read about that particular day. In these dreams I'm always trying to say something for or defend the underdog.

Question 11: Do you see themes of power, repression, oppression, anger, or anxiety in your dreams? If so, to what or whom do you believe it is related?

Power—no; repression—yes; oppression—yes; anger—yes; anxiety—yes. I believe it is related to Harold.

Question 12: Do you consider yourself to be a spiritual person? What is your definition of spirituality?

Yes. My definition of spirituality is being in tune to certain things. Not beating myself up but knowing things happened for a reason. Most of us should be more spiritual. Still believe in Catholicism. But not all of it. I believe in God.

Question 13: What do you consider to be spiritual symbols occurring in your dreams and to which ethnic heritage do these symbols belong?

The flying dream is spiritual. My mom was Hindu until she married my dad who is Catholic. I often went to the Hindu temple. The bird is a good thing to be when re-born. Always thinking I could be this bird and do whatever I want. Hindu tradition is that you be responsible for you, not what others do.

Question 14: Are there dream elements present in your dreams which you identify as African? Can you identify them as belonging to a particular tradition?

The bird dream is African but also Hindu. There is no difference between Africa and us.

Question 15: What are the themes and content of your fantasies?

I dream about being wealthy, about being in love. Being of service to others if I had more money. Would teach how to be of help, of service. Finding someone to love me and who needs to be loved.

Question 16: How do you most often experience creative self-expression in your life?

I'm always doing something. When I'm angry I clean the house. Right now I'm doing everything for the [visiting stepdaughter's birthday] party. I'm always trying to help someone and I usually get penalized for it. Criticized by partner.

Question 17: What are the ways most used and most useful in terms of your creativity?

I feel creative when I'm alone. Walking and being by the water relaxes me. Then I feel creative. When I feel wonderful and creative is when it is expressed in bringing family together.

Question 18: Are you currently receiving psychoanalysis, psychotherapy, or counseling or have you in the past?

Yes, I have in the past. But not now.

Question 19: If you found yourself in need of psychotherapy where would you seek such help?

With you [laughing]. With a person of color. At the beginning of my problems with Harold I went to the EAP (Employee Assistance Program) program for help.

Question 20: Do you believe psychotherapy to be generally helpful to those in need of psychological support?
Yes.

Question 21: What would you require of a psychotherapist and therapeutic environment before initiating therapy?
Normalcy. I wouldn't want to be separated with them on a chair and me somewhere else. I would want both of us to sit like we're sitting. Sitting and talking on a couch. It would mean talking better. Doing something about the problems.

Kyesha

Dreamer Portrait

Kyesha is a 65-year-old woman living in the Brooklyn brownstone home she moved into over 20 years ago. The magnolia tree that graces her front yard reveals an important part about Kyesha's life. Kyesha was born in Indiana, a place she calls "Klan country."

She is one of five children and is the second youngest in sibling order. Her father is a medical doctor and her mother is a housewife. Kyesha describes her family of origin as upper class.

In her present home, Kyesha lives with two of her three children. Her eldest child at home is her 24-year-old son. Her youngest daughter, Bea, will be entering Harvard in the fall and is about to leave home for the first time. Kyesha's middle daughter lives in Manhattan.

Kyesha has recently retired from teaching at City University. She had been employed there for 30 years as a psychology professor. In addition to this work, she has always had a small private practice as a psychotherapist. Kyesha says that her life is "busy" and she does not miss teaching but does intend to expand her private practice.

During our meetings together, Kyesha spoke of her relationship with the man she calls "the love of her life." She is referring to her husband who died 16 years ago. Kyesha describes how they first met.

I went to an art opening. I wasn't even sure that I wanted to attend. I was alone and was introduced to Kaba when I first arrived. I didn't pay much attention to him after our brief introduction. Within a few days the mutual friend who had invited me to the opening called and wanted to know if she could give Kaba my number. I said she could. He called within two days and we met for lunch. He told me that when he first saw me he knew he wanted to be with me for the rest of his life. I didn't think that was such a bad idea at the time. And so we were ... until the end of his life.

Kyesha speaks forthrightly about her relationship with Kaba. Shortly after arriving for my first visit to her home, I mentioned the beautiful, overhanging magnolia tree in her front yard. She explained that she and the children had planted the tree when Kaba died. It had been placed as a memorial to him but also as Kaba's Protector-Spirit watching over the family. Kyesha says the tree blooms twice a year, producing "large, magnificent-smelling blossoms." She says the tree has continued to grow just like Kaba's love and protection for his family.

The word "Kaba" means embrace. Kyesha in speaking of her relationship with Kaba sees the magnolia as metaphor. She continues to be embraced by his love.

Kyesha speaks of Kaba as if he is still alive in this physical reality. She expresses her belief that his physical death has not separated them in any way. She says just as the tree is such a presence in their lives, she continues to feel Kaba in her own life. "He is always with me." Kyesha's belief regarding Kaba is confirmed by her spiritual practice, Yoruba. According to this belief system, in the continuum of physical and spiritual life, Kaba does exist as fully as he did before. Kyesha says, "I see him. I know he is there with me."

Kyesha had her initial dream on the night of August 6th. Kaba's birthday is August 10th. "We were married three times—once in Africa, a Muslim, civil wedding downtown," she says. Kyesha and Kaba were married 12 years before his death from cancer. Kyesha and Kaba made several trips to Africa. Together they had created a "10-year plan." Kaba died just as they were beginning to implement from this plan. Trips to Africa had been a part of the plan. In discussing this plan, Kyesha says that she has been able to successfully complete all the intended goals. She indicates that the room we met in for our interviews was itself a part of the ten-year plan. Its revision and restoration varied somewhat from their original plan due to a fire in the home following Kaba's death. However, Kyesha says, "Everything is finished according to plan." Kyesha believes this has been possible due to Kaba's presence in her life.

Kyesha says her own father is still alive at 91 and calls her family "long-livers." She mentioned her mother only once in our conversations. In discussing the "guide" from the initial dream, Kyesha stated, "After my husband's death, I was trying to keep myself together as a mother. The concept of motherhood was heavy after Kaba died. I wanted to re-captivate some of what my own mother had done."

Kyesha has basically raised the children by herself. When Kaba died the oldest child was three years of age. Does Kyesha feel she has been to her children a mother like her own? She responds in the affirmative. "The children were so much of what Kaba and I had planned together—a family. He died before we could have more children."

Though she has never married again, Kyesha has been with the same lover for 15 years. She met him within a year of Kaba's death. She is 25 years his junior. She speaks of once jokingly asking Kaba if there was anything in their lives that he wanted, anything that was missing. He said he wanted to be a younger man, a younger lover for her pleasure. When Kyesha met her present lover soon after Kaba's death, she felt that he embodied the energy of her husband. She says that since Kaba's death she has had offers of marriage but has been "content" with her children, Kaba, and her lover.

Kyesha feels the "importance of relationships over materialism, spiritualism over materialism." She says that she has been well taken care of in her life, although she says at this point that she would "like to stay on track." Discussing this further, she speaks of "the race against time to refinance the house, have the tuition for college, stay focused on what's important to our lives." In her conversation about spiritualism, Kyesha says the attention it requires is the same "high maintenance" as Kaba's magnolia tree.

Kyesha maintains that her life has been "rich." The room in which we met was full of African statues and pieces of artwork. It was scented with a sweet pungent order of frankincense. Her mantle held seven candles for purification and cleansing. Kyesha burns both incense and candles everyday. She says it is love and faith that sustain her. She is reminded of this by the flame of the candles and by the protective scent of the incense.

Following is Kyesha's initial dream after our first meeting:

With the love of my life returning to Africa. Dressed in African attire—traditional dress. Trying to deliberate on whether to make the journey. Not knowing if we would be accepted without all our money and credentials. Decided to go anyway. We landed and had a long stretch of dark, uncertain, and somewhat foreboding land that we had to traverse before reaching one checkpoint. We sat on the tree stump and the brother [?] began to loosen his shirt to relieve some of the pressure. Seemingly a guide appeared, asked him certain questions, told us it was okay to rest a bit, then disappeared.

The next image was a large amphitheater-like structure with literally hundreds of people—divided first into long lines. Then once a certain level of processing within the journey, into smaller circles of 10, where we could sit down. I was at this point separated from my mate but had no doubt that we would be reunited.

Later that morning I'm holding Kivi in my arms and saying quietly to her, "I will protect you, I will protect you, I will protect you."

Kyesha

Dreamer Dialogue

Question 6: What are dominant themes in your own personal life? Do you believe they are reflected in your dreams?

I think those themes are spiritualism versus materialism. I believe this is reflected in my dreams. The subconscious comes to the fore when you're asleep. When your guard is down.

Question 7: Do you rely on your dreams in making life decisions? If so, how frequently?

When I take the time to do dream analysis, I use it. They get diverted to forgetfulness if I don't make use of them. I use unconscious content to work on my life. Dreams are important to ourselves and our issues that we are working on.

Question 8: Do you find your dreams prediction of future life events? If so how often do you see a connection between dream event and wake-state event?

Some of them have been. Not that often that I see a connection between dream and wake-state event. There are concrete elements in ordinary life—Donald, real life castle, invitation to get married.

Question 9: Do you have dreams regarding slavery? If so, describe these dreams.

Can't remember having a dream regarding slavery. When I visited Africa I went to some of the slave castles in West Africa. In one of them I took my sandals off. I stood on the stone feeling electricity through my body. It was very impactful for me. That experience reminds me of a dream.

Question 10: Have you ever had dreams where race or racism is an element of the dream?

I've dealt enough with that in reality. I was one of the first little girls in 1954 selected to go into Short Ridge School for desegregation. Can't remember dreaming about racism. I have heard and read so much about it—never dreamt about it.

Question 11: Do you see themes of power, repression, oppression, anger, or anxiety in your dreams? If so, to what or whom do you believe it is related?

I see power more than anything else. Success, power, winning. Most of my dreams support my attitude.

Question 12: Do you consider yourself to be a spiritual person? What is your definition of spirituality?

Yes. I define spiritual as having a connection with a force outside yourself, which is more powerful than yourself from which you embody a sense of oneness with the universe.

Question 13: What do you consider to be spiritual symbols occurring in your dreams and to which ethnic heritage do these symbols belong?

Pictures of the ocean, the sky, cloud formations. Spirituality combined with life experiences. Dream and reality reflect oneness.

Question 14: Are there dream elements present in your dream which you identify as African? Can you identify them as belonging to a particular tradition?

In many of my dreams I see mansions. These mansions have African art-imagery all over them. I don't recognize them as being to a particular tradition.

Question 15: What are the themes and content of your fantasies?

I live out my fantasies! [laughing] My Jacuzzi, my young lover ...

Question 16: How do you most often experience creative self-expression in your life?

I used to do that through my paintings. I do it now more through my courses on stress-reduction. Helping people to be in touch with themselves. I used to design a lot—like this house, like the one in the Hamptons.

Question 17: What are the ways most used and most useful in terms of your creativity?

Working with people, helping them.

Question 18: Are you currently receiving psychoanalysis, psychotherapy, or counseling or have you in the past?

I have in the past when I was in training to be a therapist—not since then.

Question 19: If you found yourself in need of psychotherapy where would you seek such help?

African psychologist who has Afrocentric orientation like myself.

Question 20: Do you believe psychotherapy to generally be helpful to those in need of psychological support?

Water is good for you if you have good water.

Question 21: What would you require of a psychotherapist and therapeutic environment before initiating therapy?
A person who can identify with me through training, ethnocentric, or attitude orientation. I would seek help from someone similar to myself and consonant with my belief system, identity, education, etc. Personal therapy has the potential to help with problems.

Rae

Dreamer Portrait

Rae is 50 years old. She has lived in Brooklyn most of her life arriving there with her parents at age ten. She is the youngest and only female of three siblings. Both of her brothers live in nearby communities. Her mother died 11 years ago and her father within the last three years. Rae's 22-year-old daughter Sarah resides with her in their Brooklyn home. Rae was married once. The marriage lasted for ten years.

We met in Rae's home where she has lived for 1-1/2 years. The space is mostly empty of furniture. Rae says she "cares less than I once did about furniture. This time I'm slowly furnishing the house with things I really like." She has traveled quite a lot in her life and says she is learning to "travel lighter."

Rae is presently working as a special education teacher in the New York City public schools. She has been at this position for 19 years with the exception of two sabbatical leaves. Rae has mostly taught preschoolers and first graders. More than 15 years ago she took a children's book writing and illustration class. Although she had attended the class to develop her interest in writing, the instructor identified her as a painter. She enjoyed how he described her illustrations and began to consider art as a career. She took more classes and eventually applied to graduate school for an MFA degree in painting. She wasn't accepted in this program but was offered a place in the BFA program. However, she refused, believing that she could be self-taught and achieve her artistic goals. When Rae discusses this aspect of her career, she sounds regretful. "If I had gone to the undergrad program, I would have been pretty much guaranteed admission to the MFA program."

Rae calls herself a "frustrated artist." When she married Paul, they worked out an agreement allowing her to remain home so she could focus on her art.

Paul would provide the income for the family while she was a housewife. "This worked for a time," said Rae, "but Paul would come home, look at me painting, and feel his own creative frustration." He had always wanted to be an actor but had never pursued it in a consistent manner. Seeing Rae doing her art added tension to the marriage. Rae couldn't cope with Paul's envy and eventually went back to work as a teacher. Soon after this Paul's son from a previous marriage came to live with them. Both Rae's daughter and stepson each vied for their parents' attention. The result was splitting and taking sides by Rae and Paul for their own children. The marriage ended in an angry divorce.

Rae says that she loved Paul very much. "I didn't understand about irreconcilable differences before. I thought it was just something made up and had no meaning. At my divorce I had a much better understanding." She says this with an ironic smile.

> I still miss him. We had so much passion together. But I'm still glad to have my life back. We were so close, too close. No wonder jealousy of each other's children tore our marriage apart. We only wanted each other and identified with our children too much. We were so overprotective of them because we were merged with them ourselves.

Rae has not been in another relationship since her breakup with Paul. She says that she required "many years" to take care of herself after the pain of the marriage. Paul has remarried to someone he began dating at the end of their marriage.

Rae says that she was very close to her mother. Her father was an alcoholic who was murdered by an associate. She remembers her father as being full of rage when he was drunk. Other times he was passive, quiet. For periods of time, Rae lived with her paternal grandparents. She doesn't remember these as particularly good times. She says there was always the possibility of returning home and witnessing her mother being beaten by her father.

"Though Paul nor any other partner ever physically hit me, I do feel I've been in bad relationships where men have emotionally abused me. At this point, I'm unwilling to put up with anything that's not my way." Laughingly, she continues that this probably wouldn't make a good marriage or partnership.

Becoming more serious, Rae says that she misses having a family. She says that her mother was her real family and when she died her "family" also died. Rae believes that her mother's spirit and ancestors are present in her life. Rae was raised in the African Methodist Episcopal Church.

Rae has many friends and considers them to be her extended family. "Now I wish I had had more children. I would love to have more children around. They would be my family." Rae says that by the time she felt she could be responsible for more children her marriage was ending. Rae says that she has considered adoption but doesn't feel she has the money to take care of more children. She is hopeful that her daughter will have more children and feels that she will probably be a better grandmother than she was a mother. "My mother was always tired from working as a maid. Then she came home and suffered there for almost 60 years. I don't want to live out my life like that."

Rae has kept a record of her dreams for the last 15 years. She says that journal writing came naturally to her because at some point she had hoped to write professionally. She began recording her dreams as a means to work out problems that she might be having. Following are Rae's initial dreams. Both occurred on the same night. She remembers them occurring in the order given.

Dream 1. I'm on a flying carpet with many people. We're all standing up very close to each other. When we take off we go very high. I think how we're going higher than we have before. It's exhilarating to fly so fast and high in the open. At one point I hold onto the sides of the rug when we first take off. But after that it's OK. I think there is someone there I know, maybe I've had a relationship with. There are many people from the same family. I think, if we crash so many people from the family will die. Someone named David is leading us on the ride. He is at the helm.

Dream 2. I'm at a church service where a young man and woman are being eulogized. People are looking for something to cover their faces. I suggest some of the women take off lace veils and put them over their faces. This is done, and the same white cloth is spread over both their faces. An old woman approaches me with an honorary award. She hands it to me and says there will be a celebration at some later time. This award does not seem to have to do with the funeral and seems cause for a different kind of ceremony.

Rae

Dreamer Dialogue

Question 6: What are the dominant themes in your own personal life? Do you believe they are reflected in your dreams?
Themes in my life are mostly about money. I never seem to have enough. When I do it seems to go away really fast—can't hold on to it. Missing having a family is another theme.

Question 7: Do you rely on your dreams in making life decisions? If so, how frequently?
I do rely on them but a lot of the times it's hindsight that I realize something was in my dreams and now it's come true. Things happen before I realize maybe I can influence them beforehand.

Question 8: Do you find your dreams predictive of future life events? If so, how often do you see a connection between dream event and wake-state event?
Yes, I do. I see the connection a lot. But a lot of the times it's hindsight.

Question 9: Do you have dreams regarding slavery? If so, describe these dreams.

I have never had a dream where I was a slave or saw slaves. I've had dreams where it felt like I was in the South on a plantation and there was an energy like slavery, but I wasn't a slave.

Question 10: Have you ever had dreams where race or racism is an element of the dream?

Not that I can remember.

Question 11: Do you see themes of power, repression, oppression, anger, or anxiety in your dreams? If so, to what or whom do you believe it is related?

Sometimes I'm very anxious in my dreams, especially when I dream about snakes. I have snake dreams at least once every month or month and a half. I used to have dreams where I was being chased by gangs of boys. I don't have these anymore. I think these dreams happen because there are things going on I haven't figured out yet.

Question 12: Do you consider yourself to be a spiritual person? What is your definition of spirituality?

I consider myself to be spiritual. I was always trying to get next to God when I was a kid. I used to go to Mass. I loved all that ritual stuff. I don't go anymore but I still believe in Spirit.

Question 13: What do you consider to be spiritual symbols occurring in your dreams and to which ethnic heritage do these symbols belong?

Sometimes I dream about old women who give me advice and I think they're spiritual symbols. Once I had a dream that spoke about different levels of consciousness and showed me a book of writings that looked like hieroglyphics. That dream was futuristic and from the past. I don't know who it belongs to!

Question 14: Are there dreams elements present in your dreams that you identify as African? Can you identify them as belonging to a particular tradition?

Yes. Sometimes there are drums, huts, dirt floors—snakes! I don't know enough about any particular tradition to speak on it.

Question 16: How do you most often experience creative self-expression in your life?

I would like to say painting but I don't do that anymore. I think through the kids I work with, they're so creative. Through my friendships with people. Living in New York every day is creative! You have to be creative to deal with everything here!

Question 17: What are the ways most used and useful in terms of your creativity?

Right now I think it's planning my future—money, retirement, things like that. I want to travel some more so I'm trying to save up so I can go live abroad for a year. Putting my creative thoughts together about buying another house so I can have something to support me when I get old. Is that creative? I don't know.

Question 18: Are you currently receiving psychoanalysis, psychotherapy, or counseling or have you in the past?

Yes, I am now and I have in the past. We did a lot of couples therapy when the marriage was ending. I still go now.

Question 19: If you found yourself in need of psychotherapy where would you seek such help?

It would depend on what I needed help with. Right now I'm in personal therapy but would like to join a group. That's mostly money-related but would still like some help.

Question 20: Do you believe psychotherapy to generally be helpful to those in need of psychological support?

Yes.

Question 21: What would you require of a psychotherapist and therapeutic environment before initiating therapy?

Someone fully trained. Friendly person and environment. Someone who I felt could carry the weight when things got tough. Sometime people can't even though they're therapists.

Chapter 10

African American Dreamers

Themes and Mythological Motifs

Dream Content Analysis

The contents of participants' dreams were sorted and analyzed in relation to 12 categories. In Part 2, these categories are listed and examples are provided of the various categories through presentation of dreams. The 12 comparative categories include dream themes, dream symbols, mythological motifs, therapy- and therapist-related dreams, body imagery, day residue, prospective dreams, feminine and masculine imagery, animals, children, recurring dreams, and emotions.

The total number of dreams collected was 31. Kyesha provided eight, Liz 12, and Rae 11. In Part 2, three dreams each from Kyesha and Liz are instructive in showing resultant dream content and categories. Although four individual dreams from Rae are reviewed, they are analyzed as a total of two separate dreams because they occurred on the same night.

Following each dream will be the symbols and themes from the dream (Categories 1 and 2).

Liz

Dream 2

It's a city, not like Manhattan, rather like Queens vacant lots, light industry, houses. As I walk past a house, I meet some women about my age, wearing either saris or old hippie clothes. They tell me that they're living in this ashram or Buddhist community. They have given up the external world.

I meet them later at a party. They invite me to visit. There's a gloomy entrance hall ... lots of people. They had just had a community meeting. I felt welcome but not part of it.

Then two very male men—policemen or county sheriffs—very male, very overbearing, come in. I don't know if they had guns in their hands or wallets with important documents. Maybe they were electric cattle prods. They didn't like the community. I felt threatened. I really wanted to get away. I left my handbag and my keys behind. I found myself walking through the streets at twilight. I couldn't go back home, who could help me? I resolved to go back. The men were

DOI: 10.4324/9781003219965-14

gone. The people in the community said that those men come around and try this a lot. They didn't feel as threatened as I did.

I returned again. I was thinking what it would be like to join them. Maybe I could do a project. They game me a tour. Downstairs, there were busy women working together. It was not very bright, more like a cave level.

On the second level, there was a place where they had a communal meal. There were tables with many-sided study carrels. Each woman had a specific area, with sides and ridges dividing their area from the next. Each had a saying on the front of her area. Many were Bible verses, the commonest ones, like John 3:16. It all had a monastic feel. One woman explained that their system of belief included Shakers, etc., even though it was clearly Buddhist.

The next level was the mechanics of work. It was dusty. There were men up there sitting on dusty couches. They looked like old-time kibbutzniks. They were artists, hippies, and religious-community kinds of lovers. No real sexual energy. They all seemed alive and cordial, but just sitting around. But in one section there was a foundry. I thought, "Oh, how unusual to have a foundry in the city." There was molten metal being poured into molds, big heavy, massive machines and equipment that turned out this very sturdy stuff, perhaps bowls or bells, perhaps of bronze.

I am so tired I could just lie down and take a nap. My guide says, "Oh, there are 15 empty rooms right now." The rooms are comfy, old-fashioned college dorm rooms. Someplace you could go and feel immediately as yours.

Suddenly, I am accompanied by a boy, 10 or 11 years old. He's walking exploring with me. We are perhaps on the next level up. There is an exploration I am going to do. There is a contraption, a flying machine. You have to flap its wings. It's mechanical and clunky. I asked the boy, "Do you want to join me in this adventure?" "Sure." We were in a domed room on the second or third floor. I got into the flying machine and was about to flap out the window. The boy said, "Well, if you spiral upwards you can go right up into the dome and then out from there." It was a gold dome. We got out that way. I thought it might be too tight, but no. He's in the back seat; I'm in front. We fly out. How lovely! It's comforting having him along. This is my adventure. He's not afraid. He's secure in it being an adventure. We fly over fields of gold and green, a benign landscape. I know how to get back.

Dream 2

SYMBOLS AND THEMES

Symbols	Themes
Airplane	Flying
Flying	Spirituality

(Continued)

Symbols	Themes
Golden dome	Nature
Policemen	Groups
Purse	Elements
Keys	
City	
John 3:16	
Foundry	
Guide	
Bronze bowls	
Bronze bells	
Religious community	
Ten-year-old boy	
House	
Cave	
Buddhism	
Shakers	

Dream 4

I was in one of the building with all these hallways—maybe a school, a department store. I was with some women: three sisters or a mother and two daughters. It was two generations; I was identified with both of them. One of the people had known this place for much longer than the others. "You have to see this room!" She opened the door into this glorious place filled with golden light. It's like a Victorian candy shop—windows or mirrors, wood, art nouveau frames—like a Viennese coffee house. There were baskets of chocolate, most wrapped in golden, pink and orange foil, and figures—teddy bears, Santas, baskets wrapped in cellophane with bows. There was a feeling of looking into a candy shop at night with only oil lamps, yet it was late afternoon golden light. But it was a bathroom. I said, "Oh, this is just the most wonderful place! Oh good, I have to pee."

There are two basins for toilets. They were hammered copper or brass, glowing vessels with very clean water, on marble floors. I went over to the closest basin (the others were urinating into the other basin). I open the lid on this one. It was filled with newspapers. It was unusable. But it didn't spoil my sense of the wonderfulness of this room. I should tell them that it needs to be attended to. I had no feeling of disgust. So I went over to the other one. Could I aim OK? Could I lift my skirt high enough? There was some arrangement for cleaning your shoes if they got splashed.

Dream 4

SYMBOLS AND THEMES

Symbols	Themes
Victorian candy store	Elegance/Luxury
Three women	Groups
Viennese coffee shop	Elements
Golden light	
Bathroom	
Basin/toilets	
Shoes	
Chocolate candy	
Marble floors	
Copper	

Dream 9

Today I woke up feeling very much at peach [peace] with myself. I dreamt I was in the West Indies with Regina, Harold, his ex-wife and my brothers and sisters. We were in their house preparing a huge feast and everything was really great. The feeling was peaceful. There was no animosity. Harold went outside for a walk and took a long time to come back, so I decided to go and look for him. When I was walking down this path looking for him, I finally saw him walking up towards me with this big smile on his face. When he approached me we both saw this man dressed in Indian wear, but made of leaves, riding this motorcycle. He went by us. His face was green. When I woke up I was feeling a sense of peace.

Dream 9

SYMBOLS AND THEMES

Symbols	Themes
Feast	Family
Harold	Nature
Regina	Groups
Green man	Emotions
Motorcycle	
Tree leaves	
West Indies	

Kyesha

Dream 2

In a Bedouin peasant village in Africa or Arabia. Had been entrusted by a man in long dark clothing with a raggedy, vault-like container or chest with decorative cloth over it, apparently for purposes of camouflage.

When the container was dropped through this cave-like opening into this lower depression, it opened and I was able to see that there were valuables in coins, large sums of money and jewels.

Symbols and Themes For Dream 2

Symbols	Themes
Bedouin	Africa
Peasant village	Money
Africa	Search/Find
Arabia	Spiritual
Vault-container	
Decorative cloth	
Cave opening	
Coins	
Money	
Jewels	

Dream 4

Seamy hotel-like room. Rickety stairs up to the second floor room. Inside, on wall above bed, something like a whatnot shelf with little novelties and a series of cards with envelops with handwriting on them. Could not make them out, so we were distracted and went down to the main desk to try to figure out how someone had gotten into our room in the first place to write these illegible notes on our wall.

No help. Saw no one at this unkempt desk. So we (my sister Tatu and I) return to our room and begin to try to decipher these notes. She is able to read one, it seems from a Mr. Steers, the apparent owner or lodge keeper. They appear to be amorous notes of interest for me.

As I turned and looked across the room I see a strange old black hand coming out from a door. I run over and pull the door closed. Resistance. Ask "Who are you?" In a hushed voice, a man says "Open the door. Don't worry. I'm just looking for someone." "Who?" I asked. "Just open the door; I'm looking for Mr. Steers." "I don't know Mr. Steers. How did you get in here?" "From the roof." I slowly open the door and a large old dark man is standing in a small, very small, bathroom. Actually, just a washroom. I saw no tub. About this time I realize there is another man standing on his shoulder. I reach up toward the man who hands him a knife. He moves away. The other man comes down.

At this point I open our door and he says "Take me to him." I started along with my nervous sister to lead the man down the stairs to the lobby of the hotel. The desk clerk was not there. But a small crowd of hotel residents begins to gather. A clerk comes up the stairs. I explain that I don't even know the man, Mr. Steers, who these cats are looking for. Could he help them? Tatu and I let this man and the gathered crowd become the interest group for these invaders and we ease to the back of the crowd and run back to the room, barricade it, and quickly make our getaway plan.

Dream 4

SYMBOLS AND THEMES

Symbols	Themes
Hotel room	Family
What-not shelf	Spiritual
Unkempt desk	Search/find
Sister	Love

(Continued)

Symbols	Themes
Mr. Steers	Groups
Amorous notes	Travel/transportation
Old dark man	
Knife	
Washroom	
Crowd	
Getaway plan	

Dream 6

We are at home in a rather pastoral setting. The weather was mild fall in texture and I was peaceful. I was standing on the wrap-around pillared porch and Donald was talking to me from the grassy lawn. You were telling me that you had a right to the preservation of this, your favorite or favored environment (homestead). Something or someone had challenged your holding onto it.

I shared that a similar challenge was happening with the home that I too had claimed as my own for decades. It appears that several dozen people had gathered for our wedding ceremony. But there seemed to be a problem—another nice lady with whom you had been associated for years was reluctant to leave the home. This required pastoral counseling. I was ushered into a long illuminated sitting room. You were lounging in a velvet smoking jacket (dark blue) with satin lapels on a long sofa. I was directed to sit at the other end of the sofa.

My mother it seems was sitting in an overstuffed, comfortable chair, quietly surveying the atmosphere. The pastor asked me, "What should we say to the other woman?" I responded with usual frankness and candor. "Tell her that Donald and I are being married today." Donald wore a subtle, noncommittal smile. "Then what shall we tell your mother?" I responded, "She already knows; she's my mother."

I have no recollection of the actual ceremony, which was held outside on the lawn. But afterwards I came inside and was looking out before leaving the grounds. Several women were opening a saran-wrapped package of brown cookies and handed one through the window to me.

As I left I was crossing a street and one of the women asked me if I was driving a Cadillac; I said no, I didn't like Cadillacs. Well, was I driving in a limousine? "No, I'm going to enjoy a walk." The small crowd dissipated!

Dream 6

SYMBOLS AND THEMES

Symbols	Themes
Home	Nature
Pastoral setting	Love
Fall	Marriage
Pillared porch	Groups
Donald	Family
Wedding ceremony	Luxury
Pastoral counseling	
Brown cookies	
Cadillac/limousine	
Walking	
Pastor	

Rae

Dream 9a

I'm trying to catch a train and by the time I run around the platform the train pulls off. I think that I can take a bus and catch up to the train or take another train and catch up. I don't remember exactly but I think I actually do get to another station where I'm looking for the right train.

Dream 9b

I'm sitting with a young boy, age eight or nine, pulling off sponge that has grown to his right upper chest. It is a blue rectangle sponge with a black backing. I take one sponge off but it seems another grows back in its place.

I say to the woman (mother?) who sits with us that we should try a homeopathic remedy because it would keep it from growing back. That we had to keep it from growing back—that was the solution rather than treating it.

SYMBOLS AND THEMES DREAM 9a

Symbols	Themes
Train	Travel/transportation
Bus	Emotion
Platform	
Station	

SYMBOLS AND THEMES DREAM 9b

Symbols	Themes
Boy	Spiritual
Blue sponge	Africa
Chest	Elements
Woman/mother	Search/Find
Homeopathic remedy	

DREAM 11a

A shaman stands before me dressed in ritual clothing of graying dusty almost-rags. I have just completed a death ritual, and he is doing a purification cleansing on me. I think I ask him to do the cleansing or sense that it is expected.

I put my hands out thinking that I know what to do or strongly feel this. He pours sand into my hands. From the sand he takes some and throws it over my face and forehead. Next he throws some on my chest area. Then he touches my solar plexus and stomach area. We stand as he does the ritual. Then he tells me to bury the sand in the mountains. During the ritual I hear the words—the only ones I understand—soul and clean.

DREAM 11B

I stand looking out a window. A black bull tries repeatedly to climb the wet rocks of a mountain incline. Over and over he charges up the mountain but because it is wet with water he cannot get a grip and always slides back down. But he keeps trying again and again. I think if he waits until it's dry he'll be able to climb without falling back.

Then a man comes. He too tries to climb the huge boulders but slips back. I think that he should move to the place where there is red dirt so he will be able to stand. I think he also falls back like the bull.

SYMBOLS AND THEMES DREAM 11a

Symbols	Themes
Shaman	Spiritual
Death ritual	Death
Ritual clothing	Elements
Sand	Travel/transportation
Body parts	
Mountains	
Soul	

SYMBOLS AND THEMES DREAM 11b

Symbols	Themes
Window	Death
Black bull	Sickness
Mountain	Aggression
Water	Elements
Man	
Red dirt	
Boulders	

Cross Case Analysis

The dream content was categorized for each dreamer. Following is a comparison of the dream elements found in all 31 dreams based on categories.

Mythological Motifs

Liz	Kyesha	Rae
Green Man	Baobab tree	Shaman
Twins	Treasure Chest	Bull
Flying carpet		Death rite
		Ezekiel
		Sponge boy

Images (Number of Occurrences)

Liz	Kyesha	Rae
Therapist and therapy imagery		
2	0	0
Body imagery		
1	0	3
Day residue		
0	1	1
Prospective		
1	1	0
Masculine imagery		
5	11	7
Feminine imagery		
11	11	11
Children		
2	2	3
Animals		
Worm	None	Worm
Snake		Bull
Emotions		
Fear	Fear	Fear
Anxiety	Anxiety	Anxiety
Depression	Depression	Repression
Peace	Happiness	Excitement
Curiosity	Suspicion	Repulsion
Pain	Concern	Sadness
Happiness		
Satisfaction		
Love		
Recurring Elements		
Guyana	Africa	Snakes
Family	Groups	Family
Flying	Family	

Comparison of Dream Themes

The following is a comparison of the occurrences of the themes among dreamers for 31 dreams. The respective total of dreams for each participant is as follows: Liz = 11, Kyesha = 8, and Rae = 12.

Theme	Liz	Kyesha	Rae
Africa	0	2	0
Flying	2	0	1
Family	3	5	2
Spiritual	1	1	2
Aggression	1	2	3
Search/find	1	1	0
Nature	4	2	0
Marriage	0	2	0
Love	1	1	1
Sickness	1	1	1
Groups	6	6	3
Luxury	1	2	0
Travel/transportation	6	4	5
Money	1	1	0
Bathroom	2	1	0

Comparison of Dream Symbols

The following is a comparative list of the dream symbols appearing in all 31 dreams.

Liz	Kyesha	Rae
Airplane	Wedding	Flying
Flying carpet	Baobab tree	Shaman
Soul	Africa	David
Golden dome	Child	Dead
Bride/groom	Peasant village	Gun
Green man	Cave	Ezekiel
Flying	Treasure chest	Train
Twins	Hotel	Policemen
Baby	Marble shelf	Sponge
Bicycle	Social workers	Snakes
Policemen	Shingles (sickness)	Black bull
Purse	Velvet smoking jacket	Red
City	Cadillac	Dirt
Keys	Mother	Worm
John 3:16	Palace	Mother/father
Foundry	Marble chess board	Cave

(Continued)

Liz	Kyesha	Rae
Sand	The Dakota (building)	
Guide	Pastor	
Bronze bowls	Sister	
Bronze bells	Old man	
Religious community		
Therapist		
Victorian candy store		
Bathroom		
Marble		
"F" Train		
Worm		
Motorcycle		
Homeless woman		
10-year-old boy		
4-year-old boy		
Mother		
Sister		
Cave		
Buddhism		
Shakers		
West Indies		

Occurrence Frequency of Selected Dream Images among Dreamers

Dream symbols or themes that appeared in the dreams of at least two dreamers, indicating a high frequency of occurrence, included the following:

Groups
Family
Spiritual
Biblical
Worm
Travel/transportation
Policemen
Flying
Siblings
Children
Cave
Old man
Mother

Mythological Motifs in the Dreams

The presence of mythological motifs was evident in all three dreamers. Liz in her initial dream saw twins. Kyesha's dream included the Tree of Life and

Rae's final dream was that of a shaman. Each woman had some associations with their dreams but only Rae had any foreknowledge of her particular image.

The appearance of mythological motifs was significant in their surprise appearances as well as in the subject matter. In a way similar to the emergence of the feminine images, it was not initially explored as a selected topic of this dream project. The presence of dreams with recognizable mythological themes adds to the belief of the archetypal patterns present in all humans. This position was maintained by Jung throughout his writings on archetypes and the collective unconscious.

Liz's initial dream recalled a young woman moving in a baby carriage without any noticeable source of energy. The striking element of this dream is the revelation that the woman has a four-year-old boy attached to her whom Liz describes as a Siamese twin. Liz wonders in the dream if the woman and child are actually mother and son. The story of twins is generally that of a creation myth. Liz's dream has the potential to be viewed as both personal and archetypal.

Creation

Liz's dream when interpreted from a Jungian perspective looks at a woman on the edge of adulthood. To be pushed in a baby carriage is out of place, inappropriate. Four-year-old children tend to "know it all." The adult is being controlled by a grandiose child. Clearly this child is well-nourished. She says of him that he has "sucked all the life out of her." If children show the potentiality of a dreamer's life, this child looks as if it will thrive. However, the life of one is dependent on the other. How will the young woman survive?

In the Benin myth of Mawu-Lisa, a pair of androgynous twins, the younger of the two, the boy, is described as "mischievous and unpredictable." This would fit the description of the young boy dream figure in terms of unpredictability.

The rider doesn't know where she is going or who she is in relationship to the child. She is passively being pushed along. Both girl and boy require healing.

The archetypal imaginings of this dream speak to creation. The energetic pattern is one of movement: the carriage is carrying, pushing something forward. There is movement from the unconscious. Liz is being asked to create something, perhaps a *new* life. The dream image of the woman and child are radically different, and the former seems to be suffering while the other thrives. Perhaps there is more suffering to experience in the form of sacrifice. How will the image of the two deepen? Would it lead to the death of the woman as the child grew older and stronger? Can only one survive or will there be an integration of the two forms that allow for the emergence of a third?

In *African Mythology* (1967), Geoffrey Parrinder relates the story of what he calls the "heavenly twins":

> One myth says that these twins were born from a primordial mother, Nana Buluku, who created the world and then retired. Mawu was the moon and female, controlling the night and dwelling in the west. Lisa was male, the sun, and lived in the east. They had no children when first took up their stations, but eventually they came together in an eclipse. Whenever there is an eclipse of the sun or moon it is said that Mawu and Lisa are making love. (p. 23)

When we consider what Liz wants more than anything in life, it is love, to have a "true love."

In the above myth of Mawu-Lisa we see another possibility for how the archetypal energy of Liz's dream may move. In this myth, children are created, and there is a continuous creation and recreation of love. This is Liz's heart's desire. Is it possible that in the deepening of images the young woman and boy will come to match one another and be loved?

Liz's dream shows how both a personal and an archetypal approach provide her with insight into her life. As we spoke about her dream, she experienced a sense of "openness" and possibilities. At first, she had been startled and dismayed by the dream. Noting the appearance of the woman she related her own tiredness about her current relationship. We spoke of how the woman is actually being pushed—Liz feels pushed by her own desire for a different life and worn out by her failures in trying to achieve that life through relationships.

The image of twins is an archetypal one appearing in many cultures. It is a prominent one in African tradition. Within African culture, twins have been treated in different ways—from being worshipped and recognized as special to being segregated from their communities because of their twinning. The fact that Liz had such a dream speaks to the universality of psyche and its ability to create stories that mirror, confirm, and deepen our understanding of who we are in both conscious and unconscious realms.

The Tree of Life

Kyesha's dream of resting at a tree in Africa brought to the mind the Tree of Life. Leading up to her arrival at this tree was a journey to Africa. It was a journey for which she is unable to carry any money or identification. When we spoke of this dream, in her associations, Kyesha said this dream reminded of the baobab tree. This is an iconic tree in Africa, and in African mythology represents the Tree of Life. Rituals and ceremonies are conducted under these trees, which have overseen the traditional for centuries. Before Kyesha reached her dream tree she and her husband passed through "dark ...

foreboding land." After this they reach the "checkpoint" and sit on the tree stump to rest. The tree in Kyesha's dream is only a stump. It has been cut down.

In *The Myth of the Goddess* (1993), Baring and Cashford said in their description of the Tree of Life that it "was one of the primary images of the goddess herself, in whose immanent presence all pairs of opposites are reconciled" (p. 496). Baring and Cashford further stated that "the ritual cutting down of the tree signified the dying phase of the totality of being, seasonally celebrated as the 'fall,' which, far from preventing rebirth, acknowledged its perennial possibility" (p. 498). What is important, as the dream continues, is that Kyesha becomes separated from her husband. Just importantly, she says that she "had no doubt that we would be reunited." Later in that same dream, she is swearing protection to her granddaughter.

Archetypally, the Tree of Life holds three levels of consciousness: the roots that are beneath the earth, the trunk on the earth, and the branches and leaves reaching to heaven. It has been portrayed as the connection that allows one to reach the God. In many African myths, it is the cutting down of this tree that signals the end of human immortality or the end of direct human contact with the gods. It is now only the shaman or diviner who can reach the heights and provide divine messages for humans.

Kyesha associated the tree with her African ancestors whom she believes have given her much in her life. In the dream she said it is the guide who loosens her shoes and offers comfort on the journey. They are in the desert, and it is hot. When I asked if she saw herself as a guide, she spoke about her work in bringing students to Africa, especially the first trip in 1972 when she came with 50 students. She believed that this was spiritual work and believed herself to be a "student-learner, teacher-student."

When we discussed the circle of 10, Kyesha spoke of her husband's birthday being on the 10th of August and mentioned the unity of the number 1 with God.

She said that she has always seen herself as a part of a circle of knowledge, sharing with others. "The circle is always important to me, ... the African tribal circle, Indian dancing circle, the universal concept of circle, the lotus of a thousand petals," she said.

Depending on the tradition one follows, 10 may be considered in a positive or negative view. The Maya believed the number 10 to be unlucky because it represented the day of the death god. The Bambara of Africa thought it a good number because it was composed of the number representing creation (4) and held other numbers of luck to total 10. The number is indicative of movement and indicates completion in the journey from the number 1 to the completion equaling 10. On the journey in Kyesha's dream, the guide asked Kyesha's husband certain questions, and advised him that it is okay to rest. The guide does not speak to her, only her husband. Later it is her husband who disappears as the guide as done.

In discussing the foreboding feeling of the landscape, Kyesha said it has to do with the historical perspective always given to Africa. She said it is not her personal experience of it or what she consciously thinks of it. She developed this while describing that in spite of the darkness of the sky there is a stretch of opening that is red and purple. She said she feels no anxiety at being separated and suddenly on this journey without her husband, credentials nor money. The dream ends as she whispers words of protection and reassurance to the child she holds in her arms.

I disagree with Jung's ideas pertaining to Black people as expressed in his essay "The Psychology of the Child Archetype" in *The Archetypes and the Collective Unconscious* (1968, pp. 122–175), because of his negative equating of "primitive" man to children.

He basically said of the former that, lacking psychological development, he cannot produce what Jung calls the third, or the "child." "Primitive" man, in his view, is unable to move toward producing a transcending "third" that offers possibilities for transformation. However, when I overlook the apparent racism in the essay, I am able to accept several of Jung's points regarding the child as archetype. "Child means something evolving towards independence. This it cannot do without detaching itself from its origins: abandonment is therefore a necessary condition, not just a concomitant symptom" (1968, p. 168 [CW 9, para. 287]). Kyesha is on a journey where she sits on the stump of the Tree of Life. She sits without her husband and vows protection to her child. She is without money and identity. It appears to be a time of renewal. The tree in her associations is located in the desert, a place of renewal and shedding of the old. It is a place where one learns a new "reality," a place to grapple with sacrifice and abandonment. In her dream Kyesha does not run away from this place but swears protection. It is both acknowledging of what has come to pass and taking a stand—for or against what remains part of the mystery of the journey.

Shamanic Ritual

Rae's final dream at the close of our work together imaged a shaman performing a purification cleansing following her completion of a death ritual. Rae said that she had met with two different shamans in the past but never received a ritual such as the one in her dream. She said that the shaman appeared to be from a place such as Polynesia. His clothing was gray rags and it seemed that he was covered in gray. His skin complexion was gray, almost matching exactly the color of his clothes.

Through the ritual of cleansing, he spoke words that Rae could not understand. Only at the end of the rite was she able to understand the words "soul" and "clean."

Rae said she felt the dream to be profound. She understood that the throwing and placing of sand on certain parts of her body indicated a cleansing of the chakras. She felt that it was good to have such a "thorough cleaning." It felt that something was different for her but she was unable to identify what. She felt the change had already happened but she just hadn't caught up with it yet.

In his text on shamanism, Eliade (1964) (1951) stated the following:

The shaman is indispensable in any ceremony that concern the experiences of the human soul as such ... . The shaman performs the function of doctor and healer; he announces the diagnosis, goes in search of the patient's fugitive soul, captures it, and makes it return to animate the body that it has left. It is always the shaman who conducts the dead person's soul to the underworld, for he is the psychopomp par excellence. (p. 182)

In her dream, Rae is told by the shaman to take the sand from the ritual up to the mountain for burial. The mountain is usually identified as that place where the dead are buried, humans make contact with god and the spiritually "designated" (shaman, priestess, holy man) may visit. Rae said that she is really not a "mountain person" but is an "ocean person." She was slightly surprised by the journey she must make to the mountaintop.

A Yoruba priest described Rae's dream as a "personal dream." He said that it was a very spiritual dream showing her things about the spiritual life of a spiritual teacher. He said that the sand used in the dream is used in Ifa markings to show divination marks. He believed it to be a Native American dream and an important dream.

The second part of Rae's shaman dream showed a black bull continuously attempting to climb a mountain. It was unable to accomplish this because the mountainside was wet.

A man soon appeared and also attempted to climb the mountain. He also fails. In South Africa, a black bull is where disease is ritually placed following a healing rite. The bull is then sacrificed in completion of the ritual. The bull is an archetypal symbol of sacrifice not just in African culture but in many other societies as well. In Asia the black bull is a symbol of death. The bull is also known as an animal directly connected with the sky gods.

In *The Great Cosmic Mother* (1987), authors Sjoo and Mor speak of the development of cows from sacred animals to animals of production:

In matriarchal Crete, every cow was known by her personal name! It seems that bull-calves who were unproductive were ritually killed and eaten. This could be the origin of the religious sacrifice of the sacred bull—Son of the Cow—his annual death and resurrection being a widespread throughout the Mediterranean and Northern Africa. Surely the veneration of cattle among East African peoples to this day is a remnant of the widespread Neolithic Mother Cow and bull worship. (p. 42)

The archetypal images and motifs appearing in the dreams of Liz, Rae, and Kyesha are examples of the uniqueness and the widespread possibilities of psyche. In my initial research intent, I never ruled out the possibilities of receiving dreams with mythological motifs but, as with the emergence of so many feminine images, had not placed an emphasis on this area beforehand. The presence of all the dreams with such clear archetypal imagery stood strongly in place against the absence of dreams regarding what I had assumed would be archetypal imagery of slavery in some form or another. The archetypal images that arose did not contain this theme, although many other universal topics emerged, including marriage, children, death, and mothers.

I believe it to be significant that there was such a strong and varied revelation of archetypal material in the dreams of these three women. It speaks to the power and imagination of psyche, moving and revealing and truly holding us in its image.

Following are my dreams, that occurred at the end of my last interview with the women dreamers.

1   *Sarah and I are driving on the road to find something or someone. It's in the country and the road is very dark; there are no lights. We wonder if we're on the right road.*

2   *I'm waiting to perform. I'm going to sing. A lot of time goes by. There are different people moving around backstage. My dress is tight, short; I wonder about keeping it down so the top of my stockings doesn't show.*

   I think I've forgotten the song and wish the musicians were there so I can hear the music; then I would know the lyrics to sing. I try to remember the song. I'm anxious about this not knowing. I pace in my tight dress, trying to remember.

3   *I dream again, me and my daughter are going to the school. This time we break in. But the people who live there arrive. We are looking for something. The woman gives us some information. We begin to leave the building. It had been difficult knowing what street was the right one to be on. It had taken a lot of energy trying to locate the right street, remember the name, see it in the dark on the street signs. On the drive from the school, I see the street sign. It says King Street.*

Dream Participants Feedback

All participants believed that our dreamwork together had been beneficial to them. They all indicated that they were now more conscious of dreaming and had a greater understanding of the meaning of their dreams. Though two dreamers had kept a dream journal for several years, both indicated that the project had helped them see their dreams in different ways. All dreamers expressed an interest in participating in an ongoing dream group.

Kyesha, Rae, and Liz all felt that the dreamwork project could have been improved upon in the following ways: (1) more frequent meetings during the one-year research period, (2) all participants meeting as a group in addition to one-to-one interviews, (3) participants being provided with a bibliography about dreaming, and (4) participants receiving more of my interpretations during our interview meetings.

It was emotionally gratifying for me to hear what the women gave as their response to my final inquiries to our dreamwork together.

Their full attention to the work for the months that we were together proved to be beneficial to all of us. Seeing the group imagery in their dreams was suggestive of their wish to be closely connected to family. Wake state familial relationships and dream images reflected one another.

Chapter 11

Africanist Cultural Symbols and Dream Interpretation

Cultural Symbols

What is the meaning of dreams, dream imagery, and dreaming to African American women? The dominant themes present in the dreams of the three women participants included family, groups, and travel motifs. Related areas of interest were investigated and reviewed to further develop an understanding of the quality of the themes that emerged in the dreams. The results regarding these questions follow.

What are the implications of African American women's experience of dreams and dreaming for the practice of analytical psychology or any psychological therapy practice? All respondents indicated that they rely on their dreams in making conscious life decisions. These decisions usually revolved around family issues. All participants indicated that they believed acknowledgment of their dreams and using information from them or "seeing" information from them affected their level of self-improvement in all areas of life.

What are the indications for an Africanist-centered clinical practice in analytical psychology, based on the examination of dream content, associations, and symbols of African Americans as understood within a traditional African cultural framework? Based on the results of the dream symbols, content, and associations of participants, there are indications for consideration of these elements from a cross-cultural perspective when engaged in clinical practice with African Americans. Though only one of the dream participants reported having dreams related to racism, the possibilities for dream interpretation are subjective and particular to the interpreter. In addition, the most standard methods of dream interpretation rely on symbol interpretation which is Eurocentric. It was my experience during the course of the dreamwork project I observed that dreams may be interpreted in different ways and with different considerations, as to diagnostic information based on one's knowledge of symbols. There are instances whereby a symbol may have an interpretation that is universally recognizable, including from an Africanist perspective. However, I have

DOI: 10.4324/9781003219965-15

also found that because African symbols are so sparsely used for dream interpretation, the symbolic language for determining the deeper meaning of a symbol for someone of African background may be lost.

In all the dreams of participants, there was a high frequency of dreams regarding family and groups. In looking at these dreams and considering analytic psychology's stance of the individual versus the collective, how can the dreams be interpreted when family and the collective continue to be such a major feature in Africanist consciousness? Is the path of individuation more difficult to travel because of racial group oppression requiring members to remain more closely attached to the cultural group and is this not just a natural aspect of survival and identity?

The dreams resulting from the interviews showed archetypal patterns that claim universality. One dream was of the "Green Man," this archetypal name known primarily from European cultures.

When questioned regarding her knowledge of this image, Liz, the dreamer, stated that she had no foreknowledge of it and mostly recalled the peacefulness she felt during this dream. There were several dreams that could be considered archetypal in their imagery.

In order to deepen the interpretation of dreams, there is an indication for inclusion of as many symbols as possible because what may appear meaningful based on one interpretation may actually prove to be limiting because of a lack of knowledge of symbology from a particular culture. Symbols are not always meaningful for everyone in the same way. Associations are important in helping to find direction for symbolic interpretation. Equally important is knowledge of the dreamer's culture and what symbols may be speaking from this culture.

When reviewing the research questions considering the dream results, I wondered if after separately going deeper into the image or symbol and finding meaning, two different cultures would have the same interpretation. Do symbols derived from mythology create a different archetypal meaning depending on the myths of each culture? Does culture influence change in archetypal patterns? Archetypes are said to be universal. When a dream image is archetypal and spiritual in one tradition is it possible that it can be considered merely a complex in another? If the interpreter has only one cultural list of symbols and meanings from which to choose, is it really a reflection of the archetypal?

Interview Results

This chapter provided details regarding the results of 31 dreams collected and analyzed over a one-year period. The dreams were collected on an individual basis from the three women dream participants. Each dream participant was interviewed, and dreams explored in consideration of a specific question. The primary question addressed was: "What are the indications for clinical practice in analytical psychology with African Americans as based on an examination of the content, associations, and symbols within the dreams of African Americans as understood within a traditional African cultural framework?" The primary question investigated themes found in African American dreams.

I developed an interview questionnaire and final interview questionnaire that provided for further reflection on and discussion of the dreamers' opinions and beliefs regarding dreaming. This chapter opened with a narrative portrait of each dream participant. The three participants in the project were all women of Africanist ancestry. Each woman provided a minimum of eight dreams for analysis. During our interviews, dream images were discussed considering life experiences, related stories or fantasies, and any other information considered relevant. This relevance included discussion of personal background information, recurring dreams as well as psychological life issues.

To develop a more depthful study, three participants were selected for this research study. Each dream participant was required to meet for the minimum time of ten interview hours. This proved beneficial in developing a more relaxed, inquisitive, open environment in which to dream tend. Each of us, working together, found that having this amount of time to meet with breaks between allowed for dreams to come forward and gave each of us adequate reflection time. There was no sense of needing to push or rush forward. Each participant was able to dream and recall her dreams without difficulty. Each participant kept a careful record of her dreams, noting as many personal associations as possible.

The dream elements were placed in comparative categories for each dream participant. Category 1 showed symbols appearing in all 31 dreams. The identification of these images as symbols was jointly determined by the dream participants and myself. Symbols that appeared in the dreams included a flying carpet, black bull, worms, and Biblical references (Ezekiel, John). Several of the images were archetypal and were explored in terms of this meaning with the dreamers. Mythological motifs included a shaman, snakes, twins, and the Old Man and Old Woman. Between dreamers there were overlapping dream images. For example, both Rae and Liz recorded dreaming of a worm, and both Rae and Liz had dreams with the threatening presence of policemen.

Fifteen themes were identified for further investigation in the dreams. Although more were noted, these 15 appeared important to the dreamer in our discussions or were repeated among dreamers and in that manner asserted some importance. Noticeable among the 15 themes was the fact that all three dreamers had frequent imagery of their mothers and other family members. Themes in this category included African imagery, flying, death, and nature. The greatest number of occurrences of imagery by theme was groups, family, and travel. Emotions recorded in the dreams were listed separately and showed the presence of fear and anxiety in the dreams of all three dreamers.

Of the other categories, the one with the most occurrences of imagery across the dreamers was that of feminine imagery. All three dreamers had the exact number of female images present in their dreams: 11. Masculine images occurred less frequently, with the exception of Kyesha, who also had 11 masculine images.

In terms of recurring dreams, the results showed that all three women had previously dreamt of these same images in the past. Rae reported a frequency of snake dreams, which occurred approximately every few months. In addition, she has had several flying dreams and dreams where guns are present and violent acts are committed. Liz repeatedly has dreams about family members and Guyana. Kyesha reported dreaming about Africa even before her first trip there many years ago.

All dream participants had dream images of children. Both Liz and Rae dreamt of boy children with whom they interacted, whereas Kyesha dreamt of a girl child: her granddaughter.

The dream results indicated that the dominant themes of these dream participants were about groups, included family members, and involved some reference to travel or transportation. This result indicated the presence of African imagery in the dreams. However, there was also present a moderate number of what would be considered archetypal imagery.

In the interview questionnaire, all three participants agreed that they do rely on their dreams for conscious life decisions. In further discussion of this positive response, two out of three dreamers noted that it has taken time to make use of dream imagery "information" in their wake state. One participant stated that it is usually in hindsight that she sees what the dream was suggesting or "recommending."

During the period of yearlong dreamtime work, none of the participants had any recorded dreams noting racism or racist actions against them. Although Liz stated that she has had such dreams in the past with racism as a theme none occurred during our research time. When questioned about the presence of states such as power, self-worth, repression, anger, and anxiety in their dreams, all dreamers noted the presence of anxiety but tied it to a personal relationship or personal trauma. When the dreamers indicated that these emotional psychological states were present in their dreams, there was no implication that these states were in anyway related to residual factors, conscious or unconscious, concerning American slavery.

All dreamers had images that indicated a spiritual presence based on African models. These models included mythology as well as epistemological systems. However, it is of value to note that these dream images, because of their archetypal nature, may have a cultural face specifically African but be recognizable in any part of the world for the essence of what they mean.

The dream study results suggest that culture and the symbolic meaning of dream imagery could be linked in a manner that require consideration when doing analytical psychological work with Africanist individuals. Due to the limited knowledge and understanding of symbols from African traditions and the emphasis on European symbology and interpretations, increased knowledge of African symbols would appear of value. If the dreams of African Americans are explored on an archetypal level, should there not be a language similar to that of "Greek" that addresses the ancestral heritage of Africanist dreamer?

The African American Family

The results of the dreams from the conversations and dream work suggest that certain indications exist for a culturally aware clinical practice of analytical psychology with African Americans that included cultural symbols. The first of these findings concern the dominant themes present in African American dreams. It was noted that all three women participants had family members present in their dreams. In addition, there were usually group gatherings. Though these groups may not be related to the dreamer biologically; they are considered "relations" due to their appearance in the dream.

The presence of family members and, by extension, groups I find to be related to the concept of community of Africanist people. However, it should be noted that not only Africanist individuals dream of family or groups. Dream studies by Calvin Hall (1953, 1966) and Robert Van de Castle (1966, 1994), and more recent studies by African American author Bynum (1993), indicate the presence of family members in dreams.

In most of the early research and studies completed about Africa and that look at African American culture, one is able to see the importance of family and groups. Over time, several possibilities have been offered for this fact.

The first is the most obvious and has to do with African communal living and all the considerations that existed for survival and safety. African families lived and worked within close proximity of each other because it also offered them opportunities to share their spiritual lives, raise their children together, and maintain an economic focus for their lives. Though this model of life has been examined by many anthropologists and others, including Jung, the "collective" came to be viewed as limited in terms of what was necessary for psychological growth. Jung believed that remaining within the collective and following its guidance was detrimental past a certain point in life. According to Jung, the path of individuation required a separation from the collective. Through this separation, one achieved increased life fulfillment and greater possibilities for wholeness. In the African tradition, however, individuals do individuate within the collective family. Joseph White and Thomas Parham, in *The Psychology of Blacks: An African American Perspective* (1990), reiterated what has been evident in African and African American culture for centuries:

The basic human unit is the tribe, not the individual. The tribe operates under a set of rules geared toward collective survival. Cooperation is therefore valued above competition and individualism. The concept of alienation is nonexistent in African philosophy since the people are closely interconnected with each other in a way of life that involves concern and responsibility toward others (p. 15).

Jung saw the benefit of the collective in the forming and shaping early life. However, he also saw the need to leave one's collective in order to attain true psychological freedom. This is in direct contrast with African thinking, cultural mores, and family practice. It appears to me that the frequent presence of family members and groups in the dreams of participants reinforces this aspect of Africanist culture. When I asked Liz what was creative in her life, a part of her response was her ability to be with her family and be of service to them. It was clear from Kyesha's responses to the interview questions that family (which continues to include her dead husband) is of utmost importance. Rae spoke of missing family as a personal theme in her life. All three women recognized the value and importance of family and I believe this is reflected in their dreams.

Another important related theme of the dreams was the number of occurrences of female images. The presence of female images in that of women re-affirms previous studies that show women dreamers have a high frequency of female dream imagery as compared to males. Each dreamer provided 11 separate images of females from her total number of dreams. It was an interesting fact that they each had the same number of female images. In creating the interview questionnaire, I did not include questions regarding the feminine. However, during the course of my readings it was clear that the feminine was excluded in many discussions of African philosophy, mythology, and even in African healing practices—although, in the latter, there was somewhat more inclusion due to the number of women who have traditionally been health practitioners in Africa. It is of value to notice the presence of the feminine where there was no deliberate intent to bring this forward as the primary focus of the study.

African American women are generally seen as carrying forward a matrilineal African tradition. A contributing factor to this circumstance that is often pointed to was the disruption of African American families by American slavery. Perhaps the tradition of women and the feminine asserting itself has to do with the archetypal presence of the feminine and its push for reestablishment in today's world. The emphasis on group and feminine imagery suggests the power of this consciousness in these three women dreamers. The women never met each other and had no opportunity to discuss their dreams with each other. I was the container for their dreams throughout the times we met. One of my own dreams from this time period follows:

*We go on a trip together—the She Crabbers and some men. At first it seems
that we've met them on our travels, then it appears they've been with us all
along. We're in transit on our way to Hawaii.*

*At first it's fun with the men; then they become irritating and bossy. They
seem to divide the women against each other. I want the women to meet
together without them. They don't want this and I'm trying to decide if I
should just leave them and go on by myself to Hawaii or go back home.*

*Now the women and I are walking on the street and I begin explaining my
point of view to them. They seem to understand.*

The She-Crabbers were a group of women friends who met every six months.
We traveled to various communities, as each of us lived in a different town or
city. Dreams of this group are not unusual for me and occur with some
frequency. I have dreams involving groups on a consistent basis.

The dream imagery of the feminine, family, and groups of participants
indicates to me that collectivism continues to be an important element in
female consciousness. Perhaps, in a small way, this is evidenced by the
number of referral clients at the New York CG. Jung Institute requests
female therapists. The request rate for women therapists was 90% higher than
for men therapists at the time of this dream study.

The dreams of the participants indicate to me that the power and influence
of the patriarchal collective, that held somewhat negative elements, continues
to have a strong hold on consciousness as expressed in the women of this
study. This is consistent with African American psychological belief regarding its own cultural group and the importance of it in affirming a positive
African American life.

An African Unconscious and Ego Consciousness

All dreamers in the study spoke of their reliance on dreams in making conscious life decisions. They all indicated that because of our study they had
increased the attention they paid to their dreams and were more trusting of
using information when thinking of life problems or situations. Most of the
literature regarding Africans reviewed in the book has addressed the belief
of oneness of Africans, not only within their group consciousnesses on an
ancestral level, but also with everything in nature. This philosophy is echoed
in most of the spiritual teachings of Africans. In his book *The Heart of Soul*
(1990), John Bolling discussed his view of this interconnectedness:

These Natural Soul Forces of the mandala are organizing forces of the
Innerself (unconscious mind). They lead to concepts, ideas, values, and
behaviors being organized into some coherent context in conscious
behavior. This process of organizing concepts into the context of
meaningful conscious patterns of behavior could be referred to as

"contexualization." This process allows the participant to undergo the mystic transformation from instinctual human to divine human. This process of contexualization of the Soul Forces constitutes the African Science. The African Science is the accumulated knowledge in the collective consciousness of Afrocentric people of how to live in tune with the non-human work of Mother Nature and the invisible spiritual world of God. This African Science comprises the Heart of Soul (p. 3).

Bolling is commenting on a most basic and recognizable aspect of African philosophic thought and existence. The unbroken unity of spirit and nature exists in African consciousness as one. Jung in his writings regarding psychic energy spoke of Africans and Native Americans views regarding "spirit" and its presence in the world.

Hetherwick reports the same thing of the Yaos of central Africa who cry *mulungu!* when they see something astonishing or incomprehensible. *Mulungu* means (1) the soul of a man, (2) the entire spirit world, (3) the magically effective property or power inherent in any kind of object, such as life and health, (4) the active principle in everything magical, mysterious, (5) the great spiritual power that has created the world and all life (1970).

For a long period of time after the initial exploration of Africa, Europeans involved in the "study" of Africa were critical of the African concept of inanimate object as "spirit possession." Although Jung valued the concept of libido and psychic energy in his own theories, he took an African attribute (Spirit) and denied the "correct" use of it by those from whom he borrowed the concept. His belief seemed to be that Africans and Native American people were unable to move forward in consciousness because they were stuck at the "concrete" level of infusing objects with spirit. Further, he stated that they were capable of understanding "representation" as it related to spirited objects but were incapable of developing concepts regarding the same.

When I consider the concept of unity between levels of consciousness, it seems reflected in the dreams of the participants as well as in my own dreams. In further consideration of African belief regarding this issue, as individuals and societies become more cognizant of the earth and its resources, an ecological movement has developed that accepts the spirit of everything on the planet and sees the connectedness between all things in existence. The African experience of life and respect for nature in all its aspects continues to be a standard, although until recently an unrecognized and at times a disrespected one.

Ethnicity, Culture, and Dreams

Ethnicity was one area of interest the dream study attempted to review as a factor or experience in the dreams of African Americans. Of the three dreamers only one, Liz, stated that she had dreams that she could easily identify as related to racism.

However, all the dreamers had dream images of individuals of color in their dreams. It seemed important to explore the area of ethnicity with dreamers due to the lack of available research studies in this area and also because of the presence of negative racial "scholarly" psychological work that has been completed about Africanist people. The fact that Liz had dreams with racism as a theme following an awake-state experience of racist contact, may only indicate day residue without any significant meaning. However, when there is day residue it can point to important psychic energy that later forms dream patterns. This would add confirmation to the co-influence of wake and sleep consciousness interacting with each other at all times.

My curiosity in seeking feedback from dreamers regarding the question of race in African American dreams was also in large part due to the many instances of racial biases in Jung's writing. These biases, although disavowed in clinical practice by Jungian analysts, continue to be reiterated in some Jungian institutes of training. The percentage of African Americans who attend post-graduate training programs in psychology or counseling is less than 10%, and there are only five African American Jungian analysts. I believe a part of the reason this situation persists in Jungian communities is because of a continued reluctance to decrease reliance on outdated Jungian concepts such *participation mystique*, continued use of offensive and pre-judiced words such as "savage" and "primitive" in the training curricula and a heavy reliance on only Greek mythology in the analysis of patients.

America is becoming more racially "colored." The America that Jung visited in the first part of the 20th century has changed. He commented that white Americans could be secure in their position of power over African Americans because whites outnumbered them.

This situation has changed and is continuing to change. Jung believed that white Americans had already been "overcome" by the music and physical behaviors of African Americans and that in these areas the former had taken on the negative characteristics of the latter. I have heard Jungian analysts say that Jung was "just a man of his time" and that his racism was a result of socio-historical circumstances. Even accepting this as containing some element of truth, why is it that Jungian analytical communities continue to be unable to connect with and attract individuals of color? Can the training programs be so strenuous, so difficult? Are admission requirements so strict and African Americans so unprepared academically and psychologically to be admitted? This doesn't seem to be the case for other training institutions, where the requirements are equally as stringent. So why then are there not more African Americans becoming Jungian analysts?

Perhaps, American Jungian psychology holds too tightly to the language and tone of Jung's theories without understanding the offensiveness of this language to African Americans. I am not speaking of the language of psychology per se but of the Jungian position that there needs to be an Other to serve as opposite. Unfortunately, the language of Jung, along with theories of hierarchy with indigenous people (in America, this translates as African and Native American) at the bottom, for all of their valuable information and forward-thinking in terms of the unconscious, remains basically racist and insulting to individuals of color. Some Jungians and other professionals in the field of Psychology defend the use of the word "primitive" not just as a psychological state. I believe this word remains basically unacceptable to African Americans because of its past usage and meaning.

In fact, not long ago I saw a full-page newspaper advertisement for Haitian art at a local New York gallery and printed all around its borders were the words "Haitian Art is Not Primitive Art!" I think this speaks to the increased level of consciousness that African Americans and other people of color are exhibiting regarding their cultural heritage. Yes, the word "primitive" may have initially been used to describe a psychological state—but who was the "primitive" of reference? It is generally recognized that the word had multiple meanings and was equally used as a noun referring to Africanists and other indigenous people. To think that this fact goes unnoticed by those interested in doing psychological work as Africanist clients or analysands is an error.

I was unable in my search to find or read about Africanist dreamwork of merit. I was curious to see how and what African Americans dreamed about. Unfortunately, Jung's work on this subject and that of other psychoanalysts in this area is so slim that it did not satisfy my curiosity. In fact, I became more interested to go into the shadow and darkness surrounding a lack of knowledge regarding Africanist dreaming. I sought to find out the underpinnings of the African unconscious and that led me to philosophy, mythology, and spirituality. Unable to find details about African Americans and dreaming, I considered completing my doctoral studies with this as a focus. I continue to believe that Africanist dreamlife is an area of exploration as relates to dreamwork and psychology. This is particularly true considering the above discussion regarding Jungian psychological theory and practice.

Africanist Dream Interpretation

I reviewed selected dream symbols and themes to determine if they indicated the presence of a psychological or spiritual state that was based on traditional African models. In comparing several of Rae's dreams between Jungian and Yoruba perspectives, differences did occur regarding interpretation.

The Yoruba tradition has a long history in terms of dream interpretation. Dream interpretation is a part of the lineage commencing with Esu, the diviner god. Divination is considered a sacred art form by the Yoruba, used to help humans remember their spiritual and psychological tasks in like. The belief is that prior to birth we knew who and what our purpose was on the earth; that, in fact, we have chosen a particular life. At birth, we forget this purpose but with the constant help of divination are able to understand our life's purpose.

Dreams are within the realm of Esu. When diviners conduct divination readings and do dream interpretation, Esu is the spiritual being they consult for guidance in providing the best interpretation of Ese Ifa. The written poems (odu) that tell the diviner what the dreamer needs to know are all contained in Ese Ifa. The diviner listens to the questions of the dreamer, hears descriptions of the dreams, and provides interpretations based on the dreamer's life circumstance and what Ifa shows in odu. The dreamer is able to contribute or retract any information she believes is not accurate during this time with the diviner.

The basis of dream interpretation in Yoruba is spiritual. Jungian dream interpretation has as its basis symbols of Christianity. One of the criticisms made about Jung was his reliance on the Christian "myth" for development of his psychology theories. In some regards, Jungian psychology is also spiritual because of its reliance on Judeo-Christian symbology.

The following is a description of three of Rae's dreams based on Yoruba, a traditional African model. Baba Ifa Adetunde is an African lineage *Babalawo* in the Yoruba tradition. He provides interpretations for the dreams based on his training and experiences as a Babalawo.

Rae's initial dream was of riding "on a flying carpet with many people." Baba Ifa Adetunde said that this and most of Rae's dreams are spiritual dreams. This initial dream of a magic carpet speaks of spiritual elevation. Baba Adetunde said that the dream is specific to Sufism. The images of others on the carpet are of the ancestors from that part of the world. He believed that those on the carpet were there to offer support in Rae's spiritual development. He said that they provide her with the comfort of their presence and physical direction. The fact that there is someone there who Rae thinks she has an intimate relationship with and that there are so many others "from the same family" indicates the potential for "great support on her spiritual path."

Baba Adetunde believed that there was no connection between Rae's initial flying dream and her second dream of the night with the young dead couple. He stated that when we dream, we enter the spiritual world, and dreams may become fragmented. It is not necessary to attempt associations between dreams from the same night as each dream will have its own message and intention.

The beginning of the second dream of the night opened with these words: "I'm at a church service where a young man and woman are being eulogized. People are looking for something to cover their faces." Baba Adetunde said that "this is the dream of someone who will help a lot of people." Similar to the above dream with others on the carpet, this dream has imagery that includes many people congregated in a church.

The place itself is considered to be spiritual, and Baba Adetunde said that this emphasizes the importance of the dream in providing spiritual direction for the dreamer. The dreamer said next, "I suggest some of the women take off their lace veils and put them over their faces. This is done, and the same white cloth is spread over both their faces." In facilitating the covering of their faces, the dreamer is serving as a priestess. "The placing of cloth is a ritual. It means that they are being protected from death."

Rae's dream continued: "An older woman approaches me with an honorary award. She hands it to me and says there will be a celebration at some later time. This award doesn't seem to have anything to do with the funeral and seems a cause for a different kind of ceremony." Baba Adetunde said of these final dream images that they spoke of the potential for Rae to be a priestess. In fact, he said that the dream is stating that he is her destiny if she wishes. Being offered an honorary award in this dream, coupled with the other images, shows the highest award—which is to be a spiritual teacher of Ifa.

Baba Adetunde's interpretation of the first dream would differ from the Jungian, not as it relates to the meaning, but what it indicates for ego and awake state functioning. Oftentimes, flying has to do with inflation. This is both a Jungian and Yoruba interpretation. However, in the former this is considered a "problem" in ego development. The magical aspect of flying indicates a *puer-puella* situation that is not supportive of individuation. However, the Yoruba interpretation indicates that flying places the individual closer to God. In this respect, flying is not a problem but a solution. When the dreamer can take on characteristics, like flying, that relate to spiritual beings, these suggest deeper spiritual development. In this way, a significant difference exists between the two interpretations.

However, Edinger in *Ego and Archetype* (1992) identified the circle of inflation and deflation and related it to God—the inflated stated was still considered in a negative light exactly because of the ego's identification with the god image.

Baba Adetunde interpreted Rae's snake dream, which follows:

I go down into the basement of the house looking for someone; I think it's Linda. I notice there is a snake nearby—it's orange with black stripes. Then I notice there are many snakes crawling all over the dirt floor. They're all about the same size: two feet long, either red or orange with black stripes. I become really afraid when I realize how many there are, and tell the man with me that I'm going to leave and go out of there, back upstairs.

Baba Adetunde said that this was a dream of the *egun*. The egun are the ancestors, and he explained that egun are present in basements and other places beneath the earth. "In Ifa, we understand that the invisible world of our deceased ancestors combines with the visible world of nature and human culture to form a single organic truth" (Neimark, 1993). In interpreting this dream, Baba Adetunde acknowledged the power of the egun. The location of the snakes determined how the image of the snakes would be interpreted. He stated that Rae may have to face a "frightening experience sometime in the future" because of what he saw in the dream. He recommended that she offer prayers to her ancestors, seeking guidance. He said that the exact circumstance was unclear to him but would present itself to Rae and at the time she would be able to connect it to this particular dream.

In a Benin dream interpretation manual it stated that to dream of a snake is a "very bad omen." It said that the dreamer should speak with a priest and have prayers said for the family. A part of this interpretation mentions enemies, and says that if the dreamer kills the snake he or she will be victorious over his or her enemies.

This interpretation is similar to that of Baba Adetunde's belief that snakes do not necessarily represent "good energy." Baba Adetunde clearly stated that the type of snake, its action in dreams, and its location are important elements in determining meaning when snake images are present.

My purpose in providing Rae's dreams interpreted by a priest of the Yoruba tradition is to show that cultural symbols do make a difference in how dreams are interpreted. In its almost complete reliance on European symbology for dream interpretation, there is an inherent negation of those belonging to other cultures. The theories of Jungian psychology are partially built on the "information" gathered by Europeans at the end of the 19th century. Most of this information has been translated through a racial lens that discredited or defamed African culture. Bringing African cultural symbols to Jungian psychology's dream interpretation would not only update this psychology but would also broaden its pantheon to include Africa and her Diaspora.

Chapter 12

Deepening the Dream

Initial Dream

I'm underground with a few other women. I see a brightly colored double-belly clay pot trimmed with the color red. There are other things I've seen but everything else pales next to this pot. The pot is broken off in one place but is a really nice piece.

I go outside and plan to take the pot, but a man standing nearby sees that I have the pot. I tell him I want it and he says that I cannot have it; it belong to the site. He says something about money as it relates to the pot—do I or am I willing to pay for it?

Now he has moved to a high tower with another woman standing below (who first reported I had taken the pot). The man insists that I cannot have the pot. I tell him okay, but I hold onto it tight, not intending to let go of it.

I had the above dream when I began my work on this dream study project that was the basis for the writing of *Race and the Unconscious: An Africanist Depth Psychology Perspective on Dreaming*. This dream became a leading light for me as I began the dream project with the other women. Thinking about it and re-entering this dream provided me with details about directions to take during the dreamwork with my co-dreamers, Rae, Kyesha, and Liz. Our work together was initially to collect and analyze their dreams as part of a doctoral research project. This was to be done in consideration of finding indications for psychological clinical practice with Africanist individuals. The dream content, including associations and symbols, was to be investigated within a traditional African cultural framework. Over time, since my initial research with the dreaming life of Rae, Liz, and Kyesha, there still was no publication that focused on dreaming in Africanist people.

Due to my work in depth psychology and dreamwork, after several years I continued to see the absence of dream literature on Africanist cultural group members.

One of the most obvious results from this study was the dreamers' focus and interest in relationship—particularly family relations. Various studies on

DOI: 10.4324/9781003219965-16

African American families have repeatedly shown the importance of family, family relations, and extended family. The dreams, interviews, and fantasies of Liz, Rae, and Kyesha reinforce the belief if the importance of family.

Analytical psychology includes an established school that does in fact focus on early childhood development and issues within the analytical frame. Michael Fordham, recognized leader of the London Developmental School, began his work in the 1960s following in the psychoanalytical tradition of Melanie Klein. Fordham's theories provided Jungian psychology with an approach that embraced infant and childhood development. In addition, it gave further direction to understanding the transferential relationship that takes place between analyst and analysand.

African Americans do in fact seek psychological help in the form of psychotherapy. They do not as a rule seek this service from analytical psychologists. In the African tradition of healing, families are an important element to the healing process. This is particularly true in cases of mental illness, where there is a presumption of a "calling" to be a healer or spiritual teacher rather than being considered pathological. When someone in the family is ill, it is cause for interest among all family members. Mutual support is expected and provided. In a certain way, this runs contradictory to classical Jungian analysis, wherein family members rarely are expected to participate in the psychological work of the patient. They may be imagined, dreamed about, or recollected, but not brought in directly. However, within Jungian circles a more widespread interest in Jungian psychology vis-à-vis families is beginning to appear. *Psyche and Family: Jungian Applications to Family* (Dodson & Gibson, 1996) and *Families and the Interpretation Dreams* (Bynum, 1993) both focus studies on families using Jungian theory as a foundation.

Based on the dreams of those participating in my study, it would appear that knowledge of family theory is important. Incorporating it would recognize how valued family is in the traditional African model as well within the African American family.

Looking at the dreams from this study, a second strong theme emerged that suggested indications for focus on the feminine. I do not believe that the feminine images in the dreams were there only because these were female dreamers, but rather because the consciousness of the feminine is strong and seeking acknowledgment. Classical Jungian psychology allows for gods as well as goddesses in its theories. However, as Hillman has pointed out, it is the Hero/Hercules figure that has taken the lead through its emphasis on ego development towards a central or centered self and the process of individuation. Allowing for more images to dominate, particularly female ones, provides more possibilities for psyche to mirror itself. This is one of the differences between classical and archetypal psychology that speaks to openness versus closed positioning as it relates to bringing in that which is new or different. Using the latter approach, all images that are present are experienced as permissible and of value.

The dreams of the participants were reviewed within an African cultural frame. I observed that differences do exist in terms of how a dream may be interpreted. Though Jung identified the universality of archetypal dreams, very often archetypal images were interpreted using the cultural lexicon of Europe. Sometimes this provided an accurate view of the images under the lens, but most often this was not the case. Jungian psychology as practiced in America has in many instances held to the language of Jung. This has not proven successful in convincing African Americans that Jungian psychology is compatible with their life "mythos." There was a time in Jungian dreamwork when the archetypal shadow was assumed to be a person of color—usually of African ancestry. Fortunately, this has changed, and shadow figures are no longer automatically interpreted as being negative and Africanist.

Although the dream participants had dreams that could be considered "archetypal" in both the classical and archetypal school, it is the former that could more easily recognize that which is nonbiased by its assertion that the image and the dreamer defines archetypal. It is difficult not to create archetypal imagery that is static, because over time culture solidifies the imagery and the language, excluding "new" identifying labels. The old labels, which are culturally based—in this case European—continue to be the most acceptable primarily because others are never introduced into contemporary dialogue, neither visually nor auditorily. Jungian psychology reminds me of Ralph Ellison's *Invisible Man* (1989) in this respect. It continued with the cultural lexicon of 19th-century Europe, and sometimes appears in 21st-century America's denial of the reality of the presence of African Americans in this society.

There are indications for a recognition of Africanist "consciousness," in whatever form this may take, in doing clinical work with African Americans. An unfortunate aspect of analytical psychology as practiced in America appears to be the negation of this type of consciousness. If Jungian psychology is truly a pantheon of possibilities for everyone, then Africanist cultural symbols belong within it as well as Greek symbols. However, if Jung's paradoxical position holds true-then African Americans should be recipients of this type of analysis because we live in the symbolic.

While completing this research project, it was important to explore all dream content and review it from as many perspectives as possible. This seemed essential because there has been a lack of literature that shows the collection and study of African American dreams. Noting differences that exist between Jungian schools and their approaches, I felt drawn to collect as much information about African American dreaming as possible. I am not so much interested in supporting one approach over the other as I am in identifying these approaches as best I can and "seeing" what the dreams indicate would be the best of any analytical psychological approach for clinical work. An important value of this study for me was partly "data" collection and analysis of this material—the dreams.

Feminine Imagery

Noticeably absent from the African philosophical literature—with a very few exceptions—was the voice of women. Equally present in the dreams of the dream participants were female images. Each woman in the study had an equal number of dreams with female images. This strong presence of the feminine suggests a continued awareness and need for this in our present culture. The female images of the dreamers were at times subjectively known to them. At other times the women in their dreams were strangers. In once again returning to the following dream at the beginning of the research project I note the energy of the Feminine:

> *I'm underground with a few other women. I see a brightly colored double-belly clay pot trimmed with the color red. There are other things I've seen but everything else pales next to this pot. The pot is broken off in one place but is a really nice piece.*
>
> *I go outside and plan to take the pot, but a man standing nearby sees that I have the pot. I tell him I want it and he says that I cannot have it; it belong to the site. He says something about money as it relates to the pot—do I or am I willing to pay for it?*
>
> *Now he has moved to a high tower with another women standing below (who first reported I had taken the pot). The man insists that I cannot have the pot. I tell him okay, but I hold onto it tight, not intending to let go of it.*

This dream reminds me of female desire for recapturing that which was stolen from women in the change to a masculine, patriarchy-dominated consciousness. The pot represents all that is feminine and found in the underground, once again coming to light. In speaking of African myths and culture, Holloway (1992) said that African Americans cannot retrieve that which has been lost; it is possible only to remember. She believed that in the writing of women such as Alice Walker and Toni Morrison, we can see the remembrance of that which is mythological to African Americans. I believe that in the dream, the dreams of women, and specifically within the dreams of African Americans, we can see the remembering of our myths. In our ability to "recover" rather than "retrieve," African American women can have soulfulness through writing. In looking at African myths, Holloway stated that readers must use caution in reading and accepting the interpretations of these African myths. She stated that this is due to the European influence on the interpretation of many West African myths. She suggested that these interpretations were created to suit Western points of view regarding their own society.

Maxwell (1983) wrote about ritual and myth in Bemba. Among the rituals that he described, one in particularly reminds me of my dream. "Mbusa" is a sacred pot with painted inscriptions used by young women at their initiations. The definition of *mbusa*—things handed down—suggests the importance of lineage. In this ritual, elder women give the initiates the sacred pots in a "passing down" rite.

I believe women dreaming of women reinforces the presence of the feminine in our lives. As previously stated, there was only one female citation available to me in all the books I researched on African philosophy. It is also of note that the myths that receive primary attention are those that tell of male gods. I found this to be true in texts specific to African mythology as well as European mythology. Within the last 10 years, there have been more texts that address the presence of the feminine in mythology. However, even some of these exclude African female images. The concept that men gave birth to and singularly created the earth and all things on it is more present in stories of African mythology than not. However, there are exceptions, and the following African myth is one:

MAWU

Riding in the mouth of a great snake came Mawu to create the world, making mountains, rivers, and valleys along the snake's serpentine course. The better to view creation, she made a great fire in the sky, and added to the world elephants and lions, giraffes and wildebeests in great herds, bands of monkeys, as well as people. Her work accomplished, she sent the snake under the earth, where, coiled up, it would support the weight of the creation, and Mawu retired to the lofty jungle realm of heaven.

Before long, the people began to fight among themselves, having forgotten that it was Mawu who had provided them not only with a world to live on, but, more important, with part of herself—the essence of life, their souls, a force called Sekpoli. To fight someone was thus to fight Mawu as well.

Seeing all this turmoil, Mawu's daughters and granddaughters set out through the lands of Dahomey to remind people of the wisdom of Mawu and encountered an insolent braggart named Awe, who boasted that he was just as powerful as Mawu. Among his powers of music and magic, he, too, he blustered, could make life, and many people began to believe.

To prove it, he threw three two balls of silk into the air and climbed up the threads through the clouds into the jungle of heaven, where he challenged Mawu, saying his powers were as great as hers. He chopped down a tree and carved on it all the features of a person. When he was finished, he stepped back and said, "I have created a person."

Mawu observed the wooden figure lying on the ground. "How is it," she said, "that your person doesn't smile, doesn't walk, doesn't dance and chant in thanks to you? You should breathe Sekpoli into it, the essence of life." Awe gulped an enormous breath of air and blew out so mightily that the jungle of heaven quivered as in a storm. But his person lay still and mute on the ground. Again, Awe gulped air and blew it out, so strongly that the person on the ground moved in the wind's path. But again it lay still and lifeless.

After two more attempts, Awe knew he was defeated and hung his head in shame. Only Mawu, he confessed, could make life. Only Mamu was wise. He was humbled and said he would return to the world below and explain this. But Mawu knew that Awe was at heart a charlatan and, once he returned to earth, would boast again. She made him a bowl of cereal to eat before his journey, into which she had put the seed of death.

Only when Awe had finished eating did he learn of the seed he had eaten and would carry back to earth. Mawu sent him off to explain that only Mawu could breathe the breath of life into people and, lest they value this gift lightly, could suck it out when she chose.

Two men were more responsible than many others for how African myths were translated and received outside of African society. Those anthropologists, Mircea Eliade and Claude Levi-Strauss, introduced the world to African mythology through their studies in this field. Levi-Strauss developed a technique for understanding myths that he named structural analysis. According to Levi-Strauss (1987) all myths could be identified by this technique. He was not interested in any value placed on the myth except to show patterns within myths. There does not appear to be any consideration of philosophy behind the myths that he investigated. In *The Drunken King or the Origin of the State* (1982), De Heusch, claiming to be "faithful" follower of Levi-Strauss, interpreted a number of Bantu myths. De Heusch studied these "foundation" myths, noting the connection between them and the historical development of African kingdoms. Nowhere is there mention of women or queens in the foundation or building of these kingships. This type of investigation is pronounced in most of the literature on mythology.

Africanist Symbols: Personal Dream Attributes

All three dreamers had dreams that contained important, immediately recognizable symbols. The black bull, the mountain, the Tree of Life, are all images that have developed specific meanings over time. Many cultures have defined meanings specific to their society. The interpretations that have evolved from each society generally reflect the development of the image based on its mythic and ritual remembrances.

Most of the dreams that are analyzed and interpreted are done so with the use of European symbols or symbols of indigenous peoples as translated by Europeans. Sometimes these are accurate and sometimes not. The African belief that spirit encompasses all life forms justly reflects how symbolic meaning gets created. However, over time and with cultural influence, symbols acquire new meaning.

Hall (1983), in describing levels of consciousness, addressed collective consciousness, considered to be that place in consciousness where cultural symbols are formed and identified. He identified this place a "cultural world of shared values." The participants' dreams reflected some symbols that were identifiable as symbols in various cultures, including African and European. There were symbols based on traditional African models, indicating spiritual states, found in the dreams of Liz, Rae, and Kyesha. How these symbols were interpreted and made useful in the dreamers' lives was partly determined by what the symbols-dream images meant to the dreamer.

Within Jungian psychology there are differing views regarding symbols. The broad terms for two of these differing points of view would be archetypal and classical. In *The Cambridge Companion to Jung* (Young-Eisendrath & Dawson, 1997), David Hart defined symbol according to a classical Jungian approach.

> The symbol, therefore, is not the product of rational thought, nor can it ever be fully explained. It has the quality of conscious and unconscious worlds together as a moving force in psychological and spiritual development. Any image or idea can function as a symbol in individual or collective life, as it can also lose its symbolic force and become a mere "sign," standing for something that is fully known (p. 95).

This perspective is slightly different from that of the archetypal school. James Hillman has been a leader in the initiation and development of post-Jungian thought. Hillman's belief regarding images is that they are the essence of dreaming, that images have a life of their own and require no interpretation per se. In line with this thinking is the idea that any image may be archetypal.

Following is one of Rae's dreams:

I'm sitting with a young boy, age 8–10, pulling off a sponge that has grown to his right upper chest. It is a blue rectangle sponge with a black backing. I take off the sponge but it seems another grows back in its place.

I say to the woman (mother?) who sits with us that we should try a homeopathic remedy because it would keep it from growing back. That we had to keep it from growing back—that was the solution rather than treating it (from the outside).

Rae and I together chose dream symbols from the above dream that included the following:

Eight- to ten-year-old boy	Homeopathic remedy
Sponge	Inside/outside
Blue	Women
Upper right chest	Black

In providing personal associations, Rae identified a feeling of "creepiness" at the idea of the sponge growing on the boy's chest. She said it gave her a "queasy" feeling. We looked at the purpose of a sponge: what does it do; what was it doing in her dream? Did it change, color, depth, size? How did it feel to the touch? Rae had gone to a homeopathic practitioner for the previous 24 years, ever since the birth of her daughter. So she was familiar with homeopathic medicine. Both the boy and the woman were unfamiliar. Rae said that in the dream she felt concerned and somewhat anxious at the unusualness of the sponge and its ability to keep growing back after several removals.

Baba Adetunde, in looking at the above dream by Rae, saw the image of Olukun, goddess of the ocean. He said that it was a "beautiful" dream.

In *The Way of the Orisha*, Neimark (1993) described Olukun:

In Africa, Yemonja is represented by the Ogun River rather than by the ocean as she is in the New World. Olukun has come to reflect the bottom or mysterious part of the ocean … It is here that secrets are preserved and kept, that the unknown is knowable, and that riches and treasures of the world abound (p. 118).

According to Baba Adetunde, the dream holds all the energy of the ocean goddess, Yemonja or Olukun. The boy is actually one of her children from the sea. The fact that they both appear in Rae's dream highlights her favored status with this goddess. The blue of the sponge is natural to the blue of the ocean. Sponges grow in the ocean. All the dream elements indicated to Baba Adetunde the presence of Olukun and Rae's favored status to this goddess because she is being employed in her service.

In comparison to the interpretation given by Baba Adetunde, following are possible Jungian interpretations. The sponge soaks up the emotion of the heart *chakra*; there is no flow of passion, it is stopped. The age of the child is that of latency, which is a time for exploring, adventures, and excitement. However, this child sits quietly and appears to be sad. The sponge is soaking up all of his potential for joy and passion. Lungs become more "spongy" when we are not well—is there some indication of lung-related sickness? The moisture is being held in instead of coming out as it would in a healthy psyche. What is indicated is like with like: a mirroring of sponge with sponge.

Each of these perspectives on the dream offers more information about possible considerations for Rae. This is positive, in that she is able to ascertain her own feelings, beliefs, and associations with both dream interpretations and accept both, one, or neither. If she were to remain only with the images of the dream perhaps they would take her to the intimacy of Olokun's world. Perhaps, a focus on the sponge as soaking up joy and passion would bring her to the same place. Only the dreamer knows the possibilities because of her lived experience of the dream and its images.

It is possible that a dream will be interpreted in a spiritual light in Yoruba, Jungian, or other frames.

On further exploration of the dream, there may emerge possibilities introduced by the dreamer that suggest an archetypal interpretation. Jung was in favor of having a broad-based knowledge of mythology available so that the analyst would have knowledge with which to understand dream images. He felt that this knowledge should come from different fields: mythology, religion, and alchemy. When dreams can be viewed in this kaleidoscopic way, with the dreamer providing guidance, dreams become more meaningful.

In Rae's dream above, one of the identified symbols was the opposite of inside-outside. One of the key features of classical Jungian psychology is identifying symbols within this context of the opposites. It is also a feature that differentiates it from archetypal psychology, wherein a multiplicity of images is supported over a theory of opposites. If opposites come alive as a result of the deepening of imagery, this is fine. However, it is not considered acceptable to have predetermined considerations of opposites before understanding what the image is indicating.

In homeopathy, inside and outside are viewed as reflections of each other. The symptom provides the direction for which the remedy is required. When discussing the dream with me, Rae recalled going to the doctor a few months earlier because of a sinus problem. When the homeopathic doctor asked her how she felt, she remembers reporting one of her symptoms as having lungs that felt "spongy." When she received her list of remedies, one of them was a remedy called "sponge." Because of this and other similar experiences, Rae was more readily accepting of the concept of inside and outside as reflections of one another.

Chapter 13

Closing Reflections

The Dream Family

My attention was initially drawn to investigating the dreams of African Americans because when I attempted to find such information in books, I was unable to do so. I had a desire to see in writing that focused on members of this ethnic group in terms of their dreams, their psychology as related to the dreams, and the influence of African culture on African Americans in terms of dreaming. In my readings regarding African Americans, I found texts related to their psychology, but none whose theme was a discussion of African American dreams except for Bruce Edward Bynum.

In formulating ideas concerning the structure of this writing project it became evident that details informing my main question would come from a variety of literature sources. Although I could remain within the area of Jungian psychology for details regarding dreaming—a wealth of information exist there—very little related to Africans in a positive manner (except for Vera Buhr), and none of it related to African Americans, except for what was previously mentioned regarding Jung's visit to America in 1912. The literature search involved finding a frame in which to place the dreaming life of African Americans. This structure became African philosophy. Even with all its questioning regarding the actual existence of African philosophy, I believed this was the place from which to begin this writing and dreamwork study. In fact, the philosophical questioning regarding the existence of African philosophy suggested the African American struggle with "superimposed" identity and was an added indication for this choice as a beginning point.

Ifeanyi Menkiti in his essay "Person and Community in African Traditional Thought" (Wright, 1979) pointed to the key significance of the community in Africa. This emphasis on the group does not negate the individual but provides a lifetime structure of development and support for the individual. According to Menkiti, it is this community that offers the true, realistic definition of an individual. He says that within the folds of the community "wisdom" develops over time through the experiences of aging,

DOI: 10.4324/9781003219965-17

rituals, and societal influence. In *An Essay on African Philosophical Thought* (1987), Kwame Gyekye discusses the Akan people of Ghana. Gyekye believed that communalism is essentially an African quality that determines the standards by which Africans live. He noted that in the Ghana philosophy of life, it is the lived experience that is highly valued. In the hierarchy that Gyekye said existed and was inclusive of a Supreme Being, as well as the element of nature, is the concept of the communalism that exists between all things in this matrix. The quality of *sunsum*—spirit—is a part of all things. This essence holds the communal together.

The frequency of group images appearing in the dreams of the three dream participants was consistently high for all three women. As I studied the dreams and saw emerging patterns, it was clear that groups were a theme with some importance. Liz and Kyesha each had six images of groups in their dreams. Rae had three. All women indicated in their interviews that family groups were important to them in some way.

Serequeberhan, in *Hermeneutics of African Philosophy* (1994), pointed to the "lived inheritance and tradition" as a structure for establishing philosophic thought. Serequeberhan recommended that Africans draw upon African concepts for the development of philosophy. One of the major concepts is that of communalism, which has often been labeled "collectivism."

Upon arriving in America, African Americans were able only temporarily to maintain contact with members of their group—if at all. Factors of slavery determined where groups and individuals would be sold. One of the most painful and far-reaching effects of American slavery was the destruction of social and family groups. The reasons for this separation varied but the outcome was the same: division of African family groups. One evident contrasting circumstance exists in the Gullah community off the coast of Georgia. This group of African Americans, whose ancestors arrived centuries ago, claims title to many customs and linguistic patterns recognizable as West African. The ability of this group to survive as a group occurred because the whites who their African ancestors were often not living on the island. This permitted the survival of African traditions that could not realistically continue on plantations elsewhere, where there was the constant presence of owners and overseers.

It is my belief that the women dreamers had communal dreams because this is a part of the Africanist psyche being reflected. It is true that most of us dream of groups at some point. However, the frequency of this imagery, coupled with the psychological and social history of Africans, reinforces the possibility of its relatedness to African American group dreams. One natural aspect of African communalism is the extended family. Children "belong" to everyone, not just those in the immediate family. In the dreams of the participants, it did not matter so much that there was no apparent blood connection because the appearance of the group suggested that a relationship did exist that may be identified as "extended." This is not unusual in African American creation of family, where not only blood relatives but also "outsiders" can become family through association. This was an African practice developed among slaves to support children who were sold off and who arrived at new plantations without kin.

However, even prior to this, it was traditional African custom to welcome strangers and incorporate them into the family.

> Civilization began in Africa .... Families and tribes worshipped their gods, gods who took to themselves favored families and favored cities .... Their voices bound the families together as much as the need for food, collective protection, and the perpetuation of their kinship lines (Bynum, 1993, p. 167).

In the dreams from the study, there were instances of family imagery present for all the dreamers. Both women who have sisters dreamt of at least one of these sisters. Liz had one dream that included her brothers. Rae, who has no sisters, dreamed repeatedly about her daughter. The fact that there were these images present indicates the importance of family to these dreamers.

Conscious and Unconscious Life Connections

The three dreamers all expressed their belief in the interconnection and interplay between conscious and unconscious life events. They more often than not felt it was in the area of family-relatedness that the dreams showed them difficulties, unresolved problems, or "advice" on how to proceed. Rae believed that the shaman dream she experienced was an indication of a need for more spiritual guidance. She said this was validated by her meeting with Baba Adetunde. His insistence that most of her dreams had a spiritual theme gave support to her own sense of lacking a spiritual community in which she could regularly participate.

Of the three dreamers, Kyesha was the one who continuously expressed her spiritual reverence for her ancestors, her belief in the presence of spirits in her life, and her willingness to consider spirit over matter. In reviewing her dreams, and in her discussion with me, she stated that they validated certain problems she was experiencing in her life. The dream where her husband isn't there when things get difficult reflects what is true in today's reality. Her husband is dead. But, as in the dream, Kyesha stated very firmly that they will be reunited. It is this acceptance of dualities between conscious and unconscious that appears to be present for all the three dreamers.

Liz was the dreamer who reported seeing the least connection between the conscious and the unconscious. However, she did believe it was there, only that she lacked the sight to see the connection on an ongoing basis.

She indicated that our mutual work together on her dreams had been helpful in this area. Her initial dream at the start of this project held very strong body imagery. In fact, Liz said she felt "overwhelmed" by the image of the woman and attached child.

In *Body and Mind in Zulu Medicine*, Ngubane (1977) wrote about her work with Zulus in South Africa. In her study, she discussed what was considered to be the cause of illness: psychological and physical are noted to be the same. Ancestors are believed to cause sickness as well as health. Ancestors form an unbreakable linkage with the living. In this way, they offer a connection to the unconscious. When individuals do not give proper respect to ancestors, then sickness occurs. This is the conscious aspect of the connection. For a long time, Africanist peoples' belief in spirit(s) was criticized and demeaned among non-Africans. More recently, there is a recognition of the value, the spiritual and psychological importance, of remembering those who have preceded us. It is no longer considered "heathen" or backward to acknowledge the spirit world.

African Americans have always recognized the importance of remembering the spirit world. They have always felt the necessity of keeping their conscious lives in connection with their unconscious states—ancestors being a part of that state. Dreams are accepted as a place where we may once again have union with relatives who have passed away. In this sense, African American understanding of the connection between conscious and unconscious is very strong.

In describing Zulu healing practices, Ngubane provided insight into how in their awake state Zulus make conscious choices regarding healing practices that reflect reliance on the unconscious. Ngubane stated that there is a structure for the practice of medicine. Because the practitioner or healer and the patient believe in the symbols of the healing ritual, healing takes place. She described this as a movement from "a mystical place of darkness to one of mystical light." The classification of illness, commonly named "pollution," is extensive in Zulu traditional medicine. This pollution is a mystical force. In this sense, it is a part of the unconscious realm. However, the work of the healer and the physical body that requires healing exists in both conscious and unconscious worlds.

Vera Burhmann lived and worked with a Xhosa healer, Mongezi Tiso, and his community for several years. Burhmann (1986) reported that these healers saw no difference between the conscious and the unconscious. They said that their healing work involved the use of dreams on an ongoing basis. In fact, the way one was recognized as a potential initiate into the community was through dreams of being sick or having images that indicate one is being called to that work.

In quoting the Xhosa Burhmann (1986) said, "When part of me is ill, the whole of me is ill." This is in direct agreement with African beliefs regarding the interconnectedness of all things. In addition, Burhmann recalled that for the Xhosa what is important is survival, but it is group survival. The continued emphasis on this concept underscored the interconnectedness in all things that Africans perceive. This also pertains to conscious and unconscious.

Liz, Kyesha, and Rae are all capable women in various stages of their lives. They all considered themselves to have had some experience of both conscious and unconscious coming together in ways that proved satisfying, disturbing, insightful—all the many ways possible that can ensue from such meetings. Jung reasoned a major purpose of the conscious was to make the unconscious more visible, more meaningfully understood in life. Keeping a record of dreams, exploring these dreams, and attempting to understand their meanings, becomes an avenue for bringing forward images from the unconscious that are meaningful.

In African culture the *griot* was the storyteller, the teller of the myths of the community. It is possible through mythology to see the workings of the conscious and unconscious. In looking at the dreams, stories emerge. In Liz's dreams, particularly her shaman dream, it is possible to see a mythic ritual present itself in a clearly recognizable manner. A further possibility for Liz, in conscious life, would be further exploration of this image and working at deepening it in her awake state, looking at all the nuances of the shaman and how the cleansing he gave affects her being. If she is able to create rituals from this dream, she will be doing the work of connecting the unconscious with consciousness. In this way, she also is "remembering" the myths of her ancestors.

Malinowski, an early 20th-century anthropologist, lived with the Masai for many years, researching their society. In this research he found that myth was used in a functional way.

In all the literature I reviewed, Malinowski's position on mythology seemed most reflective of African culture. Malinowski (1963) attempted through his writings to get others to discontinue their emphasis on exploiting the "exotic" differences of Africans from Europeans. He stressed that there were basically no differences between the two cultures—they both had societal rules, customs, and rites that assured the continuation of their society. He sought to show how "magic," myths, and dreams were used in a functional manner by Africans. Malinowski noted that Europeans had similar functions; they were just called by different names.

Looking at dreams and creativity in *Writers Dreaming* (1994), Epel interviewed writers discussing their dreams. The connection between conscious and unconscious was clearly displayed in the stories of these writers. Isabel Allende (Epel, 1994) spoke of how books come to her from her "belly," in an organic way. She considered dreams a storage house of elements: smells, colors, and so on that add to story making, all of which are only available through dreams.

The results of the dreams from my research study indicated that the dreamers believe there is a connection between their conscious and unconscious lives. The literature supports this claim in a variety of ways. It can be seen through the body. This is made especially evident by African healers, who see no separation of body and mind and use dreams for understanding all aspects of life. Mindell's (1985) dreambody work echoes that of the African healer.

Through mythology one is able to see the connection between the conscious and the unconscious. Holloway (1992) wrote about this, particularly as it relates to African American women writers and their ability to connect the two worlds. Epel (1994) did the same with her focus on the creative process.

Malinowski (1963) through his behaviorist lens continues to provide an important understanding for us decades later of how myths and African "magic" served the community on a conscious level.

Sylvia Perera (1991), author and Jungian analyst, recommends a "multifaceted approach" to an understanding of dreams, with which there is more likelihood that a dreamer will understand more meaning and thus be able to apply more dream material to daily life. It is through the dream that dreamer and analyst learn how to proceed in doing psychological work from session to session and for the length of time that analysis continues. If dreamer and analyst restrict themselves only to the concept of opposites, the images from the dreams become more predictable and more like "signs" than living symbols holding energetic potentialities.

The following is Liz's Dream 9:

> *Today I woke up feeling very much at peach [peace] with myself.*
>
> *I dreamt I was in Wisconsin with Regina, Harold, his ex-wife, and my brothers and sisters. We were in their house preparing a huge feast, and everything was really great. The feeling was peaceful. There was no animosity. Harold went outside for a walk and took a long time to come back, so I decided to go and look for him.*
>
> *When I was walking down this path looking for him, I finally saw him walking up toward me with this big smile on his face. When he approached me we both saw this man dressed in Indian wear, but made of leaves, riding this motorcycle that went by. His face was green.*
>
> *When I woke up I was feeling a sense of peace.*

Liz's dream brought to my mind a matching image of the Green Man. In another dream, Liz was standing in an open field in Alabama. As with Wisconsin, she has never traveled there. However, from the dreams, she says she knows what it would be like.

In associations to this dream, Liz said that what she remembers the most was the sense of peace that she felt through the dream and upon awakening. This sense of peace carried her through the day. This was the first time that Liz had had an image in her dreams like that of the Green Man. She said of him, "He had a distinguished nose. If I see him I would know him. He was 40-something."

As I reviewed her dreams, I noticed a pattern of nature images. The frequency of these images in her dreams seemed to demand their own accounting, and so I created a theme category for them. It was of note that Liz had the highest occurrence of nature images. Kyesha had half as many, and Rae had none. Liz's nature images were always expansive, flying over "fields of gold and green," lying on grass and looking up at the sky, running outside in green pastures.

Liz's dream of the Green Man was one of the surprises of this project, as was the strong emergence of female imagery. I have not found any written commentaries or myths regarding a figure in African mythology resembling the Green Man, except Osisis in Yoruba mythology. However, in Jungian psychology, he is easily recognizable as the archetype of the Earth. Perhaps the occasion for his appearance in Liz's dream was the same or similar to that of female imagery: offsetting our neglectful, sometimes abusive treatment of the Earth. In his text *Green Man: Archetype of our Oneness with the Earth* (1990), William Anderson discusses the Green Man.

Liz mistyped the word "peace" in her written version of the dream, typing "peach" instead. One of the meanings for the word peach is immortality; the Green Man is associated with rebirth, fecundity, and the cycle of nature. Liz's dreams frequently caused me to think of the southern United States with all of its lush vegetation and fruit.

Perhaps her imaging him in her dreams spoke to a personal need for more nutrition, more focus on a "vegetative" process in her life. Liz said that she felt the need for more "nurturing." When I asked more about the image of the dream, she said it made her want "a home; a home with a white picket fence and children."

Liz dreamed of a recognizable archetypal figure. It seemed relevant to bring this dream into this section of the writing on cultural symbols. The Green Man is associated primarily with European culture. Of note is this comment, "The Green Man in the form predominantly shown in this book is unknown in civilizations other than those of the Mediterranean basin and North-Western Europe" (Anderson, 1990). This does not mean that a Green Man does not exist in African mythology or other places, but it is here that we mostly find him. In researching more I found Oshosi, Yoruba god of the woods and forest. He is also the Hunter with shamanic powers. The Green Man image in Liz's dream spoke directly to her own need to be fed and loved. She repeated throughout our interviews her desire to be taken care of and nurtured. Taken on personal and archetypal levels, she has received psyche's mirroring offering a source of potential nurturing.

In arguing for deepening the image, archetypal psychology may avoid the difficulty of symbol interpretation that classical Jungian psychology experiences, wherein symbols can sometimes become signs and "new" symbols are less likely to be granted recognition. Quoting Hillman in his essay "The Archetypal School," Michael Adams said, "Any image may be considered archetypal; … [it] is a move one makes rather than a thing that is" (Young-Eisendrath & Dawson, 1997, p. 112).

What is of importance is that any image may have archetypal "value." Describing Hillman further, Adams continued, "He does not posit or infer the metaphysical existence of archetypes prior to the image" (p. 112).

Another area of interest that examined particular symbols or dream content, identifiable as indicators for the presence or absence of a related psychological or spiritual state, based on traditional African models, found that such symbols do exist. However, as evidenced by Liz's Oshosi dream and personal or subjective dreams, any kind of dream may emerge. American Jungian psychology uses almost exclusively European symbols and interprets those belonging to Africans and others of color with exclusively European lenses and translations. African American dreamers may require the understanding and creation of a dream field that is inclusive of their cultural symbols.

Clinical Practice

The focus of *Race and the Unconscious: An Africanist Depth Psychology Perspective on Dreaming* has been consideration of analytical psychology as applicable to dreamwork clinical practice with African Americans. As I began this study, I considered possible frames.

I anticipated laying a foundation that placed African Americans in a "house" that suited them culturally as I began to explore the dreams of the interviewee participants. This house was the traditional African model. As I proceeded with our work together, I discovered that the threads of Africanism were divergent but also interwoven with European culture. The information that developed as I explored the literature reflected this circumstance.

I believe that the implications for clinical practice with analytical psychology require careful consideration of the theoretical frame of classical Jungian psychology. Although there is an effort being exhibited in contemporary Jungian analytical professional circles to include African American culture in the arena of analytical psychology, this effort is sometimes questioned by some. It appears that Jungian teaching institutes in America are beginning to train analysts though still using the racist terminologies and framework that Jung employed, but with some attempts at deconstruction. Is it impossible to be both an upholder and advocate of the classical Jungian perspective on the language and concepts describing Africanist people in Jung's *Collected Works* and simultaneously expect that there will be open acceptance of analytical psychology by African Americans or the African Diaspora?

The irony of the situation is that Jung did include Africans in his theory. The problem is that he kept them at the bottom of the "consciousness" hierarchy. I do not believe that African Americans should distance themselves from Jungian psychology without first exploring and seeing for themselves how much of what he advocated was based on African principles. I am not implying that it was only African principles that guided him, but rather that they were a contribution to his theoretical work. Jung was attempting to show that Africans were in a desirable state—"primitive"— with access to the unconscious readily available to them, unlike Europeans who had alienated themselves from their unconscious by becoming "civilized." It would be beneficial if Jungian psychology, as has Freudian psychology, fully claimed Jung's racialized shadow as it relates to African Americans. Once this is done, I expect that it would open African Americans to being more receptive to Jungian psychology at least as an idea, if not yet in clinical experience.

In his text *The Healing Wisdom of Africa* (1998), Malidoma Some wrote about the concept of community, healing, and ritual. He underscored the value of the individual within a family or community context.

> When an outsider looks at indigenous culture and sees the devotion to community held by its individuals, it looks to them as if the individual self has been annihilated. For the person inside such a community, however, the sense of respect and value for one's own original and unique identity is tremendous, and it results in the desire to remain in the community because that is where your genuine identity is guaranteed the right to blossom fully (p. 301).

Clinical practice with African Americans opens the door to a more freeing view of the archetypal—if cultural symbols can be identified and recognized. However, even if this does not occur, a Hillmanian approach to working with dream images, which allows everything to be archetypal, permits the most accessible experience of spirit working directly with the imagery of the dream.

The most noticeable change in American Jungian psychology has been in its ideas regarding the feminine. Women writers within the Jungian community have been giving voice to their concerns regarding the false and patriarchal concepts of the feminine that existed in Jung's writings and theories, particularly concerning *anima* and *animus*.

With the predominance of female imagery in the dreams of Liz, Rea, and Kyesha, there would appear to be a direction indicated by psyche for more emphasis in recognition of that which is feminine.

I hope that my study of women dreamers contributes to the field of depth psychology by providing an in-depth look at one group, that of African American dreamers. I believe an additional contribution is that this viewpoint was initiated by an African American woman.

I believe my interrelatedness with the dreams preceding and during our work together greatly influenced my conscious awakened state as well as my dream life. My ability and willingness to see the individual dreamers as well as the dream were important aspects of this research study. In researching Africanist themes and symbols in the dreams, I found them to be moderately present. The dreamers indicated the value they themselves placed on particular symbols, and this in turn determined the importance or ethnicity of a symbol. The dreamers and I jointly reviewed dream imagery and drew conclusions following discussion and mutual agreement. In taking this route, I allowed the dreamer to provide the lead in our work, in respect for the dream and psyche.

I believe that the findings from this study are specific to the dreamers and yet offer the potential for broadening the discussion regarding African Americans and dreaming.

The instances of archetypal motifs in the classical Jungian approach suggest that this approach may be applicable to African American dreamers. However, the lack of Africanist cultural symbols continues to reinforce European symbology. It speaks of universality when in fact it is very particular to Europeans. In this arena, racist language and outdated psychological concepts continue to be used and applied without "consciousness" regarding the place and times in which we now live. I find that archetypal psychology as put forth by Hillman, and feminist psychology as developed by mostly female Jungian analysts such as Polly Young-Eisendrath and Marion Woodman presently offer more in terms of the possible inclusion of African Americans in clinical practice. I say this with an understanding that these individuals draw on the theoretical framework of Jung. It is their ability to reach beyond the "classical" that provides some possibility for deconstructing analytical psychology in terms of race.

The philosophical frame of this study relied on African philosophy for direction at its beginnings. As I proceeded through this literature, I noticed differing opinions among Africans, mostly regarding the nature of African philosophy. Many questioned its very existence. I recognized the question of identity as relevant to African Americans in their ongoing attempts to be accepted and gain recognition in American culture. Both Africans and African Americans experienced a violent intrusion by Western culture. Because of this intrusion and all that has followed for centuries, concepts of identity, community, familial group, and individual remain restless undercurrents in the Africanist psyche. This is possible in societies where racial color continues to ride the waters of consciousness in daily life.

Where is the feminine in African mythology? Where is the feminine in African philosophy? Are we to believe that so few stories existed of the feminine in African mythology? Why do the few with female goddesses often portray them functioning at the behest of male gods?

In this study, traditional African medicine was explored in consideration of its influence in African life. I found that this form of medicine, in particular the ngoma practices, continues to offer healing to Africans. This healing addresses psychological, physical, and spiritual aspects of the African.

The ability to see each of these aspects as one is clearly accepted as being in tune with African culture. In my consideration of the three dreamers and their belief regarding conscious and unconscious connections, I saw the spirit of traditional African medicine at work.

Further Dream Studies

This study has provided me with an exceptional opportunity to review literature that I find meaningful in both my personal and professional life. It has also allowed me time to rethink my own beliefs regarding psyche and the psychology of the individual and the collective group.

More widespread studies of the general population of African Americans would produce the beginnings of a lexicon of cultural symbols that are non-European centered. In this way, Africanist culture would become a more accepted reference for those dreaming and those working with dream interpretation. If dream symbols are important—as all dream research appears to indicate—then the application of cultural knowledge in the form of dream interpretation is equally important.

I began this dream research project after seeking to find written information on the dreamlife of African Americans. I consider my attempt a beginning effort at researching this particular group of dreamers. As of this writing, there remains no comprehensive study of African American dreamers. My study has reiterated for me the necessity and value of inclusion of Africanist people in the clinical, archetypal, psychological realm in a manner that respects their heritage and traditions. Continued dream research would add to the literature and the understanding of the psychology of Africanist dreamers in service of healing.

I believe, and am hopeful, that researching the dreams of Africanist people will influence us all in ways that enhance our conscious and unconscious lives.

Let there be a meeting ground between our awakened life and that of the dream.

References

Adams, M. (1997). The archetypal school. In P. Young-Eisendrath & T. Dawson (Eds.), *The Cambridge Companion to Jung* (pp. 101–118). Cambridge, UK: Cambridge University Press.

Akomolafe, A., Asante, M., & Nwoye, A. (Eds.) (2017). *We will tell our own story: The lions of Africa speak!* New York: Universal Write Publications LLC.

Akomolafe, B. (2017). *These wilds beyond our fences: Letters to my daughter on humanity's search for home.* Berkeley, CA: North Atlantic Books.

Alston, T., Calogeras, R., & Deserno, H. (1993). *The dream reader: Psychoanalytic articles on dreams.* Madison, CT: International Universities Press.

American Psychological Association. (2001). *Publication manual of the American Psychological Association* (5th ed.). Washington, DC: Author.

Anderson, W. (1990). *Green Man: Archetype of our oneness with the earth.* London: Harper Collins.

Ayoade, J. A. (1979). Time in Yoruba thought. In R. Wright (Ed.), *African philosophy: An introduction* (pp. 71–85). Washington, DC: University Press of America.

Baring, A., & Cashford, J. (1993). *The myth of the goddess: Evolution of an image.* London: Penguin Books.

Baton, M. (1967). *The structural study of myth and totemism.* London: Tavistock.

Boas, F. (1994). *The way of the dream: Conversations on Jungian dream interpretation with Marie-Louise von Franz.* Boston: Shambhala.

Bolling, J. (1990). *The heart of soul: An Afrocentric approach to psycho-spiritual wholeness.* New York: Mandala Rising Press.

Bosnak, R. (1997). *Christopher's dreams: Dreaming and living with AIDS.* New York: Dell.

Bourdillon, M. (1993). *Where are the ancestors: Changing culture in Zimbabwe.* Harare, Zimbabwe: University of Zimbabwe.

Boyatzis, R. (1998). *Transforming qualitative information.* Thousand Oaks, CA: Sage.

Boyd-Franklin, N. (1989). *Black families in therapy: A multisystems approach.* New York: Guilford Press.

Brewster, F. (2019). *African Americans and Jungian psychology: Leaving the shadows.* London & New York: Routledge.

Brewster, F. (2020). *Archetypal grief: Slavery's legacy of intergenerational child loss.* London & New York: Routledge.

Brooke, R. (1991). *Jung and phenomenology.* New York: Routledge.

Buhrmann, M. V. (1986). *Living in two worlds: Communication between a white healer and her black counterparts*. Wilmette, IL: Chiron.

Bulkeley, K. (Ed.) (1996). *Among all these dreamers: Essays on dreaming and modern society*. Albany: State University of New York Press.

Bynum, E. (1993). *Families and the interpretation of dreams: Awakening the intimate web*. New York: Harrington Park Press.

Bynum, E. (2017). *The dreamlife of families: The psychospiritual connection*. Rochester, NY: Inner Traditions.

Cassier, E. (1953). *Language and myth*. New York: Dover.

Chavunduka, G. (1986). Zinatha: The organization of traditional medicine in Zimbabwe. In M. Last & G. Chavunduka (Eds.), *Professionalisation of African medicine* (pp. 71–85). Manchester, UK: Manchester University Press and London: International African Institute.

Courlander, H. (1973). *Tales of Yoruba gods and heroes*. New York: Crown Books.

Coxhead, D., & Hiller, S. (1990). *Dreams: Visions of the night*. New York: Thames and Hudson.

De Heusch, L. (1982). *The drunken king or the origin of the state*. Bloomington: Indiana University Press.

Desmangles, L. (1992). *The faces of the gods*. Chapel Hill: University of North Carolina Press.

DeToit, B., & Abdalla, I. (1985). *African healing strategies*. Owerri, Nigeria: Trado-Medic Books.

Dodson, L., & Gibson, T. (1996). *Psyche and family: Jungian applications to family therapy*. Willamette, IL: Chiron.

Downing, C. (2018). *Mythopoetic musings: 2007–2018*. Santa Barbara, CA: Christine Downing.

Dunlea, M. (2019). *Bodydreaming in the treatment of developmental trauma: An embodied therapeutic approach*. London & New York: Routledge.

Edinger, E. (1992). *Ego and archetype: Individuation and the religious function of the psyche*. Boston: Shambhala.

Eliade, M. (1964). *Shamanism*. New York: Bollingen Foundation.

Eliade, M. (1967). *Myths, dreams and mysteries*. New York: Harper and Row.

Ellison, R. (1989). *Invisible man*. New York: Vintage Books.

Epel, N. (1994). *Writers dreaming*. New York: Random House.

Falola, T. (Ed.) (2013). *Esu: Yoruba god, power, and the imaginative frontiers*. Durham, NC: Carolina Academic Press.

Ford, C. W. (2000). *The hero with an African face: Mythic wisdom of traditional Africa*. New York: Bantam Books.

Freud, S. (1913). *Totem and taboo*. New York: W. W. Norton.

Freud, S. (1965). *The interpretation of dreams*. New York: Avon Books.

Gates, H. L. (1988). *The signifying monkey: A theory of African American literary criticism*. New York: Oxford University Press.

Glissant, E. (2010). *Poetics of relation*. Ann Arbor: University of Michigan Press.

Gonzales-Wippler, M. (1989). *Powers of the orishas*. New York: Crown Books.

Good, C. (1987). *Ethnomedical systems in Africa: Pattern of traditional medicine in rural and urban Kenya*. New York: Guilford Press.

Greenson, R. (1993). The exceptional position of the dream in psychoanalytic practice. In T. Alston, R. Valogeras & H. Deserno (Eds.), *The dream reader: Psychoanalytic articles on dreams* (pp. 106–132). Madison, CT: International Universities Press.

Guthrie, R. (1976). *Even the rat was white.* New York: Harper and Row.

Gyekye, K. (1987). *An essay on African philosophical thought: The Akan conceptual scheme.* Cambridge, UK: Cambridge University Press.

Hall, C. (1953). *The meaning of dreams.* New York: Harper and Row.

Hall, C., & Van de Castle, R. (1966). *The content analysis of dreams.* New York: Appleton-Century-Crofts.

Hall, J. (1983). *Jungian dream interpretation: A handbook of theory and practice.* Toronto, Canada: Inner City Books.

Hallen, B., & Sodipo, J. (1986). *Knowledge, belief and witchcraft: Analytical experiments in African philosophy.* London: Ethnographics.

Hambly, W. D. (1937). *Source book for African anthropology.* Chicago: Field Museum of Natural History.

Hart, D. (1997). The classical Jungian psychology. In P. Young-Eisendrath & T. Dawson (Eds.), *The Cambridge companion to Jung* (pp. 89–100). Cambridge, UK: Cambridge University Press.

Heidegger, M. (1962). *Being and time.* San Francisco: Harper and Row.

Henderson, J. (1980). In J. M. Natterson (Ed.), *The dream in clinical practice* (pp. 369–403). Lanham, MD: Jason Aronson.

Hernandez, J. (1993). The subjective meaning of crack in black females: A phenomenological study based on dreams and early recollections during detoxification (Doctoral Dissertation, Union Institute, 1992). *Dissertation Abstracts International, 53*(09), 4955B.

Herrnstein, R., & Murray, C. (1994). *The bell curve: Intelligence and class structure in American life.* New York: Simon and Schuster.

Hewat, M. (1970). *Bantu folklore.* Westport, CT: Negro University Press.

Hillman, J. (1979). *The dream and the underworld.* New York: Harper and Row.

Hillman, J. (1997). The seduction of black. *Spring 61: A Journal of Archetype and Culture, 61,* 1–15.

Holloway, K. (1992). *Moorings and metaphors: Figures of culture and gender in black women's literature.* New Brunswick, NJ: Rutgers University Press.

Hountondji, P. (1983). *African philosophy: Myth and reality.* Bloomington: Indiana University Press.

Ilechukwu, S. (1989). Approaches to psychotherapy in Africans: Do they have to be non-medical? *Culture, Medicine and Psychiatry, 13,* 419–435.

Jackson, L., & Greene, B. (Eds.) (2000). *Psychotherapy with African American women: Innovations in psychodynamic perspectives and practice.* New York: Guilford Press.

Janzen, J. (1992). *Ngoma: Discourses in healing in central and southern Africa.* Berkeley: University of California Press.

Jensen, G. (1973). *The doctor-patient relationship in an African tribal society.* Assen, Netherlands: Van Gorcum.

Jung, C. G. (1968). *Analytical psychology: Its theory and practice.* New York: Pantheon Books.

Jung, C. G. (1968). *The archetypes and the collective unconscious (The collected works of C. G. Jung, Vol. 9, Part I)*. Princeton, NJ: Princeton University Press.

Jung, C. G. (1970). *The structure and dynamics of the psyche (The collected works of C. G. Jung, Vol. 8)*. Princeton, NJ: Princeton University Press.

Jung, C. G. (1973). *Memories, dreams, reflections*. New York: Pantheon Books.

Jung, C. G. (1977). *The symbolic life: Miscellaneous writings (The collected works of C. G. Jung, Vol. 18)*. Princeton, NJ: Princeton University Press.

Karade, I. B. (1994). *Handbook of Yoruba religious concepts*. York Beach, ME: Samuel Weiser.

Keita, L. (1979). The philosophical tradition. In R. Wright (Ed.), *African philosophy: An introduction* (pp. 35–50). Washington, DC: University Press of America.

Kvale, S. (1996). *Interviews: An introduction to qualitative research interviewing*. Thousand Oaks, CA: Sage.

Kyles, T. (2021). Yemonja and the dark waters of the unconscious: Reflections on an Africana archetype. In L. Simpson-Wilkey, S. S. McKoy & Eric M. Bridges (Eds.), *Recovering the African feminine divine in literature, the arts, and practice* (pp.11–18). Lanham, Maryland: Lexington Books.

Last, M., & Chavunduka, G. (Eds.) (1986). *Professionalisation of African medicine*. Manchester, UK: Manchester University Press and London: International African Institute.

Levi-Strauss, C. (1987). *Anthropology and myth: Lectures 1951–1982*. Oxford: Basil Blackwell.

Levy-Bruhl, L. (1960). *How natives think*. New York: Washington Square Press.

Lincoln, C., & Mamiya, L. (1990). *The Black church in the African American experience*. Durham, NC: Duke University Press.

Lincoln, J. (1935). *The dream in primitive cultures*. New York: Johnson Reprint.

Lipschutz, L. (1954). The written dream. *Journal of the American Psychoanalytical Association, 2*(3), 473–478.

Love, V. (2012). *Divining the self: A study in Yoruba myth and human consciousness*. University Park, PA: Pennsylvania State University Press.

Makinde, M. (1988). *African philosophy, culture and traditional medicine*. Athens, OH: Center for International Studies.

Malinowski, B. (1961). *Argonauts of the western Pacific*. New York: Dutton.

Malinowski, B. (1963). *Sex, culture and myth*. London: Rupert Hart-Davis.

Maxwell, K. (1983). *Bemba myth and ritual: The impact of literacy on an oral culture*. New York: Peter Lang.

Mbembe, A. (2017). *Critique of Black reason*. Durham & London. Duke University Press.

Mbiti, J. (1969). *African religion and philosophy*. Portsmouth, NH: Heinemann.

McLean, H., & Cole, A. (2002). *The dream-working handbook*. New York: Carlton Books.

Meier, C. (1967). *Healing dream and ritual: Ancient incubation and modern psychotherapy*. Einsiedeln, Switzerland: Daimon Verlag.

Menkiti, I. (1979). Person and community in African traditional thought. In R. Wright (Ed.), *African philosophy: An introduction* (pp. 157–167). Washington, DC: University Press of America.

Mbiti, J. (1967). African religions and philosophy. Portsmouth: Heinemann Educational Books.

Mindell, A. (1985). *Working with the dreaming body*. London: Penguin Books.

Morris, J. (1985). *The dream workbook*. Boston: Little, Brown.

Morrison, T. (2002). *Sula*. New York: Knopf.

Moustakas, C. (1990). *Heuristic research: Design, methodology, and applications*. Thousand Oaks, CA: Sage.

Moustakas, C. (1995). *Being-in, being-for, being-with*. Northvale, NJ: Aronson.

Mudimbe, V. (1994). *The idea of Africa*. Bloomington: Indiana University Press.

Myers, W. (1977). The significance of colors black and white in the dreams of black and white patients. *Journal of the American Psychoanalytical Association, 25*(1), 163–181.

Natterson, J. M. (1980). *The dream in clinical practice*. Lanham, MD: Jason Aronson.

Neimark, P. (1993). *The way of the Orisha: Empowering your life through the ancient African religion of Ifa*. New York: HarperCollins.

Ngubane, H. (1977). *Body and mind in Zulu medicine: Ethnography of health and disease in Nyuswa-Zulu thought and practice*. New York: Academic Press.

Oguah, B. (1979). African and Western philosophy: A comparative study. In R. Wright (Ed.), *African philosophy: An introduction* (pp. 169–182). Washington, DC: University Press of America.

Oruka, O. (1990). *Sage philosophy*. New York: E. J. Brill.

Oyewumi, O. (1997). *The invention of women: Making an African sense of western gender discourses*. Minneapolis MN: University of Minnesota Press.

Parrinder, G. (1967). *African mythology*. London: Hamlyn Books.

Patton, M. (1990). *Qualitative evaluation and research methods*. Thousand Oaks, CA: Sage.

Peirce, P. (2001). *Dreams for dummies*. Foster City, CA: IDG Books.

Perera, S., & Whitmont, C. (1991). *Dreams: A portal to the source*. London: Routledge.

Rice, A. (1976). *Interview with the vampire*. New York: Ballantine Books.

Romanyshyn, R. (1988). Psychotherapy as a creative process in psychotherapy and the creative patient. New York: The Haworth Press.

Rudestam, K., & Newton, R. (1992). *Surviving your dissertation: A comprehensive guide to content and process*. Thousand Oaks, CA: Sage.

Sela-Smith, S. (2002). *Heuristic research: A review and critique of Moustakas' method*. Thousand Oaks, CA: Sage.

Serequeberhan, T. (1994). *The hermeneutics of African philosophy: Horizon and discourse*. New York: Routledge.

Sjo, M., & Mor, B. (1987). *The great cosmic mother: Rediscovering the religion of the earth*. San Francisco: Harper and Row.

Sogolo, G. (1993). *Foundation of African philosophy: A definitive analysis of conceptual issues in African thought*. Ibadan, Nigeria: Ibadan University Press.

Some, M. (1998). *The healing wisdom of Africa: Finding life purpose through nature, ritual, and community*. New York: Tarcher Putnam.

Spring, A. (1985). Healthcare systems in northwest Zambia. In B. DeToit & I. Abdalla (Eds.), *African healing strategies* (pp. 135–150). Owerri, Nigeria: Trado-Medic Books.

Staugard, F. (1986). Traditional healthcare in Botswana. In M. Last & G. Chavunduka (Eds.), *Professionalisation of African medicine*. Manchester, UK: Manchester University Press and London: International African Institute.

Strenski, I. (1987). *Four theories of myth in 20th century history*. Iowa City: University of Iowa Press.

Stukane, E., & Van de Castle, R. (1985). *The dream worlds of pregnancy*. New York: Quill Books.

Sullivan, B. (1992). *Psychotherapy grounded in the feminine principle*. Wilmette, IL: Chiron.

Sunmola, A. (1994). The pattern of dreams of a sample of Nigerians. *Journal of Analytical Psychology, 39*, 361–372.

Temples, P. (1945). *Bantu philosophy*. Paris: Presene Africaine.

Tick, E. (2001). *The practice of dream healing: Bringing ancient Greek mysteries into modern medicine*. Wheaton, IL: Quest Books.

Van de Castle, R. (1994). *Our dreaming mind*. New York: Ballantine Books.

Van Den Berg, J. H. (1989). *A different existence*. Pittsburgh: Duquesne University Press.

van Manen, M. (1990). *Researching lived experience: Human science for an action sensitive pedagogy*. Ontario, Canada: State University of New York Press.

Vaughan-Lee, L. (1998). *Catching the thread: Sufism, dreamwork and Jungian psychology*. Inverness, CA: The Golden Sufi Center.

von Franz, M.-L. (1979). *Alchemical active imagination*. Irving, TX: Spring.

Wangyal Rinpoche, T., & Dahlby, M. (1998). *The Tibetan yogas of dream and sleep*. Ithaca, NY: Snow Lion.

Wehr, D. (1987). *Jung and feminism: Liberating archetypes*. Boston: Beacon Press.

White, J., & Parham, T. (1990). *The psychology of blacks: An African American perspective*. New York: Prentice Hall.

Wiredu, K. (1996). *Cultural universals and particulars*. Bloomington: Indiana University Press.

Wiredu, J. E. (1997). How not to compare African thought with Western thought. In R. Wright (Ed.), *African philosophy: An introduction* (pp. 133–144). Washington, DC: University Press of America.

Wright, R. (1979). Investigation of philosophy. In R. Wright (Ed.), *African philosophy: An introduction* (pp. 19–32). Washington, DC: University Press of America.

Young-Eisendrath, P., & Dawson, T. (Eds.) (1997). *The Cambridge companion to Jung*. Cambridge, UK: Cambridge University Press.

Index